DISCARDED

Decade of Destiny

Judah L. Graubart
and Alice V. Graubart

E
747
G7
1978

Lamar University Library

588847

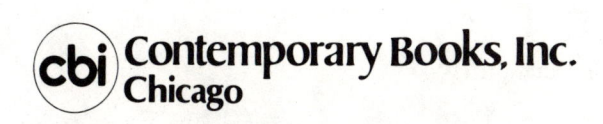

cbi Contemporary Books, Inc.
Chicago

Library of Congress Cataloging in Publication Data

Graubart, Judah L.
   Decade of destiny.

   1. United States—History—1933-1945—Biography.
2. United States—History—1919-1933—Biography.
3. United States—Biography.   I. Graubart, Alice V.,
joint author.   II. Title.
E747.G7   1978   920'.073   78-57436
ISBN: 0-8092-7729-8

Interview with Art Hodes copyright © 1978 by Art Hodes.
All rights reserved.

Interview with Thomas A. Dorsey copyright © 1978 by Thomas A. Dorsey.
All rights reserved.

Interview with Alan Lomax copyright © 1978 by Alan Lomax.
All rights reserved.

Copyright © 1978 by Judah L. Graubart and Alice V. Graubart
All rights reserved
Published by Contemporary Books, Inc.
180 North Michigan Avenue, Chicago, Illinois 60601
Manufactured in the United States of America
Library of Congress Catalog Card Number:78-57436
International Standard Book Number: 0-8092-7729-8

Published simultaneously in Canada by
Beaverbooks
953 Dillingham Road
Pickering, Ontario L1W 1Z7
Canada

To our parents, David and Eunice Graubart,
and Myron and Shirley Vision,
and our sister, Gale Graubart.

CONTENTS

Acknowledgments xi
Introduction xiii

1 A NEW DEAL FOR AMERICA . . .
James Roosevelt 1
Dorothy Rosenman 11
Alger Hiss 15
J. Douglas Brown 24
Wilbur Cohen 32
Milton Eisenhower 38
Ralph Helstein 46
Robert C. Weaver 51
Louis Simon 57
Carl Gottfried 63

2 POLITICIANS AND PERSONALITIES
Hamilton Fish 67
Jennings Randolph 77
John McCormack 82
Emanuel Celler 87
Leon Keyserling 89
Jacob Arvey 93
Earl Dickerson 97
Joe Rauh 101
Marquis Childs 105

3 MOVEMENTS AND MINORITIES
Roger Baldwin 111
Clarence Mitchell 115
John D. Elliott 123

Milton Cohen	127
Richard Criley	132
Simon Weber	137
Paul Novick	142
David Graubart	147

4 THE UNION MAKES US STRONG

A. Philip Randolph	151
Patrick Gorman	154
Abe Feinglass	156
Hannah Haskell Kreindler	159
Morris Yanoff	163

5 THE SPORTING LIFE

George Halas	167
Charles Gehringer	171
John "Jimmie" Crutchfield	174
Effa Manley	181
Henry Armstrong	185
Edward Froelich	190
Thomas "Gumbo" Gibbs	196

6 STAY TUNED FOR . . .

Edgar Bergen	201
Ann Elstner Matthews	206
Al Hodge	211
Shirley Bell Cole	216
James Ameche	221
Herbert Morrison	226
Dan Seymour	231
Archibald Crossley	240

7 THAT WAS ENTERTAINMENT, TOO . . .

Joe Smith	245
King Vidor	248
Carmen Nigro	254
Spencer Gordon Bennett	256
Ward Kimball	260
Gordon Sheehan	269

8 . . . AND ALL THAT JAZZ

Lionel Hampton	277
Earl "Fatha" Hines	282
Red Saunders	285
Edith Wilson	288
Art Hodes	291
Thomas A. Dorsey	296

9 A CLOSING MONTAGE

George Gallup	301
Edward Bernays	306
Alan Lomax	310
Samuel Insull, Jr.	321
Virgil Peterson	325

Index   *333*

ACKNOWLEDGMENTS

We would first like to thank the many men and women whose careers and contributions spanned the Decade of Destiny for sharing their reminiscences with us. It is most of all because of their generosity that this book has reached fruition.

We also want to thank our agent, Arthur Gould, for his insightful criticisms and his skillful critiques of the initial stages of our work, and for his assistance in so many of its most important aspects.

Locating the interviewees and arranging appointments was often a difficult and complicated process, and many people made that process a little less difficult and complicated. We would like to thank some of the people who were particularly helpful with that aspect of the book: Hyman Bookbinder; Gere Brown; Tom Dillon, president of the Lambs; Harry Fleischman; Barry and Marge Greenwald; William Katz; O. J. Pocok of the Lambs; Susan Rubin; Bob Sakamoto, formerly of "Action Answers" of the now defunct *Chicago Daily News;* and Chuck Schaden, Chicago's resident radio expert and program host of "Those Were the Days."

There were a number of people who helped us in preparing the book and we'd like to express our thanks to them: Eunice Graubart; Sandee Luchowski; Marc Francik and Carmen Merino of Search School; June Sochen of Northeastern Illinois University; and Normal "Tweed" Webb, noted black baseball historian.

Many thanks, too, to the New York chapter of the American Federation of Radio and Television Artists (AFTRA) and the Des Plaines and Skokie, Illinois, Public Libraries.

April, 1978

INTRODUCTION

The thirties—what were they really? Bread lines and box cars; apples for a nickel; "brother, can you spare a dime?" Yes, the thirties were these things, but they were much more. They were years in which the fantasy of the American Dream was replaced by the reality of the Great Depression, years in which the old ways of American society had to be discarded. For with the collapse of the economy—and of the political and social fabric as well—ideas and institutions that had served so well for so long suddenly became outmoded and useless. If American society was to survive, new ideas and institutions had to be developed. And this is what *Decade of Destiny* is all about. For we believe that in terms of societal contribution, the decade of the thirties was one of the most productive in our nation's history and, of equal importance, was one that left a legacy whose influence is felt even today. Indeed, many of our contemporary social, political and cultural ideas and institutions are either a direct result of the rebuilding process of the thirties or an indirect but still integral outgrowth of creative process that enveloped the United States between Black Thursday and Pearl Harbor.

But our purpose in writing this book was to do more than chronicle the way in which America rebuilt itself. We wanted to re-create a sense of what it meant to be a part of that experience; of how it felt to be among those to whom Franklin Roosevelt referred in his 1936 Inaugural Address when he said, "This generation of Americans has a rendezvous with destiny."

To achieve our goal, we first prepared a list of hundreds of people, both famous and unknown, who we felt were representative of the thirties generation. That list was then narrowed down to those people we felt were *most* representative of the issues and circumstances with which we were concerned. The interviewees were questioned at length about their roles and experiences in the thirties and also about their perceptions of what took place and why.

In presenting these reminiscences, we make no claim to historical objectivity. Indeed, we have attempted, through a minimum of editing, to present as much of the subjectivity—as much of the *essence*—of each person's memoir as possible. For history, in the final analysis, is not so much the record of the events of the past as it is the way in which people understand those events to have happened.

1
A NEW DEAL FOR AMERICA...

While Franklin Roosevelt provided a father image to a nation that, in the thirties, was in deep distress, he was literally a father to the man whose memoir follows. Thus James Roosevelt had a "great life" and viewed the Roosevelt era from a personal vantage point with which few others were gifted. Having been in such a position, he gained intimate knowledge of his father's personality, his marriage, his campaigns—and of some of the people who exerted great influence from behind the scenes.

A former two-term Democratic congressman, James Roosevelt now heads a public-relations firm in Newport Beach, California.

JAMES ROOSEVELT

I went with my father to the Madison Square Garden convention in '24, when he first nominated Al Smith and called him "the Happy Warrior." Then, in '28, the convention was held down in Texas, and my brother Elliott went with my father. Of course, it was then that Father was invited by Governor Smith to run for governor of New York. I don't think it marked a turning point so much as a grand strategy that a fellow named Louis Howe had worked out. It did, however, mark the full enlistment of Jim Farley into the team of Howe and Farley. But I think Howe had made his mind up many years before that the grand strategy was to pick the right time and work your way into a position so that you could launch a stronger base for a campaign for the presidency. I don't really think my father was much involved in it until the end of '29 or early '30, especially upon his re-election as governor in '30 by a rather wide margin, better than 700,000 votes. At that time, he began to think that maybe Howe hadn't been having pipe dreams and that it might just work out.

I couldn't and wouldn't say that he and Howe had never talked about the presidency, because Howe had certainly talked to a lot of people about it over the years from '24 on, and maybe even before that. But I don't think anybody, including Father, took it seriously until '28 and especially in '29 and '30.

I think the economic crisis gave him a clear opportunity to put into practice the unemployment measures, the emergency measures of different kinds, the relief measures (what I would call the human measures) that became part of the New Deal in '33. So I think the New Deal foundation certainly was being laid. Not that the presidential use of it was the main objective, but it was fortuitous because of the large size of the state of New York, that practical experiences were being handled which could be adapted to the national situation in '33. It also gave him the opportunity, in '29 and '30, to bring into close association as part of his managerial team, so to speak, what was known as the Brain Trust: people like Tugwell, Moley, Harry Hopkins, Frances Perkins, Judge Rosenman and Bob Sherwood, who became such valuable assets to him.

The decision to go ahead with the effort was reached pretty soon after the re-election in '30. It was sort of a team effort. Farley, of course, crisscrossed the country, talking to potential delegates, state chairmen, people like that. Howe was looking at the weak points of the Hoover administration, wondering how the people's despair over the state of the economy would be translated vote-wise into active support for the Democratic candidate in '32.

No, I don't think they were ever positive that the nomination could be won. At the '32 convention, you had to have a two-thirds majority in order to get nominated, and I think they recognized that that was going to be a difficult accomplishment.

The strategy was in the hands of Howe and Farley; my brothers and I didn't really participate in the policymaking. For instance, we didn't negotiate any of the McAdoo-Garner-Hearst discussions at the convention that finally produced on the third ballot the necessary votes for the two-thirds majority. We were there, but in all honesty, we weren't the catalyst that helped produce the results. I think we ran errands and maybe filled in with some useful legwork, but it was the senior people who made the decisions. We were still pretty young and unpracticed in the political world.

That campaign was an interesting and exciting experience. But I don't think we felt the impact of it till much later, because I don't think we realized what a great change it was going to make in our lives. It was a tiring event, a strenuous experience, no question about that. I went on just about all the campaign trips, and my sister went on some and was very active. Elliott was pretty much out west, and my two younger brothers weren't quite as active because they were still in school.

On the campaign trip, everything was laid out very systematically. You knew what kind of cities you were going to be going through and what kind of interests the people in the area would generally have. You knew what people were going to be boarding the train—what candidates, state chairmen, congressmen or senators.

I'd get up and have breakfast around 7:30 A.M. Father would rarely make an appearance much before 9:00. Then my job was mostly to be with him and to help him walk out to the back end of the platform, to make sure that as he was drawing near the close of his remarks, the train was ready to start. You didn't want too much of a lull between the end of his speech and the time the train pulled out. Then I'd watch the newspapermen scramble from the end of the train, where they had been listening, to the middle, where the club car was located. They used to get a lot of exercise!

We'd go through the country, stopping at scheduled stops, which usually took place once an hour. Normally, you'd have a big noon occasion; depending on the size of the city, it might be a county fair, a ball game or a parade. There were evening meetings, too, and rallies, usually held indoors. I remember an agricultural area around Des Moines or St. Louis was picked as the place to make the anti-Prohibition speech in which my father came out for beer and the repeal of the 18th Amendment. There were, of course, special things, where there would be more formality and bigger crowds and a motorcade.

There was certainly no feeling that the election was a foregone conclusion. You've got to remember that there had not been a successful Democratic presidential campaign since '16. This was now '32, and there was a strong feeling that the country was basically Republican; therefore, you took nothing for granted at any time. And actually, if you look at the figures, there wasn't that much margin between the two candidates. It's true Mr. Hoover lost, but he probably suffered more *after* than during the election as a result of the continued depression.

I think Mother probably had greater adjustments to make than the rest of us. Of course, she had lived in Washington before, but being in the White House was an entirely different matter. I think adjusting her own activities and not just becoming a First Lady who lived in the White House was a traumatic experience for her. I don't think it meant so much to us children. My brothers were all going to college, so it didn't change their way of life very much; my sister was married and had her own plans, I was married and had my own plans, and Elliott had been out west for years and had always been a kind of free spirit, so I don't think it bothered him at all.

There isn't much question that Mother had made up her mind to be as helpful to Father as possible, and that the efforts she put into that were partly compensation for lack of a more emotional relationship that might have existed otherwise. Louis Howe helped prepare her to fulfill her role as a public figure who would constantly be making appearances before groups, generally by bolstering her confidence, which was never very strong. I think she found that she enjoyed these roles and got tremendously interested in her work. It gave her an opportunity to have a position of influence and to express her interest in the areas she was concerned about. It may have been compensation, yes, but you have to remember: It was also a wonderful thing for my father, because she became his legs. Her reporting was good; it always had an element of the humanistic touch and was invaluable to Father because it wasn't tinged with political considerations. There's no question that she had a great influence on him.

Yes, Mother grew to have a great affection for Louis Howe, and for his wife and children, owing to her great admiration for his contribution to what Father was trying to do.

It's hard to describe Louis; he was a very complex, difficult man in many ways. He smoked Sweet Caporal cigarettes when everybody else smoked Camels or something else. He burned incense in his room, which smelled to high heaven. He was a gnome of a man and he was sloppy, always had ash marks on his suit, and yet he had a way, a confidence about him that made you respect him. So, although he would sort of sink into the sofa and you'd hardly see him when he sat down, the minute he began to talk, you'd listen carefully.

He was one of the few people who would come in and argue with my father, saying, "By gosh, that was a stupid thing you did yesterday!" He had a very unusual relationship with Father and with our whole family. My grandmother couldn't stand it, but my mother, as I said, grew to have tremendous affection for him. He lived in the White House, only a few feet away from the rest of the family; he was a part of it and doubled as a constantly available confidant.

Howe didn't want to be an actor on the stage; he wanted to be active behind the scenes. He wanted to have a low profile. The less his name appeared, the happier he was. He really felt—and I think he was right—that if he kept a low profile, Father could always count on him to be available.

I think his death in '36 left a void nobody could fill in the same way. He was a very unusual, extraordinary fellow. Part of the reason I became Father's secretary was to give him someone he could talk with as closely as he did with Louis Howe, someone with whom he could "let his hair down." But nobody could fill the political vacuum Howe left. He had a tremendous instinct about political issues and groups that were important in the making of the coalition of the Democratic party. He would say, "We have to have a program on unemployment," and he would keep after it until it emerged. Then he knew where to go and would say, "Why don't you use——?" and it was they who got the credit historically. I've always felt that he should have gotten more credit than he did.

The "fireside chats"? My feeling has always been that a number of factors came into being, which were then used advantageously. One was that Father's voice was particularly suited to broadcasting, and when this was realized, and when it was also realized how many people could be reached by radio, this helped develop the basic concept of the chats and radio addresses. Then too, considering Father's polio problem, radio seemed suited to him, something he could do sitting down, because, unlike television, people wouldn't see him being helped in and out of his chair. It was just a thing that seemed to naturally fit into radio. Of course, it wasn't the only way. There were always the newspapers.

By and large, I think the press felt that they were treated fairly and honestly. There was a degree of mutual respect, which built up a certain camaraderie. I think the press thought they were included in the political goings-on almost from a family view, so that there was a closeness. Father enjoyed the members of the press, and my mother did, too. They were on a first-name basis with the press, their family problems were familiar, and yet it never detracted from their professionalism. I think were it not for this honesty, there never would have been that kind of rapport.

Also, credit has to be given to Steve Early, who was the press secretary and a rather unusual fellow in many ways. He was a strong-willed, strong-voiced fellow who had Father's confidence. He may have made a few mistakes down the line, but again he had the respect of the newspaper people. They felt that if he told them something, they could count on it as true, that they were not being fed stuff just for propaganda purposes.

As far as his polio was concerned, I think Father was mentally adjusted to handling it. This sounds odd to say, but it almost became an asset in many ways. While he couldn't move around freely, which must have been a very difficult thing to get used to, the polio gave him a reason for not being forced to go here or there. It thus gave him more time to study and confer than perhaps he might have had if he had never had polio. He came to think of the polio as you or I would of a lost limb. We'd learn to get along with the other one, and as you do that, you become less and less conscious of the one you lost. I don't think it bothered him consciously at all, in his relationships with people or in his ability to do things. I think the only aspect he felt there was no answer to was his fear of being caught in a fire.

I would say he was optimistic about the polio until around '38. He really felt he would eventually get the use of his legs back to the point where he would be able to walk a bit without the braces or with very much smaller ones. But I think that life got so much more difficult for him, he realized he couldn't be in Warm Springs enough to get the exercise he needed. So I think he just finally resigned himself to the fact that he was going to stay the way he was and that the main thing was to stay well as far as the rest of his body was concerned.

One of the things that stood Father in good stead and enabled him to relax at certain times with his sense of humor. He liked to tease people, particularly people like Henry Morgenthau, who he felt didn't have much of a sense of humor, or at least was very vulnerable to teasing.

I recall we were on board ship once, just sitting around, wondering what solution Edward VI would find regarding Mrs. Simpson. Everyone had a different idea. Some thought he would abdicate, which of course he did. Some thought that he would marry Mrs. Simpson but that she would be his morganatic wife. Others thought he would insist that she become the queen. As I remember, Father suggested that Pa Watson (his military aide) hold the stakes and that we all chip in $5 to the pool and then *he* (Father) would be the judge as to whose solution came out the nearest.

Another time, we were on a cruise down the Caribbean on a fishing trip and were approaching one of the islands, which had been a fort, just south of the Florida Keys. Now, Father knew that the army no longer controlled the old fort, that it had been turned over to the Department of the Interior, but he found out that Pa Watson didn't, so he let Pa Watson signal that the president would be coming ashore and they should render all proper courtesies, but no formalities of an official nature were to take place. As we approached the fort, Pa Watson was standing on the bridge to see that everything was in readiness, but he couldn't see anything, because there was only one old caretaker on the island. Pa got more and more worried, and finally he came down and said, "I don't think my message has gotten through. You think I'd better go ahead first and alert them to the fact that you would like to go ashore?" Father kept a perfectly straight face and said, "No, no, when we get there, we'll handle the situation." Well, when we got there and pulled up alongside, there was this old black man who came out in a dirty shirt and pants, and Father said, "Is he the commanding officer?" Pa Watson then realized that the Department of Interior was in control, and not the whole War Department!

As to my relationship with Father, when I became his secretary, it meant that I had as responsible a position as one could dream of, and from a very personal point of view, I could be with him, be closer to him, understand both his personal and official problems. It was something that was a tremendous experience for me to have.

There were three secretaries, and we had administrative duties. Mine were mostly to be the liaison between the government agencies that did not come under the supervision of a cabinet officer, like the Civilian Conservation Corps. And, of course, for me, there was always the worry that I would do something wrong or that would cause embarrassment to Father. Being a public official with a public responsibility and, at the same time, having that responsibility intertwined with the personal relationship I had with my father, which was closer than it had ever been, was a tremendous pressure. I remember, when Alva Johnson, in the *Saturday Evening Post,* began to attack me *personally* as a means of embarrassing Father, it was very annoying. The things I was accused of would really be classed as "conflict of interest" in today's atmosphere. I got a fellow to answer the Johnson articles in *Collier's,* making public all my income-tax returns, which nobody did in those days. I remember my father saying, "You know, it really isn't worth the effort. The defense never catches up with the accusation. You just get a tough skin and go about your job." I don't know whether I can blame having ulcers in '38 totally on those kinds of situations, but, as I said, it was a tremendous pressure.

As far as the third term goes, I feel strongly that when Father looked around and saw the alternatives in leadership to get the country ready for what he felt was inevitable, he felt that the survival of the country, as well as the life of a free people, were things that imposed on him an obligation to stay on the job. Of course he tried to make it appear as though he hadn't made up his mind, as though there was great question, because that was the wise political thing to do. And if he kept everyone guessing, he also kept people like Jim Farley from launching himself into a campaign, because Farley didn't really know whether Father would run again. That way my father kept all potential opposition eliminated and, at the same time, went right ahead and got things ready to go for the next campaign. I think it was tough on Jim Farley, and perhaps unfair, but nevertheless, from a political point of view, it was wise. I would have to say that Father knew exactly what he was doing.

Now, if the world situation hadn't been what it was, probably he wouldn't have felt that his political strength was such as to overcome the popular resistance to a third term. Under other circumstances, I don't think he would have run for a third term—not because he thought the job was done, but probably because he thought that, under normal circumstances, it wasn't a bad idea to have a two-term limitation.

Looking back on it all, I think I have a lot to be thankful for. True, I've always said there were disadvantages, but I think the advantages far outweigh them, and I feel I've been very fortunate to have a great life. I used to resent it when someone would say to me, "If you're only half as good as your father, I'll be satisfied with you as my congressman." I'd say, "Why do you expect me to be only half as good?" But now I look back at those experiences and say, "Look, it would have been great if I could have said that I have within me as many good qualities as he had, or as many fortunate qualities as he had for public service." But I know I don't have them. However, if I hadn't been born to my father and mother, maybe I would have had a much less interesting life.

The Roosevelt presidency, the Roosevelt family, Roosevelt and the Jews, Roosevelt and the third term—these are just a few subjects that have occupied many students of history for the past 30 years. Discussing them here is a woman who is not a student of the historical process but a part of it. Dorothy Rosenman, the widow of Judge Samuel Rosenman, one of FDR's closest friends and advisors, was herself intimate with the inner workings of both the Roosevelt administration and the Roosevelt family, a circumstance that lends added dimension to this memoir.

Mrs. Rosenman, a housing analyst, has served on a number of state and national housing commissions and is the author of one book on housing and co-author, with her late husband, of another, on five American Presidents. She lives in New York City.

DOROTHY ROSENMAN

It was fairly apparent that a Democrat would win in '32; therefore, everyone of any possibility sprang into the field. Al Smith figured that this was the time he could win, and he was the most prominent candidate. Others were Newton Baker, who had been secretary of war, William McAdoo, and John Nance Garner.

Roosevelt had been thinking of running for some time. He had always wanted my husband with him during crucial moments, so he got in touch with Sam to make sure he'd be with him the week before the nomination. Then, quite characteristically, he said, "Tell Dot"—he was the only one who called me "Dot"—"to come up the day the nominations begin." So I was there that first night of the nominations, when they lasted into the wee hours. We all were sort of half dozing around the little den, listening, and there was nothing. It didn't look as if he'd been nominated, and the next morning it was still uncertain, and Mama, the president's mother, and her sister-in-law, Mrs. Rosie Roosevelt, left for Hyde Park, because Mama just couldn't take it.

The next night at dinner in the private dining room, there were just the governor and Mrs. Roosevelt, Elliott, the governor's two secretaries, and Sam and me. Louis Howe and the others were in Chicago. The governor had sent a special wire to the convention, and during dinner he got a call (which he took at the table). When he'd hung up, Missy LeHand said, "You look like the cat that swallowed the canary." He didn't say anything, but it was at that time that Garner and McAdoo gave their votes to Roosevelt and sealed the nomination.

By the way, Mama was a great lady. I spent many an hour with her. She had great dignity, great curiosity and understanding, the same sort of curiosity and understanding her son had. She went along with him and never balked at any of his new ideas that were offensive to the people with whom she'd grown up. If you go to her house in Hyde Park, you'll see the little table in the dining room that was always expanded when Governor Roosevelt was there. That was because he would have all kinds of people there, people from all walks of life whom Mama had never met but to whom she was gracious.

Eleanor was so antagonistic in later years that this has left a wrong impression of her. You see, in the early days, Eleanor had no confidence in herself and was very dependent upon Mama. Then—I think it was after the Lucy Mercer thing, and also after nursing Franklin—she became more independent and assertive and stood on her own two feet. So for Mama and for Eleanor, there was complete and understandable change, this natural difference between the two. But as far as I'm concerned, Mama was a great human being.

Now, as for the stories about Missy LeHand: In the first place, I want to say that it was only Elliott who wrote those stories. The other children I talked with said there was absolutely nothing to them. I lived with them on the *Sequoia* and at Warm Springs, and at the Executive Mansion in Albany and I was frequently at the White House and never once did I see anything that suggested an intimate relationship and neither did Sam. And anyway, if anything *did* happen, it was their own affair.

I think that, like Mama, Missy will never have her due. She was a woman who came from very simple surroundings and had an innate sense of grace. She saw to it that Franklin had people around him with whom he could relax and enjoy life. Missy had great judgment—he could always talk with her—and she and Eleanor were close friends (which certainly wasn't true of Eleanor and Lucy Mercer).

I'd say that the relationship between Eleanor and her husband was a very good one. The only thing that wasn't good was that if she wanted something done and the timing for it wasn't right, she would nag about it. But that was the only thing. In those days, Eleanor was a great advantage to him, because she would travel all around and come home and tell Franklin what she had seen and heard, and he loved it when anybody would go places he couldn't and tell him what was happening.

The third term? People think that he was expecting to run all the time, but I know from my experience that it isn't true. In the spring of '40 we were invited to Hyde Park on a Saturday for lunch, and as we were finishing, a real-estate man was announced. The president was taking Sam and me to look at houses in the area. We had no intention of buying there, but because the president was planning to spend his time in Hyde Park and write, he wanted Sam near him. Now, he wouldn't have gone to all those lengths if he had really expected to run again.

And I remember how Sam used to come back from Washington and say, "He just definitely won't run." But I guess he finally realized that we were going to get into the war and that there was no one else with his experience. I think he would have much preferred to go back to the Hyde Park he loved.

As far as the war and anti-Semitism goes, I still get letters saying that Roosevelt was a Jew-hater, because of that boat incident in Havana [when 906 German Jewish refugees were refused entry into the U.S.]. Now, I don't know anything about that, but I do know that none of these people have taken into consideration the forces Roosevelt had to deal with. He was trying to get Hitler to change, but he was mistaken; he couldn't have gotten him to change. Nevertheless, he was trying; therefore, he didn't want to do anything that would be drastic and that would keep him from dealing with Hitler. That was the main objective, to deal with him. Insofar as Roosevelt was concerned, the man didn't have a bone or muscle of prejudice in his body. I'll tell you of an incident in our own family that illustrates the situation.

Sam brought over a cousin of his from Poland who had decided not to bring his family over until he'd got himself settled first. He was here a year or two when he got a letter from someone in Poland saying that he had better get his family out, because things were getting tougher. So Sam went to the State Department, and they said, "Well, we can get them out, but they'll have to come through Berlin, and Berlin will know there's someone very important in back of them. So we don't know what will happen once they get there. We could fly them out of Poland, but they'd still have to come out by way of Berlin." So we put it up to Sam's cousin, and he decided not to do anything. We never heard of any of them again. That's what I mean. They're very delicate decisions. You may guess right and you may guess wrong.

The president was really an extraordinary man. I remember, every time I would go into his presence, if I may put it that way, I would feel a glow. He was glad to see you, he was glad to see people.

The whole thing was a very broadening experience and a very delightful one, particularly since it wasn't just a question of working with someone. Rather, as Jimmy Roosevelt wrote when Sam died, "I feel as if a member of the family had died, because you and Sam had been members of the family." That was the relationship, and it was very lovely.

Few people held as wide a variety of sensitive government positions during the thirties (and forties) as Alger Hiss. Serving in the Works Progress Administration, the Department of Agriculture, on the Nye Committee and in the State Department, he was witness to and participant in much of the formation of America's prewar foreign and domestic policies. Indeed, it is Mr. Hiss's belief that it was because he was so integral a part of the New Deal era that he became the personification of it for Roosevelt's posthumous enemies.

Today Alger Hiss lives in New York City, where he works for a paper company and has a private law practice.

ALGER HISS

I think the extent, the depth, the fury of the depression caught most people of my generation by surprise and taught us, more than anything else, the importance of politics. When I graduated from college, I paid very little attention to such matters; those who were in politics seemed to me rather grubby and corrupt people. But while at law school, and then immediately after, the depression began and it indicated that things were not right with our country. The collapse, the whole economic picture was widespread devastation.

In New York, the Hoovervilles were on Riverside Drive, in Central Park, everywhere. One couldn't move around without seeing them. On Wall Street, where I worked, the famous men who were too proud to beg were selling apples for a nickel apiece. Once employed, sometimes running their own businesses, they got steadily more and more threadbare. The soup kitchens were much too inadequate.

In '33, after Roosevelt became president, I was invited by

Jerome Frank, the general counsel to the Agricultural Adjustment Administration, to come to Washington. I was not carried away by the idea, because I had only very recently come to the job I had in New York and was in the middle of a case. But a telegram from my former teacher, Felix Frankfurter, who had influenced me in law school, sparked my decision to go. The telegram read: "On basis national emergency, you must accept Jerome Frank's invitation."

Well, it was like a call to arms, being told that the nation was in danger. I think many of us who went down in those first few weeks thought of ourselves as civilian militia going down for the duration of a real emergency, as if we were going to war. Roosevelt, in his Inaugural Address, used the sacrifices of war as an analogy. I think we believed that in a few years the emergency would be met; I know I always expected to go back to civil law. Practically none of us were in the civil service. We were going to be there only a short time and certainly weren't interested in a government career as bureaucrats. Therefore, the furthest thing from our thoughts was retirement benefits at the end of lengthy bureaucratic lives, and all the people in government—the civil servants—recognized that in us.

We formed a good working relationship with the civil servants, who, we soon realized, were as much in favor of personal self-sacrifice and of working long hours for the public good as we were. Whereas we found them to be invaluable because of their knowledge and experience, many of them regarded us as reinforcements, to use the military analogy, since all their bright ideas, not unlike ours, had been refused by the Republicans. Now came people who would be sympathetic, and they were cheered up.

When the New Deal came in, we pretty much had a free hand. Things were not working out the way business leaders had been led to believe they would; so we had public support. Roosevelt said he would experiment and if one thing didn't work, he would try another. The whole thing was improvised. We had some success and we had some failures, but certainly the bitterness of the depression was for millions of people ameliorated by the benefits paid to the small farmers by the Works

Progress Administration, by the relief funds and by the Federal Emergency Relief Act. The whole spirit of the New Deal, of such people as Hopkins, Ickes and Miss Perkins, was so idealistic, so humanitarian, I think the public as a whole felt as it has not felt since—that the government cared about its duties and about individual citizens. There was a genuine sense of participation in the farm program where I worked. There were county committees set up for the farmers that not only handled a great deal of the administration—checking the acreage and so on—but also sent recommendations for improvements. It was an extraordinary period of public confidence in the government.

The incident with Senator "Cotton Ed" Smith occurred while I was with the Department of Agriculture in an official capacity. I helped draft the cotton contract for reducing cost on acreage and we had provided that some of the payments made in exchange for reduction of the acreage should go to tenant farmers when the farm involved had tenants as well as an owner. Senator Smith had expected that all those payments would go to him as the owner. He came to see me in my office and was very angry, because the payments, as we had drafted them, applied to him as well as to his tenants and were to be made directly to them. He said something to the effect, "You can't send checks to my niggers," as if they were hardly human and sending payments to them would be like sending them to his horses or mules, who wouldn't know how to handle checks. I explained that this was what was required under the statutes and that I assumed that my superiors accepted this view or they wouldn't have approved it in the first place. I was as polite to him as I could be, but I was in no way frightened. It wouldn't have meant much to me if I had been fired; I could have gone somewhere else or back to practicing law, and this was a matter of principle. It just seemed to me to be no big deal. The New Deal was the big deal.

I should add that a year later, when the purge over the cotton contracts occurred, not only Senator Smith but also the cotton producers and their representatives in Congress changed things. In the second cotton contracts, we insisted not only that the payments go to the tenants but also that the same number of tenants be kept on the farm. It wasn't going to help the country, and it wasn't going to be fair, if the owner, in order to get the payments himself, dismissed some of the tenants. This we lost out on.

During the purge, Jerome Frank, my boss, was asked to leave, as were Lee Pressman and a number of others, much to their shock, for they thought Secretary Wallace was supporting their position. But, when push came to shove, Wallace felt that there was too much opposition to his position in Congress and, in effect, backed down and jettisoned them. They became not scapegoats but something pretty close to it. Other people didn't resign but were fired only a few days later. Since I was then mostly on loan to the Nye Committee on the Munitions Industry as their counsel, I had no occasion to get involved in the purge. Nevertheless, my interest in the Department of Agriculture lessened from day to day, since the people I had worked with were gone, as were the idealism and innovation they had supplied.

The reason I had been sent to join the Nye Committee was that at least two of its members were on the Senate Agricultural Committee and so Secretary Wallace tried to do them a favor. The objectives of the former committee were twofold. The first was to limit the actual trade in arms. something that is of interest again today, though on a much broader scale. The arms trade was considered then, as now, immoral. It was also thought that the arms trade maximized the danger of warfare between small countries. We found, for example, that the salesmen for a great arms firm would do their best to convince the officials of, let's say, a Latin American country that a neighboring rival country had military designs against them, and would encourage them to buy. They would then run to the neighboring country and say, "Look, your rival has just bought this much."

I remember a particular letter that came out in the hearings, in which a local representative of one of the American munitions companies complained that the State Department was "fomenting peace." We had always thought of the word "fomenting" as being used for war, not for something desirable, like peace.

The committee's second objective was to take profit out of

war. In that effort, it was supported by the American Legion and other veteran associations, which felt that it was unfair for businessmen to make big profits while the individual soldier should be expected to give up a job, in which he might have been receiving increased pay, to run the risk of being injured or killed.

We explored that. We found that after every major American war, even the Civil War, there had been congressional investigations into the wastes, the corruption, etc. We found that war does tend to encourage and promote corruption, and certainly extravagance. After all, when the issue is possible defeat, money doesn't seem so important. On the other hand, a lot of people benefit corruptly and greedily at such a time. But we were unable to figure any way to take the profit out of war, and the reports I helped write said this just wasn't very likely.

Yes, I was approached by one of the duPont lawyers who told me that "whatever you're earning here, you could earn more," or something like, "Your talents would be useful." Certainly it was an indication that I could get a job and I suppose that they preferred that I got the job early, rather than after I'd continued. No, I never doubted that it was an attempt, as you put it, to "bribe me."

Senator Nye? He was a friendly man with Midwestern gusto, vigor and simplicity. Not terribly sophisticated, not very learned, easy to work with, and a man of a good deal of conscience. He came from the Dakotas, where isolationism was strong. Therefore he was a spokesman for what he grew up with. He felt that Europe was less noble, beautiful, and pure than the American Middle West. That part of Washington's Farewell Address that went "Do not get involved with evil designs of foreign powers" must have been inculcated in his own thinking. In that sense, of course, he was oversimplifying the view. I found him to be very pleasant, conscientious, and well-meaning, though he was not of the stature of Senator Vandenberg, nor did he have the intellectual quickness and charm of Senator Bone or the dignity of Senator Pope.

The committee came to be known primarily as the Neutrality Committee after the period I was with it—the isolationists believed in neutrality—and it began to recommend that the United States should, particularly if war broke out abroad, refuse to trade with either side. Although when the Spanish civil war broke out, the terms of that Neutrality Act, which were not meant to apply to a civil war, did seem to apply to Spain, and Nye was willing to revise his own act, because he did not think it was proper to refuse to ship to the Loyalist government, the legal government of Spain. I think the reason was that he came from a region where populism was strong and most populists are liberals. They cared about the little man, about the underdog and about decency. And Nye had some of this populist tradition himself.

In '36 I went into the State Department because of Francis Sayre, the assistant secretary in charge of the whole economic aspect of foreign affairs, including trade. I had been working in the Department of Justice to protect the trade agreements from attacks, alleging they were unconstitutional. When his assistant, John Dickey, left, Mr. Sayre asked me to come and work on trade agreements in the State Department and continue to supervise the litigation aspect, which I did.

Concerning the Spanish civil war, I would say that the State Department was short-sighted. It was difficult for them to sense what that war meant to Italy and Germany. They took more seriously than I think was warranted the efforts of the British and French in the nonintervention treaty. And the British, and the French, too, I think, were weak-kneed. They did not foresee that this would be the first victory of the Axis, that this was the beginning of World War II. Now, of course, the State Department had the excuse of simply trying to help the British and French carry out nonintervention. That's why the neutrality approach toward Spain was allowed to continue, even though Senator Nye was so sympathetic to the Loyalists, he was willing to work for removal of the embargo.

Regarding what was happening in Germany then, the State Department officials did not think that it was their duty to chastize the Germans. Any professional foreign office tends to feel that the domestic procedures of foreign countries are less important than the governmental relationships. From my own point of view, they were not aroused enough. I saw Nazism as a mortal danger. They tended to minimize the reports of what was going on in Germany. Of course, things were not as bad as they became later, but there was a tendency with State Department officials to say that the press was exaggerating what was happening there. The reason for my attitude was that I was more New Dealish than many people in the State Department. The New Dealers used to say that the writ of the New Deal ran everywhere except the State Department, which was more conservative and cautious. For example, if you look at the memoirs of George Kennan, who's almost exactly my twin in age, you'll see that he went immediately into the Foreign Service, and the depression seems to have made no impact on him. His only complaint about it was his expression of annoyance with Roosevelt that the expense accounts of Foreign Service officers should be reduced as an economy move. Well, this was not the way people of the New Deal felt. We felt that this was a time of great suffering for the American people and everybody should pitch in and try to help. But the State Department was basically conservative; they came from a different medium. They had been protected all their lives.

There were very few Jewish people in the State Department. Herbert Feis was the only one I can remember. I do not think the State Department favored Hitlerian anti-Semitism. The State Department's anti-Semitism may have been snobbish. That's possible. It was that kind of social fabric. But that's quite different from implying that the State Department as a whole or any official within it condoned the kind of brutality that Hitlerian anti-Semitism meant. Is that the idea of *While Six Million Died?* I think that idea's very exaggerated.

I also worked with Mr. Sayre in the Far Eastern Division. The American position was that Japan's aggression against China should not only not be rewarded, but that we should not continue our shipping of scrap iron to Japan, thereby facilitating Japan's access to the oil reserves of the Dutch East Indies, almost all of which were owned by American companies. So in order to free ourselves for discriminatory action—and it would take discriminatory action to say they could not get scrap iron but other countries could—we terminated the trade treaty guaranteeing equal practices.

I always believed that war with Germany was inevitable, but not at all with Japan. I was conscious early in '35, certainly in '36, that we had reached a prewar instead of a postwar era. I spoke to my college fraternity in Baltimore, saying that I thought war was coming in Europe. I saw that Hitler lived by expansionism, that this was the only way the Germany economy could keep going, and Hitler's power depended on his being a militarized and militaristic leader. So I thought we would be drawn into a war because Germany was strong and we would have to protect England and France, as we had in World War I.

I felt quite the contrary about Japan. We never considered them a match for us, and they weren't. I don't think anybody in the State Department had anticipated the attack on Pearl Harbor. It seemed suicidal when it happened. If anybody would have said it would happen, we would have discounted it.

No, I wouldn't say the New Deal ended abruptly with Pearl Harbor. It was under wraps, minimized in many respects, particularly those where it would come into conflict with business, as in wartime production. But those aspects of the New Deal that would facilitate production, such was the morale of labor, were treated with liberalism. I would say that the New Deal didn't really end until the cold war began and this was one of the functions of the cold war and of McCarthyism—to discredit the New Deal.

I never had any doubt as to the fact that McCarthyism was to attack Roosevelt indirectly. He was too popular, even when dead, to be attacked directly. If the New Deal could be attacked, if Yalta and his other policies could be attacked, then this was one way of removing the stigmata of Roosevelt from those policies. I've never doubted that one of the accomplishments of McCarthyism was to diminish sympathy for Roosevelt, sympathy for the New Deal, sympathy for the United Nations.

But the New Deal will be needed when conditions get bad again. It only came to light when the traditional business hierarchy of leadership couldn't function anymore. That time will come again. Another depression? I wouldn't go so far as to say that. But what I would say is that the serious malformations in the American economic and social structure with which the New Deal tried to deal, when not cured or corrected, were obviated by the war. The New Deal as an improvisation, as an experiment, never succeeded in making the major changes necessary to avoid the disasters of the depression. Had it been thoroughly successful, we wouldn't have had the kinds of things that went on in the '60s, when the rigidity of American culture came up against the demands for major changes. The New Deal represented the same kind of attempt to break out of the rigidity that had led to the depression and to the inability to change the format under which American culture had grown. I think the New Deal era and the '60s had some things in common, except that the New Deal was more restrained, had a better sense of history and was more practical. But the time will come again, I think, when those things will have to be combined for major changes, though I'm not sure that many people would agree with me.

The thirties career of Princeton economist J. Douglas Brown, as he recalls it here, neatly capsulizes the political highlights of that decade. First called to Washington in the days of President Hoover's cautious attempts to revive the economy, Brown continued in government service, becoming advisory council chairman of the first Social Security Advisory Board and, later, helping U.S. industry to prepare for war.

Dr. Brown was dean of the Industrial Relations Section of Princeton University from 1926 to 1955 and is today one of its faculty associates. In addition, he is provost and dean of the faculty emeritus of that university, author of a number of books and journal articles, and an advisor to government agencies.

J. DOUGLAS BROWN

The Hoover administration was getting terribly concerned in '30: The economic effects of the Crash were growing very rapidly, and Hoover was in over his head. He picked a man named Colonel Wood, who had formerly been police commissioner of the city of New York and was well-to-do in his own right, to form a committee on the economic crisis. Wood searched around immediately for people who knew something, and I was picked from Princeton.

So I went down to Washington and worked 14 hours a day. My area was to help get the employer to take care of unemployment himself, by having employees share work. The idea was that the employer, instead of holding one person full time and laying off another, would cut both people's hours in half, so that each would work two and a half days a week. We developed a nationwide radio campaign, in which we got the presidents of the great corporations on national radio for 15 minutes at prime time to make these appeals.

Then I developed a four-page outline of the steps needed to spread the work. The printing office printed about three million and sent them all over the country. Then we did another outline, which was called "Easy Steps." We also put advertisements in subways and all sorts of other places all over the country, and got good cooperation with our campaign slogan: "Spread the Work!"

Meanwhile, we did lots of other things, and one of them was the reason we got fired. We were trying to impress upon Hoover that he had to set up an administration immediately to get after unemployment. He had argued that the Red Cross was set up for this; but it was utterly impossible to think of the Red Cross in that context. We said that we must get public works started, and asked for $450 million. Hoover just thought we were radicals. He was willing to go up to only $150 million for public works for the whole country. Just think of it. It was a drop in the bucket compared with what we thought was needed. And he finally thought we had gone too far and let us go.

Hoover was in his hair-shirt period then. He had a man who reported to him up on the Hill, and as far as we could tell, that man would never tell Congress what we were recommending; he'd play it down. Take that $450 million. I don't think Hoover ever let that go to Congress. And since we were his advisors, we couldn't go out and announce some of these things.

He was a man in a hell of a hole, and it seemed as though he couldn't fully understand why. I remember, my wife and I went to a presidential reception, and after we went through the reception line to meet Hoover, my wife said, "I looked right in his face and it was perfectly gray. I mean, his whole demeanor was just that of a very tired, discouraged man." And I think that was true.

Sure the government and the American people were scared. This was the biggest thing that had hit them except for wars—and in wartime at least you knew what to do. You knew you had to get out production; you knew you had to train troops. But in the case of the depression, the American people were frustrated, because the vast majority didn't know what to do. They felt that it was up to the government, and the government wasn't operating. Those were desperate times—which is why Roosevelt got in by such a terrific landslide.

One of the other highlights of my career occurred in '37, when I became chairman of the Advisory Council on Social Security. The agreement to set up the council was made in May, and then it took time to pick all the people, so our first official meeting was held in November. At that meeting, Gerard Swope, the head of General Electric, moved that I be made chairman. I was scared to death, but there were no two ways about it; I was a public member, and they had to pick a public member to be chairman.

From that winter through the next year or so I worked awfully hard up at Princeton, because, as chairman, I brought all my work there. We organized and we organized. The American social-security system was not built out of elaborate research and statistics; it was an idea job—an idea whose time had come.

The interesting thing was the confidence the AFL crowd had in me; they'd do damn near anything. The CIO side was represented largely by Lee Pressman, their lawyer, and he and I got along all right. Then, over on the employers' side, I had Swope, Marion Folsom (an old friend) and four or five others, and in the public group there was Paul Douglas of Chicago, Bill Haber of Michigan and others, and we could all talk together. We thrashed everything out in two-day meetings, two-day meetings—and two-day meetings. Then we had an interim with just a small group, who naturally were the key people, and then we got the committee to move along.

The trick was to concentrate on two- or three-sentence recommendations for each part, which we would discuss and debate. Finally, we got unanimous agreement, except for a couple of very limited footnotes. And our recommendations have had influence ever since.

As to exactly what happened on the Advisory Council, consider "Exhibit A"—the first draft for the social-security plan for the United States of America. Two of us did it—the late Barbara Armstrong, professor of law at the University of California (a brilliant, extremely able woman, who had studied social insurance abroad), and I. We each made our own drafts, then exchanged them.

As to the legislation, we started with principles. What elements should the social legislation have? We first decided that there was a philosophy of a right of protection. Any citizen had this right. It wasn't that he had to become a pauper, that he had to get down on his hands and knees and pray; the right of protection, we felt, should be on a dignified basis. Another basic concept was prevention rather than alleviation after the effect, which meant the right for people to be secure. Individualization of benefit rights was another concept, meaning that a person shouldn't have to go down, stand in line and then have somebody say to him, "You get so much and the person behind you gets the same amount." He ought to hold his own ticket. Then we decided the program had to be compulsory, because the very people who needed it most would probably never come into it. Next we decided it had to be national in scope.

When we got to that point, it was very interesting, because we had a battle with the Unemployment Insurance Board. We used both very fundamental analysis and a statement of impossible conditions. I will always remember saying, "Now, look, a person moves to six, eight, ten states during his life. He's worked under each state's laws. When he retires, does he get checks from eight or ten states? Impossible. Some states are better financed than others. Are you going to give each state responsibility for setting up a reserve? Are you going to require every state to hire a bunch of actuaries? That person, after working in six or eight states, will say, 'Well, four of them came through and the others went busted.' You can't do that. There are relative costs. For example, states with a lot of older people, like Vermont and New Hampshire, have horrible costs compared with those of states where there are a bunch of young people."

Then there was the problem of financing. One of the stickiest things of all was to work with what we called the "funnel principle." That was the idea that we'd collect from everybody in the beginning and there'd be only a few receiving benefits. And what were we going to do with all that money until we needed it? You can't have a trillion-dollar reserve. You can't have too many billion-dollar reserves. It had to be on a current-flow basis. In other words, in the early stages, when we collected from many and paid few, we kept the in-flow down. Then, later, at the time we began to pay many, we needed the extra money from the federal government, so we gradually increased taxes as the benefit load increased. A private insurance company, you see, would have to have that big reserve, but the government of the United States can decide when it's going to make up for a reserve. Another way of putting it is: It's the only way you can do it. Now, that may sound awfully simple, but to get that across to a congressman, well . . .

Secretary Morgenthau was the last person to see it. One winter he said, "Brown, come down on Wednesdays and you can tutor me on this whole financing." He just couldn't see it. He tried to hold up the social-security program—or at least he told Roosevelt there ought not be any tax figures, because he wasn't sure it ought to be fully financed. It sounds so righteous to say "fully financed." But that's what I call "tradesman's economics." If you're a tradesman, dammit, you ought to have money in the bank to pay off your debt. If you're the federal government, you decide what your debts are yourself, as in this case, and then you decide when you're going to pay them.

As for Morgenthau, he was a lovely guy, but I must say he wasn't the brightest fellow on earth. You know why he was there? Among other things, he was a great friend of FDR's. When Roosevelt was struck with infantile paralysis, Mr. and Mrs. Morgenthau, whose estate was right next door to the Roosevelts' in Hyde Park, were tremendously friendly to him in his hour of depression. So he always was a close friend of Henry's. He had lunch with him every Monday.

Once, when Morgenthau was supposed to report to the president on social security, I wrote a précis across the top of the full statement for FDR to read. He looked over his glasses with a twinkle in his eyes and said, "This is yours, isn't it, Brown?" I said, "Yes, Mr. President," because he knew Henry wasn't going to give him the explanation.

Yes, we had resistance within the executive branch itself. Quite frankly, I don't think Edwin Witte, the executive director of the

Cabinet Committee on Economic Security, was too enthusiastic about old-age insurance. He was desperately anxious to get unemployment insurance through and thought old-age insurance would be a drag and, anyway, it was an impossible thing and so on. What happened was that Witte and Perkins drafted a speech for Roosevelt to give at a conference to show that he had a great interest in all this stuff, and what came out in that speech was that Roosevelt was for unemployment insurance, but maybe this was not the time for old-age insurance. We were just humiliated, utterly discouraged. We had friends in the press; Louis Stern, of *The New York Times,* and Max Stern, of the Scripps-Howard crowd, were both dismayed that the president should make such a terrible blunder.

When Roosevelt read the headlines in the papers that night, he called Perkins and bawled the hell out of her, and by all accounts, Perkins bawled the hell out of Witte. So Witte came into our office, where we were working away like beavers, and asked, "Have you any idea why the president got such bad press?" We thought that was pretty funny. But actually Roosevelt got a bad press because he had done the wrong thing, and after that he was much more alert to the public concern for old-age insurance.

Yes, we were always concerned about constitutionality. We even had a formula for the Social Security Act, which said that we believe the law is a living science and because of the importance of this kind of legislation, in time the courts will approve of it as a necessary thing for the welfare of the people of the United States. And the courts did do that. But you just had to do things ahead of the law. If you wait for the courts on these things, you're behind the ball. The needs of the American people work faster than the traditions of the court.

We had four of the best constitutional lawyers in the country. So with the old-age insurance, we gave the courts an out. We used the appropriation power for the benefits and then the taxing power for the contributions. That way, we designed the law so that each power was independent, except where both were used in the same records. And Cardozo, in his opinion, shot right over it: He said, "It's a matter of general welfare," which is exactly what we wanted. He upheld the whole business on the grounds that the Preamble to the Constitution says that it shall be the function of the United States government "to provide for the general welfare of its citizens." It was a 5-4 decision, so it wasn't easy, but it's still the law.

I'll tell about one other thing I did for the president. This was in the period of the "phony war." See, I got into World War II awfully early. The ambassador to Great Britain, a fellow named Winant, was an old friend of mine, and he was there right after Britain declared war on Germany. He saw the terrible time they had getting organized for war production, and when he came back in late March or early April of '40, he did everything he could to convince the president that he ought to get started on war production. And being a good friend of mine, he said, "You ought to get Doug Brown down here."

Well, I was called down to the White House, and the assignment Roosevelt gave me was utterly secret; I couldn't tell anybody. I was to make a survey and report back to him personally on air frames, air engines and machine tools; they were the tight things in England. So I put in thousands of miles, you know, young Princeton professor-academician. There was only one person who ever broke my front: the vice-president of U.S. Steel, John Stephens. He said, "What the hell are you asking me all these damn-fool questions for?" And we began planning the reopening of all the plants in the U.S. Steel Corporation step by step.

The last of the story is that when I went to report back, I asked Roosevelt's aide, General "Pa" Watson, "how do I tell the president a tremendous amount of stuff without his interrupting me?" (Roosevelt was such a wonderful conversationalist, and it was hard to keep him from going off on sidetracks.) "Brown," he said, "start talking and don't let the boss talk." So I went in there and talked a blue streak and I told him what the government would have to do.

Then in May, '41, I became the deputy to Sidney Hillman, then the associate director general of the Office of Production Management. I became the director of priorities. I got to Washington and had to develop a staff of 20-25 economists overnight. I had a grand group, and we all worked like the devil.

I had a whole industry branch. You see, the industry guys were conservative as hell about changing over to war production. We were fighting like hell to do what we had to do. We had to supply France to keep it from falling and supply Britain so it could defend itself. Therefore, war production was vital and was demanding far more than we could produce. The shortages were there, so we had to work on every priority order. I had cleared every priority order as to its effect on labor. That was really a time when the tail wagged the dog. We even had priority orders to release labor. Three months before Pearl Harbor, a man named Adams, who was head of the auto division, and I had the final job of convincing Knudsen, the president of General Motors, that the auto industry should change over to war production.

You see, we wanted that wonderful establishment of the auto industry—their managerial, subcontracting capacity. That industry was and is economically one of the most effective and elaborate organizations in the United States. We wanted the auto industry to grab tank contracts, all those other big contracts, and farm them out to others, because that was what they were used to doing. So first we cut them out of aluminum; then we cut them out of brass, then copper, then rubber, and they *still* found substitutes. Then we cut them out of making cars completely. And that was the real rub. Finally, at the time of their October inventory, they began to change over to wartime production.

My role in retrospect? Coming out of Princeton, I wasn't a political person; I was a consultant. I had been that for years. And you never know who needs help. You gain a certain reputation of being a policy economist, and when the government gets into trouble, they don't want an econometrician to give them a whole battery of statistics. That's the trouble down in Washington: They already have 999 statistics to one good policy idea. My job has always been to draw the policy impact. Even now—and I'm 79—I'm not stopping. In terms of social security, I am making sure that they revise the act in the right way.

In a country where maxims like "Strive and succeed" and "Live by the sweat of thy brow" sum up the national norm, the Great Depression resulted in a cruel paradox: Millions of people *were* striving and sweating—not to succeed but to survive—but, with the collapse of the economy, there were few opportunities for either. Particularly affected by this transformation of the American dream into the American nightmare were the elderly—people who had lost their savings and assets and who had even less means or opportunities of self-support than younger citizens.

In 1934 President Roosevelt established a cabinet Committee on Economic Security to deal with this problem, and in 1935 the first social-security bill was enacted. Since that time, as Wilbur Cohen points out, social security has expanded considerably, from being a single relief measure to being one of the government's largest programs.

Mr. Cohen has had a distinguished career both in government and in education. In addition to his service with the Committee on Economic Security, he was with the Social Security Administration from 1935 to 1956, and then served as secretary of the Department of Health, Education and Welfare under President Kennedy. Until his recent retirement, he had been affiliated with the University of Michigan—first as dean of the School of Social Work and then as dean of the School of Education.

WILBUR COHEN

When I went to Washington, the initial impact was one of enthusiasm and optimism, a looking forward to the future.

President Roosevelt had said he was going to work on a social-security program, and thousands of young people from colleges and universities all over the United States flocked to the capital. The capital from '34 to '38 was a veritable combination of university campuses, with a lot of young people taking advantage of the opportunity for a tremendously joyous, exciting experience. Of course, there were a lot of older people who had come, too, but being young myself, I fell in with a group of other young people, many of whom have remained my friends for 40 years. There was an *esprit de corps* and a *joie de vivre* growing out of that experience that is absolutely impossible to put into words. It's like buddies who have been in the war together who continue to feel a sense of comradeship even though their subsequent lives are different. Their common experience of crisis remains a vital, inspirational, integrative force for them. My recollection of the introduction of the social-security legislation into Congress in January, '35, is that this experience was all on the positive side.

At that time, Roosevelt was showing a leadership capacity and a forward movement and this gave a new sense of confidence to the American people. The things he had done in '33, '34 and now in '35 were all leading the American people to a new sense of confidence. Nothing had yet happened, but it was all in the direction of restoring faith in the system. By '32-'33, people had lost so much faith in our system of government, economics and leadership that almost anybody could have gotten the American people to support almost any kind of political structure. I think that President Roosevelt could have nationalized the banks, wiped out the states of the Union, and changed the legislative branch if he had wanted to. People were so discouraged and pessimistic from four or five years of unemployment, from the suffering they experienced when their life savings had been lost. These were people who had been self-supporting and respectable and who felt they had gone down the drain. Roosevelt restored their confidence in themselves and in the economic and political system. And when he set up the social-security proposals in November, '34, this was another step in the reaffirmation of their faith and belief in themselves and the system.

I became involved with the development and implementation of social security when Edwin E. Witte, the executive director of President Roosevelt's cabinet Committee on Economic Security, selected me as his research assistant in August, '34. While my salary was low—less than $1,500 a year—I had a responsible position, doing a lot of things that were normally beyond the responsibilities that would be given to a 21-year-old boy. During that time I initially worked 10 or 12 hours a day, 6 or 7 days a week. And since not much was known about social security, it was relatively easy, by studying foreign systems, workmen's compensation and so on, to learn a great deal in a short time.

Then, when the committee's work was done and the Social Security Board was established in August, '35, Mr. Altmeyer, head of the board, took me as his assistant.

The Townsend Plan? Oh, yes, in '35, while the legislation was still going through, I met with Dr. Townsend and had a number of conversations with him. He was deeply disturbed by the humiliation and degradation older people had had to face, living out of garbage cans and so on, and he was tremendously motivated to do something for them. He was really a courageous man; but he had been a medical doctor and knew nothing about economics or economic policy. He wanted to have a flat pension of $200 a month, which people at age 60 would be required to spend in 30 days.

There was a tremendous amount of political support for the Townsend Plan, support that grew from the discontent of the people. But it was viewed by economists and others as a kind of "funny-money" plan; you know, tax people, spend it and so on. It was a ridiculous proposal for that time and, if anything, wound up helping to get social security passed. How?

Well, from the time we met, we would discuss the differences, in point of view, between his plan and ours. I think his criticisms of our plan had a great deal of validity and vice versa. Out of those discussions came some changes in our plan as it went through Congress. Then too, the Townsend Plan, and also Huey Long's "Every Man a King" plan, was in the direction of saying that something had to be done to take care of poor and older people, to effect a fairer distribution of the income. And in this regard, both those plans were in essence guaranteed-income plans, of which social security was a variety. So we're talking about a political and social situation in which the idea of guaranteeing income to people was widely discussed. And there's no question that in this respect both the Townsend Plan and Huey Long's plan hastened the acceptance of this unusual role for the federal government.

Of course, once the Social Security Act was passed by Congress and approved by the president, we needed the money to get it started, and it was then that there was trouble with Senator Long. You see, he originally supported FDR, but quickly became disenchanted with him when he didn't agree with everything Long wanted. Senator Long was a radical man, and Roosevelt wasn't radical enough for him. Also, Long was convinced that he was the proper man to lead the country, as opposed to Roosevelt, who was a patrician and an easterner. So, while Long helped in pushing things through in '33 and '34, by '35 there was no real chance of their working out a *modus operandi*.

It was on the evening of August 23, 1935, that I remember going up to the Senate and listening to Senator Long filibuster the appropriations bill for social security to death. He recited a lot of recipes for Louisiana stews, attacked Roosevelt and so on, and when twelve o'clock came, he was still speaking. So all the legislation that was pending failed. But what Roosevelt then did was tell Harry Hopkins, who was head of the Federal Emergency Relief Administration, to put aside enough money to employ us through the next February, when Congress could come back and appropriate the funds.

Now, when it came time to establish the agency that would administer social security, another interesting thing happened. Instead of putting it in the Labor Department under Frances Perkins (where it was originally planned), Congress made it an independent board. To understand why, you must recall that at that time Miss Perkins was the first woman cabinet member, so naturally the men in Congress, who always thought of these jobs as being male-dominated, found it difficult to deal with her. Second, Miss Perkins was a very proper, very stern, almost puritanical woman, who obviously did not fit in with the conventional male wisdom. By making the Social Security Board an independent agency, the men in Congress showed their attitude toward her.

I happen to think that out of that little strife and discontent came a good decision for, being independent, the board was *not* beholden to the president or the secretary of labor, and so social security made a favorable initial impression with the people. This was important, because in the '36 election the Republicans, the automobile manufacturers and the Hearst press all opposed the social security program; but in their opposition, they made a big psychological mistake and wound up making the program acceptable to the workers.

What happened was that, first, Landon made the tremendous tactical error, in his Milwaukee speech of September, '36, of calling social security "a cruel hoax." This is not exactly what he meant. I can say this because I had extensive correspondence with Mr. Landon some years ago in which I tried to explain what I thought was a massive mistake on his part. Mr. Landon and his Republican advisors were for a social security program that would be called a "pay-as-you-go" program, paid out of general revenues, and they attempted to develop such a plan, one that I was opposed to but, nevertheless, thought had certain merit as an alternative. However, when that speech was written, it was turned over to what I would call some Madison Avenue writers, who didn't think it had enough jazz in it and therefore added the words "cruel hoax" and "fraud." The net effect of the speech was to make people think that Landon was opposed to *any* social security plan, which was not true.

Next, the automobile companies made a mistake by putting stuffers into their workers' checks, saying their wages were going to be cut 1 percent by social security. But the workers' attitude became, "Now, why would my employer be trying to protect my interests?" Therefore, their reaction was exactly the reverse: "Look, if I'm going to get a pay cut, there must be something worse for my employer," and so they didn't vote against Roosevelt in '36.

Finally, the Hearst press put a fake photo in their newspapers a day or two before the election, showing a man with a chain around his neck with his social security number and with a "supposed" employee personnel card that told his religion, his age and his union affiliation, all of which was unauthorized. Again, I think it was a case of being so far out that people didn't believe it. So, actually, what all this did was to crystallize social security support.

Looking back on this whole period, I think one of the great achievements of social security that has not been recognized is that it was the first economic, social and political liberation of all low-income people. Putting it another way, it was the first big step in the reduction of poverty in the United States. Roosevelt used the act not only to restore economic tranquility but also to give people who had been downtrodden and discriminated against an equality of treatment that had never been present before.

I should also point out that without social security, national health insurance wouldn't be possible. The national health insurance movement began right after the act was passed, when Mr. Altmeyer got Roosevelt to sign a letter, dated about ten days after the law's passage, setting up an interdepartmental committee to study national health insurance. The staff developed a plan that wound up in the Wagner bill of '39, the Wagner-Murray-Dingell bill of '43, and led ultimately to the adoption of Medicare in '65.

It's all very awesome, because social security is probably now at a point where it's spending nearly a hundred billion dollars a year, dispensing checks to 32 million people every month and collecting contributions from a hundred million people every year. It's the single biggest governmental program we've got, and I feel proud of having been a part of something that's brought a little more dignity into people's lives. I've seen what it's meant to my own family, to people around me, to people who write me about it. But my mind is mostly on how to improve it for the future, and I'm not so struck by the successes of the past to exclude the idea that we shouldn't be able to do more. And so, though I feel that the revolution Roosevelt, Altmeyer and Witte started has come a long way, I think that in the years left in this century we will build upon that edifice. A guaranteed annual income, a national health insurance system—these will be part of the American way of life. And I feel a sense of pride at having had the opportunity to work for that.

The symbol of the underpaid, overworked laborer in the thirties was not only the guy with the hard hat and the blue collar; it was also the man with the broken hoe and the idle plow. That the New Deal had a profound effect on him was not the result of efforts by Congress and the White House alone, but also by a secretary of agriculture whose influence was profound—Henry A. Wallace.

For Milton Eisenhower, Wallace was an "intriguing man," and his department a quagmire of "enormous inefficiencies" and political infighting. Yet, from this confusion would come lasting farm legislation, the result of the work of a brilliant political figure who is yet to be completely understood.

Dr. Eisenhower's governmental career as department administrator and presidential advisor began in President Hoover's administration and continued through President Nixon's. During those years, he also distinguished himself in academia, and now serves as president emeritus of Johns Hopkins University in Baltimore.

MILTON EISENHOWER

I was in the Department of Agriculture at the time. My recollection is that it required only a short time for the president, members of Congress and the cabinet to realize that it was one of the worst depressions the United States had ever experienced.

There was some delay in the president's determining what action might be taken to alleviate the situation. At first he felt that, by obtaining the collaboration of business leaders and others in restoring confidence in the country, the psychological change would bring about improvement. When it became evident that this would not be adequate, he took several actions.

First, he established the Reconstruction Finance Corporation to make loans to banks and other business enterprises. This was a good move, but it also engendered a rather disastrous situation. When the legislation was being debated in the House, under pressure by Sam Rayburn, Speaker of the House, an amendment was put into the bill that required all loans made by the RFC to be publicized. As a result, every time a bank received a loan, the publicity so frightened depositors that there were runs on the banks, contributing to the great bank crisis that occured just as Franklin Roosevelt became president.

Second, Hoover set up the Federal Farm Board with $345 million, which the board could lend to agricultural cooperatives to enable them to purchase commodities from the market at very low prices, put them in storage, and then sell them as prices rose. The problem was that prices kept falling despite the purchases by the cooperatives, and the $345 million was lost.

Interestingly, this became a campaign issue in the next election, when Franklin Roosevelt was the candidate of the Democrats and Hoover was renominated. FDR, running on a very conservative platform, was going to reduce federal expenditures as one means of checking the depression.

If it is true that the depression was in no way alleviated under Hoover, it is also true that no one, no matter who he was or what he did, could have changed the situation at that time. It was too late. In terms of background, education, and experience, Hoover was probably the best prepared man in all of American history to be president. He possessed everything except a magic wand.

Hoover was not a Franklin Roosevelt, or even a John Kennedy, in the ability to induce people to believe in themselves—in their capacity to solve the serious problem the nation then faced. He was a man filled with facts, knowledgeable, extremely intelligent, caring deeply about this country, but he did not have the spark that enabled him to inspire people. Therefore, I think his defeat in 1932 was inevitable. However, even FDR, a genius in communicating with the American people, would have been defeated had he taken office in 1929.

The "Bonus March?" I would say that there were mixed reactions about it. Certainly a great many veterans came to Washington to demand a bonus. I remember well their being quite prominent around the Department of Agriculture when I came to work early each morning. They did no damage; they were simply exercising their democratic right of using this as a method of communication to express their wishes. And so some of us—many of us—were bitterly opposed to and disappointed by the president's decision to have them removed from the capital. Apparently anticipating a riot, he directed General MacArthur, who was then Chief of Staff of the U.S. Army, to remove the Bonus Marchers. My recollection is that my brother was then his assistant; he was opposed to such military action but did not have a policy voice at that time. So MacArthur, looking very regal on horseback, personally led the armed forces, and the veterans were driven from the city.

The editorials at the time were mostly critical. I was one of those who felt rather deeply and bitterly about the situation. If the veterans had been destroying property, interfering with traffic and committing other offenses, there might have been some justification for some moderate action.

During the first Hundred Days, President Roosevelt almost electrified the people. He spoke before the Congress; he spoke frequently to the public through the talks called "fireside chats." It was his capacity to turn the people's despair to hope that resulted in a complete change of attitude throughout the nation, having nothing to do with politics.

He appointed as secretary of agriculture Henry A. Wallace, a son of a former secretary of agriculture. Mr. Wallace had been a scientist, a plant breeder and an economist. When he first came to Washington, he possessed intellectual integrity that was almost absolute. He was very nearly apolitical. I recall that the day after he took the oath of office, he called all of his top officers into a large room. At the time I was Director of Information, therefore one of the top directors in the department. He said that all his life he had admired the Department of

Agriculture for its great efficiency in administration, for the quality of its research, and for the vast educational program it carried out through the nationwide Extension Service, which had greatly increased the efficiency of American agriculture. But the time had come when the department had to take on economic-action programs in order to solve a problem that could be traced back to '18, when we became a creditor country. We had always been a debtor before then. And so, under his direction, there was quickly prepared the Agricultural Adjustment Act.

The act provided for reduction in agricultural production, the argument being that agriculture had to behave just as industry does: When demand declines, production should decline. And since there were then six million production units, one could not expect them to act in unison on their own; there had to be incentives. So the government would pay the farmers to reduce cotton production and so on in order to reduce price-depressing surpluses.

By 1935 the act was before the Supreme Court to determine its constitutionality. Late in '35 or early in '36, Wallace made this statement: "The greatest feature of this act is that the farmers know and are proud of the fact that they themselves are paying the bill to try to rectify the situation, which has long been a great problem to them. If this is ever eliminated by the court or by any other method, and as a consequence farmers dip into the treasury to finance their program, it not only will be immoral, but it will set loose in this country forces that no one can stop."

Well, in '36 the Supreme Court declared the act unconstitutional. It was amended and its name was changed to the "Agricultural Conservation Act," but, actually, there was very little difference. "Conservation" was just a Madison Avenue kind of term; the real objective was still to improve the income of the farmers by reducing production.

Then, in 1937, a strange thing happened. By that time we had three new action programs: the Agricultural Conservation Administration, with the Commodity Credit Corporation as a supplement costing about $7 billion a year; the Farm Security

Administration, originally headed by Rexford Tugwell, whose purpose was to help underprivileged farmers who lived on such acreages that they could not really be self-supporting to enlarge their farms; and the nationwide Soil Conservation Service, under Hugh Bennett, because there was no doubt that we were permitting the rich, productive topsoil of the nation to wash down the rivers to the oceans.

There came serious conflicts in these three programs. But then, if you set up a nationwide organization almost overnight with personnel who previously haven't worked in government, haven't been centrally trained, and don't have the same philosophy, there are found to be enormous inefficiencies. Specifically, the Agricultural Conservation Administration was paying farmers to take certain crops out of production, while the Farm Security Administration was paying them to put the same crops into production, because the people whose farms had been enlarged with the money given or loaned to them had to have cash income. And cash income would come from cotton in the South and wheat or corn in other areas. Further, the Soil Conservation Service, which went out militantly to stop the loss of the precious topsoil, used such methods as strip-cropping, terracing and proper rotation of crops, and in so doing, induced farmers to plant crops the Agricultural Conservation Administration was paying them to reduce.

So the secretary came to me. By this time we had become intimate friends, and I think there was mutual respect. He asked me to set up an agency to coordinate the programs in such a way as to eliminate the conflicts that were now being criticized in Congress and were reaching the president's desk.

Now, in each of the programs, while there were national standards, nonetheless those standards were adjustable at state, county and local levels where committees of farmers had a great deal to do with the policies and the programs. And so the agency I headed set up as its objective inducing each region, each county to obtain the maximum economic return from production, consistent with conservation of the soil and water. For this purpose we had soil and conservation surveys put in their hands, which gave them expert guidance. It was one attack that began to work pretty well.

Second, I became convinced that coordination of programs could not be achieved in Washington. An effort had to be made at the regional and local levels. The region for each of the programs was different from the other two. So I felt—and the secretary approved wholeheartedly—that we should bring about a restructuring so that all programs had coterminous regions, and that we would house the regional, state and local people in the same buildings. Well, the secretary realized that this was political dynamite, because whenever you try to move up an activity, you get complaints for economic reasons in various localities. Therefore, he said, "Do two things. First, go see the president and lay this out, show him what you're going to do." (By this time, I'd been doing quite a bit of work for Roosevelt.) "Second, make sure that the first new region you set up involves my state of Iowa, so it will prove that I'm unbiased and willing to take the political heat."

I went to the White House to show the president what the crazy-quilt pattern was and what we proposed to do. He was sympathetic because he was getting a lot of criticism, and after looking the plans over, he said to me, "Milton, that is a good idea. I'll get some political heat, too, but I'll support you."

We made the first move by establishing the regional headquarters for the north central states, as I remember, in Milwaukee, which moved the Soil Conservation Service from Des Moines, Secretary Wallace's home town. Receiving very little criticism for this, we then decided to make the next move in the southeastern states, and selected Atlanta as headquarters because of transportation and other reasons. Among the moves, we directed the transference of the regional office of the Soil Conservation Service from Spartansburg, South Carolina, to Atlanta. Well, about two weeks later, a call from the White House said, "The president wants to see you." I went over and entered the president's office.

With a sheepish look, he said, "Milton, I'm terribly sorry, but you just can't go ahead with those moves in the southeastern part of the country. Jimmy Byrnes is a man on whom I have to put great reliance. He is a senator, but I have higher responsibilities in mind for him. I need his help. I have on my desk a petition signed by 200,000 people opposing this move of the Soil

Conservation Service from Spartansburg to Atlanta."

I said, "Well, Mr. President, if you direct me to stop, of course I shall stop, no question about that. But you realize that if I stop this move, I can make no changes throughout the United States, because of the news of how political opposition in one instance stopped what is purely a constructive action."

He said, "Milton, I realize that, but as you get older, maybe you'll come to realize that sometimes one has responsibilities that transcend others and that one can't have his way in all affairs. I just have to say to you that the problems of this nation are such that I need Senator Byrnes and that transcends what I realize is constructive work on your part."

I said, "Very well, Mr. President. The whole thing will be discontinued at once."

Interestingly, this apparently increased his respect for me. You see, it was said in those days that only a relatively few people could talk to the president, that he did all the talking. One of the reasons I became well acquainted with him was that Henry Wallace was one of those the president wouldn't let talk, and so at first the secretary would take me with him to see the president; then he began sending me over alone. And once I got directly in touch with President Roosevelt and saw a great deal of him, I became fond of him as a human being. I think I may have had lunch with him as often as anybody else, which many times he would have served right at his desk. They'd bring in a big container of aluminum and put it beside him. He'd take a hot plate out of one drawer, some fish out of another, and put them before you. He found that he could relax, and we would have wonderful two-way conversations about many things. He was good at humor, always had good stories to tell. But I knew that he was earnest, that he cared; always he had serious business on his mind.

About Henry Wallace—I don't fully understand what I'm going to say to you, but it's been told to me by so many people, it has to be true. He was an intriguing person. First of all, he was a vegetarian and believed in keeping physically fit. He'd take long walks. He threw shillelaghs all the time; he had a great collection of them. I'll never forget the day he wanted to urge me to become the coordinator. He said, "Let's have lunch." I said, "Fine." He said, "Let's walk over to the Washington Monument." When we got there, he said, "Let's walk up." I staggered up. Then: "Let's walk down," he said. I staggered down. Then we headed for what we called the south building of the Department of Agriculture, and the private dining room, which was on the eight floor. He said, "Let's walk up." Well, I was so tired by the time I got there, I don't remember what we ate, but that's when he asked me to become coordinator.

He would develop friendships, very close friendships, and would be profoundly affected by the judgments of others, which caused him to make some bad decisions. He was close to an economist who induced him to make a proposal that all foreign shipments of agricultural commodities abroad be carried in foreign bottoms which, he pointed out, would cost less than shipping in American bottoms. When he issued a press release advocating this, all of American labor descended upon him, because he had forgotten about the Seamen's Act, which fixed the wages on American ships that were about two or three times higher than those on other ships. He had to back down and withdraw.

Then, when he became a candidate for the presidency, he became associated with the extreme left-wing elements of our society, and here was a different Wallace. Suddenly gone was the intellectual integrity. But when he returned to private life, he reverted, almost miraculously, to the position he first held when he came to Washington in 1933.

The National Recovery Administration (NRA) did two significant things: It set the first minimum standards for hours and wages; and, in the words of Ralph Helstein, one of its state administrators, it showed that "government really cared." Today wages and hours are largely union matters, while the government's "caring" image is a pre-1970s memory. But the fact that the NRA *did* have that kind of impact is a testimony to the importance of the political legacy of the thirties.

Following his work with the NRA, Helstein became one of the founders of the Young Democrats of America and then of the Farmer Labor Party of Minnesota. As a lawyer, he was hired by the United Packinghouse Workers Union to be their legal counsel and was subsequently elected their international president. He recently retired from that office and now serves as international president emeritus. Mr. Helstein lives in Chicago.

RALPH HELSTEIN

I started working for the NRA in '34 when I was a senior in law school. I was due to graduate in June, but they wouldn't hold the job, so I had to take it and go to school. I finally found myself administering the codes of fair competition as they related to the labor section. I was the labor compliance officer for the state [Minnesota].

The NRA had been running only a few months then, and I was carried away, because here was an opportunity to bring justice and practice mercy. You know, people were earning such a pittance; those who were lucky enough to have jobs were making 25¢, 30¢ an hour. And this was never on the hourly basis. They'd have to work 50 hours and then they'd get paid $12, $15 a week; it would vary.

Most codes that were adopted provided for minimum wages.

Generally, the flat minimum was 30¢ an hour, but there were variations, depending on the particular code. I was much too naive in those days to realize that American industry was willing to agree to certain minimum wage requirements because they could break down the rules against monopoly and restraint of trade. And, of course, had the NRA remained, it clearly would have undermined the whole antitrust, antimonopoly provisions of American labor law.

I had all kinds of interesting experiences while I was with the NRA. One concerned an operation in Minneapolis called the Snider Drug Company. It had started out as a little tobacco store run by a man known as "Mugsy." He was quite a character—brought up on the wrong side of the tracks, in the Jewish ghetto of those days, never had any formal education, probably an immigrant. He had difficulty reading and writing, but he had an absolutely incredible capacity for telling you every piece of stock in his inventory. He knew every piece of merchandise, knew its value, and could tell you his daily sales. He could calculate these things in his head before most people could get them on an adding machine. By the time I met him, he owned a whole bunch of stores. Eventually, he became the largest drug store operator in Minneapolis.

As I've indicated, my main function was to enforce labor provisions of the codes of fair competition. And what would happen is that we would get a complaint from somebody that he was paid such and such and wasn't that a violation of the code—"the Blue Eagle," as some people would refer to it. And we'd check and maybe find that it was, in which case we'd insist that the employer pay him back wages, and in most cases he did. Of course, there were some cases where we had to threaten to take away the Blue Eagle and we did. But then, some employers didn't mind having the Blue Eagle removed, since they were big enough not to have to worry about nonsense of that character. At any rate, in Mugsy's case, we established a relationship over a period of time. And it got so I would call and say, "Mugsy, I've got a complaint. This guy called and said he was paid ——." So Mugsy'd say to me, "Well, do I owe him?" And I'd say, "Well, if his claim is correct . . ." And he'd say, "Look, I don't care if his claim is correct or not, so what difference does it make if I give him a few dollars? Tell me, should I pay it?" I figured that if I was going to redistribute a bit of wealth anywhere, it was worth it. So I'd say, "Sure, pay it." Unless, of course, there was something that gave me pause in the complaint. Finally, it got so I just had to call him; he didn't even bother to come to the office after the first few times.

Every once in a while, though, you'd come across a character who was going to chisel every chance he had, and so many times there were complaints that were not properly filed. An individual would be trying to pull something and using us to do it, and I'm sure that we often permitted ourselves to be used. But what was it we were trying to be careful of? It amounted to so little in the scheme of things that my attitude was, if there was a doubt I couldn't resolve on its merits, I would be disposed to resolve it in favor of the guy who needed it, not the one who had it.

We were able to create an atmosphere in which people quit fooling around with the minimum wages a code provided. Generally, I think of it as 40¢ an hour, but I may be confusing it with the first Wages and Hours Law, which went into effect in '38. In a more important sense, this wage was for a fixed number of hours, so it forced the keeping of records that showed how many hours a man worked and got him paid for those hours. Most codes began to make provisions for overtime rates. In this respect, then, we were able to make an impact. People really felt that government cared, that it did make a difference how they lived and how they managed.

I don't know of a single case of the NRA's having to enforce the minimum-wage provisions through the courts. The problem was that they were not about to do anything about enforcing the right of people to join unions. By the time the Schechter decision [*Schecter Poultry Corp.* v. *U.S.*, in which the Supreme Court ruled that the NRA was unconstitutional] came around, I had a feeling that it was probably just as well.

After the Schechter decision, I was asked to come to Washington for the purpose of making a general evaluation of what had gone on during this period. After I'd lived in Washington for seven or eight months, I began to see things through different eyes. I had very grave doubts about centralizing everything there. I felt removed from what went on and realized that Washington was literally removed; everything was second-hand. But Washington did give me an understanding of the skills or art of manipulation. I learned what people did when they wanted to get a job in government, the political game. How you went to see this man and that man and how terribly important it was to find out who the cut-off guy was for a job in a particular agency—"cut-off guy" being a slang expression that began on Coney Island. It meant the man who called the shots. He was in a key spot. He might not make the decisions, but he knew how to go about influencing the people who did. Harry Hopkins was the key guy in that period when Roosevelt decided he was opening up. So I learned those skills. I also learned that there was generally a gap between the word and the deed, and that you could use all kinds of rhetoric and get people to respond to the rhetoric, but if you never really acted on it . . .

It is very difficult for someone who didn't live through it to be able to capture the spirit of that age, or for a person who did live through it to do justice in projecting it. For me, this is over 40 years now. It was a multicolored tapestry. There was an excitement about it: You could dream about anything you wanted and have the feeling that somebody was sitting somewhere in Washington and dreaming about the same thing. It was really a glory road in lots of ways, because nothing from the past could tie you down. You were on a road that seemed to have an endless horizon. I *knew* because I'd met the people who had all kinds of ideas about how to build a better society. Some of them were people of importance: Harry Hopkins, constantly pressing, searching; Hubert Humphrey—I first came in contact with him when he was speaking for the workers' education program of the WPA; Wagner; Black; George Norris, a great man, a man of real vision, quality, intellectual quality, who could be tough-minded as hell on an issue but who also had a great gentleness. It was an atmosphere, a spirit of intellectual opening, a climate of creation. I was in the House the day John Lewis walked in and denounced John Nance Garner as a whiskey-drinking, poker-playing, evil old man. That sort of thing stands out in one's mind, too.

Essentially, the New Deal was a reform movement, and one of

the products of its being reformist and our being taken in by it was that we had a very romantic, almost Rousseau-like notion of the goodness of man, the noble savage. We assumed that if we took care of his physical needs and gave him more than that in the process, that would take care of the kind of man he was going to become. You know, the *Talmud* says, "Where there is no bread, there is no learning." Roosevelt had another way of saying that: "Necessitous men can't be free men." But, while it's true that necessitous men can't be free men, and that where there is no food, there is no learning, the fact that there *is* food doesn't guarantee that there will be learning and that you'll have free souls. However, we didn't realize this. We thought it was almost an automatic axiom. But you began to sense that the spirit of reform was running out—at least I did, in '37, with the Neutrality Act, which resulted in no support for Spain. That Spanish thing had a great deal to do with the disillusionment. It required a fundamental negation of all the things the New Deal stood for.

And then finally—I guess it was at the end of his second term—Roosevelt was asked about the New Deal, and he said, "Oh, Dr. New Deal is dead; it's Dr. Win the War now." Essentially, that gave rise to a whole new world. The reality became that as you got into the war business, things began: The economy spurted, jobs were there, everybody wanted more, everybody wanted his piece, everything was cost plus.

I think that when the opportunity presents itself, you should take advantage of it. The American people in '33-'34 were ready for fundamental changes in their system. They would have accepted redistribution of wealth, redistribution of power, modernization of the political system. They would have accepted those changes, but those changes weren't forthcoming, because no one in leadership was prepared to push for them.

As time went on, there were all kinds of blandishments and it became harder and harder to reject them. And once it became harder to reject them, fewer and fewer people were willing to fight. Once you're back at the old stand and it's working, you can't recapture something in the same form; you have to find something new that will respond to the needs of that time.

Though we associate such phenomena as black political power, affirmative action and quota systems with the sixties and seventies, they were already extant in the New Deal era. For, as Robert C. Weaver, then a Department of the Interior officer, explains, by utilizing newly established programs and key executive contacts, he and other "black cabinet" members made significant gains for American blacks—gains that were unprecedented in their political and economic impact and would affect generations to come.

In addition to serving as Advisor on Negro Affairs in the Interior Department, Mr. Weaver held a variety of other government positions. In 1966 he was appointed Secretary of Housing and Urban Development, the first black to hold a cabinet-level post.

ROBERT C. WEAVER

Clark Foreman had been appointed Advisor on Negro Affairs in the Department of the Interior. He was a dollar-a-year man, with the Rosenwald Fund paying his salary. Although he was a liberal southerner, he was under great attack from blacks, because, number one, they didn't want whites in the Rosenwald Fund deciding who would hold the position, and, number two, they didn't want a white person holding it. Clark then got in touch with me to ask if I would become the Associate Advisor on Negro Affairs, which I did in November, '33. Then, after about a year, he resigned for another job and I became the advisor. That was how I got involved in the New Deal.

When I became advisor, I gave recommendations to Ickes about what policies should be adopted to encourage the participation of blacks equitably in the New Deal programs, most of which were in the Department of the Interior.

You see, the New Deal was not designed to benefit blacks but the men who were lowest on the totem pole. So I had to recognize that the problem of black Americans was an accentuation of the problem of *all* Americans. There were extremely high rates of unemployment and they were much higher among blacks than whites, so that the job was the primary issue. What this meant was that if the New Deal was equitably administered, there would be a wider participation of blacks, not as blacks *per se* but as *people* covered by the programs. Therefore, I had a function not only of trying to get close to equal participation in the programs for blacks but also of maintaining their morale so that they would participate. Subsequently, one of my functions was to help get the administration re-elected, but in the beginning that was a secondary interest of mine.

We were concerned primarily with interpreting to black Americans what these programs were. I wrote a series of articles, did a lot of public speaking, went to meetings urging blacks to participate. I also handled complaints where blacks were turned down or got unfair treatment. It was not a situation where there was no discrimination, but we minimized it, reduced it materially, and made blacks feel that they were getting something out of the New Deal.

After a while I became particularly active in the Public Works Administration Division of Housing, and asked Mr. Ickes if I could become a consultant to it. He said, "What do you know about housing, young man?" (I was only 25 at the time.) I said, "Very little." He said, "You'll do fine. The rest of them don't know a damn thing about it, either."

Ickes? He was a very gruff person. I can tell you another story about him. At that time, all the departments had black and white cafeterias; they had been that way since Wilson's administration. A friend of mine, Bill Hastie, and I decided we were not going to accept that, and we went to the Department of the Interior white cafeteria. We tossed a coin to see who would pay for lunch; I lost and had to pay. The cashier looked at me as if ten years had been taken off her life and said, "Do you work here?" I said, "Yes." She said, "Do you mind giving me your name?" I said, "Certainly. Do you mind giving me *your* name?" Well, for about five or ten seconds she couldn't quite remember it, but then she gave it to me. I got out a little book, wrote it down, then told her our names and that we were both employees of the Department of the Interior.

We didn't think much of the incident, but the grapevine reported back to me within 20 minutes that a group of ladies had gone to see Mr. Ickes about it. Now, he had just found somebody stealing some federal money and so he was not in a good mood. He said, "Good afternoon, ladies. What can I do for you?" They said, "Mr. Secretary, Negroes are eating in the cafeteria." He kept on working, and one of the women said, "What are you going to do about it, Mr. Secretary?" He said, "Not a damn thing, ladies!" And that was the end of that. Many people were quite frightened of him, but he was a very decent human being and a good administrator.

At any rate, my concern in housing was primarily with getting equitable participation for blacks as construction workers by working out a particular technique with labor unions. You see, Ickes had issued an order that there be no discrimination in employment in public works. Well, that had been done by Ogden Mills earlier under the Hoover administration, but it was nothing but a paper statement. In large construction, most of the labor was union labor, and most of the unions either excluded Negroes from membership or had them in separate locals where they were *de facto* kept out of jobs. So I worked out an agreement with the Department of Labor, largely through Isador Lubin, whereby we would get membership or work permits for blacks on PWA jobs and housing jobs in particular. I then worked with William Hastings, who was at that time assistant solicitor with the Department of the Interior, a *prima facie* formula for measuring discrimination. This formula said, in effect, that unless X percent of the skilled-labor payroll, Y percent of the semiskilled payroll and Z percent of the unskilled payroll was paid to blacks, it was *prima facie* evidence of discrimination. This became the first affirmative action in the federal government.

My office then reviewed every single payroll each month to identify the race of the people to see that the program was being carried out. The resident engineers and the federal employees were charged with the responsibility of seeing that this was done. There were two reasons we took the payroll figures: First, I was afraid that if we just took the actual numbers of people, they would hire one guy today and fire him tomorrow; second, by taking the figures we did, we could get a larger proportion of blacks in those trades—plastering, cement finishing, bricklaying, sometimes carpentry—in which they were concentrated.

I was also concerned with seeing that Negroes were put on the advisory committees, which were the local groups that were sponsoring the programs. So I was in charge of laying the groundwork and setting up the procedures for getting people into the management aspects, where we had blacks as managers from the very start. This was something particularly new in the South. We also got Negro architects to design the housing projects, which was also unheard of in those days, especially in the South. In all, we got about a third of the projects for nonwhite housing.

Another thing I did was to set up a survey of Negro white-collar and skilled workers. The purpose of it was twofold: First, we wanted to find out what happened to trained blacks in white-collar, skilled and trained occupations; second, we wanted to resolve the terrible problem we were having getting Negroes employment in research projects in the WPA. Even where blacks were employed, it was at the state level, where they usually were paid lower wages than whites. This survey was set up as a federal project, and, as administrator, I was able to get equal pay and hire about 200 professional people, many of whom became quite prominent as time went on. All told, I employed about 1,500 people in about 31 states, and we got two volumes published from the research—a very interesting aspect of that job.

In addition, there were millions of routine matters that came up in my work: preparing court drafts, preparing speeches for the secretary, sometimes even for the president, and seeing what happened to them afterward, constantly pressing the administration to go further in the matter of equality.

Opposition to my work came from three sides. Blacks felt that not enough was being done and criticized me for being without power, then criticized me for not using the power they said I didn't have. Whites, particularly southern whites, objected to Negroes being in any type of government job, particularly in an executive position, which was the result of my efforts to break down discrimination within public works. Then I was also resented in some parts of government, as was the whole of the PWA, for moving too fast. I was encouraging blacks to get out of the kitchen, to refuse to work for so little money, and, of course, I was going to cause riots and that sort of thing.

I dealt with congressional opposition in two ways. First of all, I was a behind-the-scenes operator, not a flamboyant, charismatic guy who went out, made big speeches and attracted a great deal of attention. This stood me in good stead, because many congressmen didn't know what I was doing until after it had been done. I was in a position where I could go to the person in charge and say, "This is the policy," and if he didn't do it, I could go to Ickes or Strauss to see that the person followed the policy. You see, in a job where you don't have a line of authority, where you don't have a political base and backing, you really don't have clout. So you have to have the support of someone at the top, and I think it was Ickes's and Strauss's confidence in me, their support and their agreement with what I was trying to do, that made it possible.

There was also the so-called black cabinet, which Mrs. Mary McLeod Bethune, of the National Youth Administration, had organized and in which I became more or less the secretariat. She had had a long-time friendship with Mrs. Roosevelt and had access to her whenever she needed it, and occasionally to the president, too. She used to say, "I have the contacts. You boys get out there and get the program," which we did. When we had problems, she went to Mrs. Roosevelt, who then called up the head of the department or agency and had the problem straightened out. For instance, when the Sojourner Truth Housing Project was built in Detroit, it was built in a Negro area; but the whites wanted it. The black cabinet took it to Mrs. Roosevelt, who got it changed for Negro occupancy. One of the congressmen on the floor said, "Who are these Negro advisors? Where do they get their power? Why do they get to decide what's going to be the racial occupancy of these projects? I object to this." But we won the issue.

My contacts with the president were few and far between. I don't think he would have known me if I had walked into his office. On the other hand, my contacts with Mrs. Roosevelt were very close. As I said, it was through her that most of the things done in this area got done. She would pick up the phone and call this one, that one or the other one. I don't know whether she cleared it with the president, but I have the feeling that he said, "You go ahead and do as much as you can do, but don't get me involved in it."

Roosevelt himself did not take a firm position on any of this. I think his attitude was, "Well, if we can give these people a fair break, fine. But I'm not going to endanger the administration or my larger programs, nor am I going to fight segregation in the South." He accepted the Warm Springs, Georgia, pattern. He was not a racist, but he was certainly no burning proponent in this area, either.

Looking back, I feel that I worked very hard and got some satisfaction. Sometimes it was an enjoyable process and sometimes it wasn't. But when I came back to Washington in 1961, I think it all stood me in good stead.

Again and again the themes of creativity and invention echo through the New Deal era. And nowhere is this more apparent than with the Federal Theater Project. For though it had a limited budget, it emerged as an impoverished nation's answer to a costly legitimate theater, becoming a center of dramatic originality, and even controversy, while also helping to launch the careers of future theatrical greats.

Louis Simon was director of both the New Jersey and New York Federal Theater projects and is presently the executive director of Actors' Fund in New York.

LOUIS SIMON

The Crash occurred exactly three weeks after I started on my first job. I think everybody really expected that there would be a recovery and did not treat the situation seriously until the late spring of '30, when they realized that the whole economic system of the country was vastly upset. Thus, while the famous headline in *Variety,* "Wall Street Lays an Egg," had created sympathy, initially it was almost humorous, and that was indicative of the times.

There were interesting sidelights about the Crash—for example, wealthy stockbrokers who were keeping showgirls suddenly had to drop them. I remember getting into a taxi in New York two days after the October crash and the driver, who had just come from the Vanderbilt Hotel, saying, "Jeez, you should've seen the gals checking out of there. They were checking out like flies!"

In 1930 I wanted to get a permanent job at the Theater Guild, where I was a stage manager working from show to show, but they were beginning to retrench. I'd always had a theory that if you wanted to be in the theater, you either had to be a genius or have an outside income. And since I wasn't a genius, and since my family had lost what money it had in the extended depression, I thought it was time to get out of the theater. But, as it happened, I managed to get enough theater jobs to keep going.

About '34 I landed a job as supervisor of the New Jersey Federal Theater Project. I got $250 a month, while the actors got $24.60 a week. These were considered prize jobs, because the normal relief client doing day labor got about $18 a week. These were all people who were on relief but who had a history of being professionals. You see, in the Federal Theater, 90 percent of your project, which included the technical people, had to be chosen from relief clients. With the other 10 percent, you could engage people who were not on relief to play leads or those parts you had to justify as not being able to cast with the relief clients.

In the beginning, there was a great division of opinion. Many New York producers and actors were vehemently against using nonprofessionals. They felt that it was a leveling down. But we weren't looking for excellence; we were looking for a social solution to taking care of people who otherwise hadn't been able to make it, so to speak. It wasn't until people like John Houseman, Orson Welles, Elmer Rice and Edward Goodman began to do things that were innovative and high level, and latent talent began to come forth, that the Federal Theater began to get notice from the critics and public.

There was a gradual change, during which educational institutions, for instance, were very glad to have the classics brought to high school auditoriums. And there was an enormous untapped audience that could pay 50¢ to $1.00 for a seat, while in those days a Broadway play was about $3.50 and a musical about $4.00. So here were people who now had access to the theater who hadn't had it before. And many of the plays were done in the schools for children particularly and there was no admission charge for them.

In New Jersey, for example, we had a Children's Theater Project, which was cosponsored by the Young Men's Hebrew Association, so we did *The Emperor's New Clothes, Treasure Island* and a great number of other plays that were particularly suited for children.

In New York it was different, because you had a very theater-oriented audience. Tickets to the plays that got good reviews were so low priced and became very hard to come by. Yes, Brooks Atkinson took the Federal Theater very seriously, as did the other newspaper critics. They came to the Federal Theater productions just as they went to a Gilbert Miller or Theater Guild opening. Things like the *Negro Macbeth, Horse Eats Hat* and the *Living Newspaper* were sell-out performances for quite a number of weeks. Another big hit was *Murder in the Cathedral* at Eddie Goodman's Theater. You see, in New York, the owners of the Maxine Elliot Theater and the Biltmore Theater, where they had the *Living Newspaper,* were very glad to rent these theaters to the government, because they were getting revenue from their real estate at a time when commercial productions were very much narrowed down from what they had been in the late '20s.

Yes, the *Living Newspaper* did involve some controversy—for example, the time they wrote it on the subject of Ethiopia just when Mussolini was going in and taking over. The Italian embassy put in a protest, and the State Department said they would have to tell Elmer Rice there were things that were offensive to the Italian government and they would have to be cut. Rice said, "Look, if we're going to have this kind of censorship by the government, I'm quitting," and he resigned, creating sensational headlines.

There were pros and cons in the reactions. Some people felt that, because of the high visibility of things like the *Living Newspaper,* the Federal Theater was interfering with the normal diplomatic processes of government reserved for the State Department. Others felt that we had a free press in this country and therefore had a right to speak out. If *The New York Times* came out castigating what Mr. Mussolini was doing in Ethiopia, the argument was that the government had no control over the privately owned press. But now it posed a very difficult problem, because the situation involved a government subsidy. And this, of course, was the argument the people who were totally opposed to the Federal Theater used—that in any expression of opinion—and the theater is an expression of opinion in certain types of plays—the government should not be involved.

Now, I must say that when it came to the writers on the project criticizing our *own* government, while there was uneasiness in Washington about it, there was never a direct intervention, with the exception of the Marc Blitzstein musical play *The Cradle Will Rock*. And that wasn't a direct intervention; it was the government's way of trying to get around the problem—i.e., that *The Cradle Will Rock* was considered extremely left wing. Let me explain what happened.

I had a considerable part in steering *The Cradle Will Rock* to the Federal Theater, because I was a friend of Blitzstein's. He had written a very witty series of musical sketches ridiculing the so-called respectable professions—education, law, etc. Due to personal circumstances, he had decided to abandon his career as a composer. I tried to interest him in going back to his musical writings and nothing seemed to interest him until suddenly I said, "What did you do with that series on the respectable professions?" He agreed they might be worth developing but he wanted me to do it in New Jersey. I told him, "The only singers in the Music Project up there are typical old-fashioned operatic singers, and that is not what you want. You're dealing in very witty lyrics that have to get across, and those people can't do it. We don't have the facilities to do your kind of show. Let me call John Houseman and Orson Welles."

Well, Welles fell in love with the whole thing and he worked with Blitzstein. They got it together and it was to go on at the Maxine Elliot Theater when Welles and Houseman were ordered not to do any new productions until it was time for new budget allocations; Washington was reported to have issued a nationwide order that only performances of works already opened could be done—no new productions.

Being suspicious, I investigated New Jersey and found out there was no such prohibition about new productions. As a matter of fact, word filtered back to us that the play was regarded as bad propaganda for the government, that it was too critical of the establishment.

Anyway, they had gotten through to their dress rehearsal and decided they were going to go ahead anyway and have their opening night and defy the government. Then Equity, afraid that the actors would be chopped off the program or might be subject to charges, ordered them not to appear in the project. However, there was a technicality in the Equity order that they could not appear "on the stage" in this production. So Houseman and Welles pulled a brilliant coup: They managed to get the use of the old Al Jolson Theater on Seventh Avenue and Fifty-eighth Street. Then they asked the audience that was waiting outside the Maxine Elliot Theater to come to the Jolson Theater, which was 20 blocks away. So this whole parade of the cast and about a thousand people trooped up to the Jolson Theater. Houseman and Welles had rented a piano, and Blitzstein was going to play the score and sing the parts himself, with Welles doing a kind of narration, filling in the dialog portions. The Equity cast found themselves seats in the audience, and, to Marc's and everybody else's surprise, first one Equity actor and then another stood up in the auditorium and sang his or her part. After all they were not performing "on the stage." So the production was both on the stage and in the audience. And, of course, the whole affair made headlines. There were stories on the front page of *The New York Times* and other newspapers about this defiance of the federal government that had taken place. But, as a result of that experience, Houseman and Welles quit the Federal Theater and established the Mercury Theater. That's the only case I know of where there was an actual denial of appropriation of funds to an individual production.

By '37-'38, more and more employment was opening up and people had the general feeling that the worst of the depression was over. There were less people to take care of and that in turn cut appropriations back. As a matter of fact, there was a congressman from Iowa during that time who came to Hallie Flanagan, director of the Federal Theater Project. He was logrolling for a particular constituent to get him on any project. Mrs. Flanagan said, "The project isn't going to go on, there isn't any funding for it; it was eliminated in the cutback. As a matter of fact, you were one of the people who voted for the cutback." And he said, "I did? I didn't know that was part of the bill I was supposed to vote for!" So the Federal Theater just got phased out.

There were still groups that felt that in the four or five years of the WPA's existence so much had been done that was of permanent value that there should be a permanent federal arts program of some sort, but it never got off the ground, and despite much agitation for it, when we got into the war it was forgotten. Then it took many years after the war until we finally did get some sort of federal subsidy for the arts, the National Endowment for the Humanities, which is even today very modest.

Sure the program was controversial. If it had not been for the relief aspects, I don't think there ever would have been an arts program. So the primary consideration was getting people fed and housed, but I must say it was a much healthier situation when certain skills were developed, careers were preserved and opportunities were given to do creative work than if those people were simply to accept money for food and rent.

It was in the Federal Theater Project that many actors got their first chance. A perfect example is the man I cast in the role of the pro-Nazi in *It Can't Happen Here.* The authorities tried to bump him off the project because he didn't qualify as a professional actor (he had done some boxing, wrestling and amateur theater work), but I told them, "Whether he can act or not is not the point; he's physically the type I need for the bully in the play." Through various kinds of pressure, I finally got this "stay of execution," and he played the part and got brilliant notices. I then used him in some of the children's plays and, later, in a play called *The Trial of Dr. Beck,* which was good enough to go to New York. And in New York this actor got good notices and was offered a Hollywood contract. This was William Bendix. There were countless others given this kind of opportunity as well: Welles, Houseman, Paula Lawrence, Hiram Sherman, and Joseph Cotten all went on to the Mercury Theater, and from there to very substantial careers in Broadway and Hollywood. So many got their starts then.

The New Deal penetrated to all levels of society. More than any other set of government programs in history, it made a *personal* impact on countless Americans. This impact was especially so in the case of the Civilian Conservation Corps, the agency that put young men to work restoring the country's ecological balance (as we'd say today).

In this memoir, Carl Gottfried recalls what life was like for him and tens of thousands of others who were part of that "back-to-nature" program.

Mr. Gottfried, now the manager of a large men's clothing store, lives in Skokie, Illinois.

CARL GOTTFRIED

It was the summer of '35. I had just graduated from high school, where I'd led a very sedentary life—no gymnastics, just woodwind rehearsal, brass rehearsal, section rehearsal—and thought I'd go into the Civilian Conservation Corps and build myself up. It was a big ego trip—get out in the open, be a lumberjack, prove to myself that I could be a man. Also, having four sisters and being the baby of the family, I had to make the break somehow, so I falsified my age, since I was only 17 and you had to be at least 18, and before I knew it, I wound up at Jackson Barracks, Missouri.

Of course, "Jackson Barracks" was a misnomer. The camp was mostly tents, red clay, humidity and rain. We had fellows from all walks of life, but mainly the working, blue-collar class. By the way, we were integrated; we had quite a few blacks. We didn't know about segregation; the blacks were accepted. We all worked together, were all part of the crew, were all in the same boat. Some of us were there for the three meals a day, some for the challenge.

For me, it was adventurous getting away from the city into a new environment—a different country, a different town—all expenses paid. We didn't know where we were going to be assigned. I was rather disappointed that I was finally assigned to Carrollton, Illinois, because I wanted to go to the Pacific Northwest and see the states of Washington and California. But in a way it worked out fine, because I was able to get home for the holidays. Our camp was brand new, and they were just building barracks to house all the men. We had no facilities for shampooing, and since we were out in all that mud and dirt, a lot of us shaved our heads to keep our scalps clean.

We got up every morning about six-thirty, seven o'clock. First there was roll call, then calisthenics outside, then breakfast in the mess hall, after which we'd be assigned to our trucks for certain details. We went out in the trucks every day except when the temperature was below zero.

We had the lumber detail, where we had the two-man saw to cut down big trees. Some of us used axes to split the trees into logs or rails; others dug post holes and then hammered the posts into the ravines. You see, in southern Illinois there was a soil-erosion problem with these deep ravines, and our function was to fill in these lands. We would dig a post hole on each side and on the bottom of the ravine, hammer the posts in, and run a wire screen across them, all along the ravine. Naturally, when it rained, the water would wash the soil down into the ravine, but the wire fence would hold the soil, so that the ravine would build up until it became level.

We'd ride about 20-25 miles a day to various farms—finish one project, go to work on another farm, knock off for a half-hour lunch in the field, and finally get back about five o'clock. On cold days we couldn't have water with lunch, because it would freeze in the keg. But we had warm clothing and warm GI underwear. And we also had a doctor on the post.

Wages were $30 a month; $25 was sent home to your dependents and you kept $5. But in those days you could exist on $5 a month. A dollar was worth a dollar, and besides, there was a post exchange and anything you purchased had no taxes on it, no federal, state or city taxes. For example, cigarettes were 8¢ a pack; in town, they were 21¢. That's where I started my habit; there was no diversion. A package of Camels was 8¢

and there I was.

Incidentally, whenever you have a bunch of boys thrown in together, there are bound to be fights every once in a while. So what they did was have these "grudge" fights on Friday nights, when they had boxing shows. The boys would get in the ring with boxing gloves for three rounds and vent their anger. In the end, they would shake hands and become good friends. It was a fine idea.

Saturdays and Sundays we had free. On Saturdays we'd go to the dayroom, where there'd be Ping-Pong, horseshoes and very little other recreation. We'd have our main meal in the afternoon and then we were permitted to go into town in the evening, where we were invited to church socials. It was a typical small town: there was the canyon and the courthouse and the smell of jasmine in the evening.

The boys would carry a half-pint of sloe gin fizz in their back pocket whenever they went into town. It bolstered their egos, made them bolder. Of course, you always had a few trollops in every town, and the guys sought them out.

At first there was a little tension because we were the new element coming into town, and some of the townspeople who had daughters were a bit fearful. But as time went on, the people saw the work we did on their farms, saw that we were helping them, and they in turn warmed to us and accepted us. So there were no incidents with the civilians. Yeah, they were civilians and we were part of the military. It was called the Civilian Conservation Corps, but we lived on army posts; we had a captain for a company commander; we had the American flag; we had reveille and a bugle; we even had K. P.

Military supervision? We had to keep the barracks spotless—make our beds military fashion, etc.—and we had inspections every so often. We also had bed check every night. You had to be back before it, at 10:00 P.M. They'd come in with a flashlight, and if there was an empty bed, they would question the fellow in the morning and he might be disciplined. For instance, he might lose certain privileges and be quarantined to the post. If you requested it, they'd let you go home for a national holiday. In those days, our mode of getting home was by freight car. No, we never had any trouble: We were wearing the army uniform, had our khaki overcoats, our overseas caps. The railroads were very cooperative. In fact, in cold weather we'd be given a car that had a lot of straw to keep us warm. The trip took about six or seven hours, because the train would stop and go and change tracks, but you just stayed on it because you were told, "This train is going to Chicago."

The enlistment period was six months and was renewable every six months. You couldn't just quit whenever you wanted to, as with an ordinary job. I don't know what the penalty was, but if you signed up for a six-month term, you had to stick it out. I was in for eight months, but I got out because of a special request for dependency. Hitler was beginning to rumble in Europe, and the big rumor was that the CCC was going to trade in its shovels for guns. That was a big rumor in camp; we heard that we got in a big load of guns, which were stored in the supply room, and they were going to put them in our hands and ship us overseas. This rumor kept growing. My parents were worried, and finally I turned in my shovel and came home.

What did that CCC experience mean to me? For one thing, it prepared me for my regular army career. I was able to adjust more readily when I went into the army, because I had learned how to live with men. You lose your privacy when you're in a group. You go into the latrine and there's no privacy. So when the big war came and I went in, I was very well adjusted, while a lot of other guys had problems.

For another, it helped me learn how to cope with life. It was a hardship and I was able to endure it. It helped me later in my business, too, in my dealings with different kinds of people. It taught me to give more. In my present job, I always give more than people expect and I get results; it pays dividends if you really extend yourself. I got that from the CCC.

2
POLITICIANS AND PERSONALITIES

He was a cautious conservative who became a radical reformer; he conspired to draw America into war by provoking a foreign attack. Who was he? According to former Republican Congressman Hamilton Fish, he was President Franklin D. Roosevelt.

As his party's leading conservative spokesman, New York Representative Fish was one of Roosevelt's most bitter political foes. Indeed, in the 1936 election, Roosevelt labeled him one third of the Republican triumvirate ("Martin, Barton and Fish") that was blocking his program. Throughout the rest of the decade, Fish remained his party's principal conservative and noninterventionist leader.

Mr. Fish is now retired and lives in New York City.

HAMILTON FISH

I think the depression was unexpected in Congress. Things were going so well; people were employed, and everybody was making money. The stock market got out of hand, and I guess that's what caused it.

As soon as we began to get into a serious situation, the president, who wasn't much of a politician but was a sound person and saw what was happening, tried to do everything he could to prevent it. Unfortunately, the Democrats had come back into power in the House.

Then, in '32, there was FDR, one of the shrewdest politicians we ever had and a little unscrupulous, too. He refused to cooperate with Mr. Hoover, who was trying to save the banks and head off further disaster. But I knew from my Democratic friends that they were playing politics. They thought, "Well, if it all collapses, it will be the fault of Mr. Hoover and we'll benefit." All those senators and congressmen, who had been out of power for some time, saw that if the Crash became the responsibility of the Republicans, they could take full advantage of it. What they did was wrong, but, from a political point of view, that's what it was, and maybe the Republicans would have done the same thing.

In '32 I made the keynote speech at the Republican state convention. It was a question of whether Governor Miller or I should deliver the speech, and I was chosen because I was in Congress. The speech was very well received, and the leadership offered me the nomination for U.S. senator in the next election; but I told them I didn't want it, because they would be Democratic years.

That speech, telling what we stood for as opposed to Roosevelt, was probably the most important one I had delivered up to that time; it was carried on the radio and published in the press. One feature of my original draft was that there should be a referendum on the question of light wine and beer. I took the position that it was a moral issue, that the people were entitled to say if they wanted to drink those beverages, and I thought that coming out and saying that we should have a referendum was a proper way of doing it. But leaders thought that I should submit the speech to President Hoover first to see if there was anything that should be stricken. He approved everything but that part about light wine and beer. He said, "I don't know about that. I think it's a very important issue and I'd like to think it over tonight. Do you mind if I take this speech back to the White House and see you at ten o'clock tomorrow morning?" I might have known his answer, because his wife was a White Ribboner; she was one of the driest of the drys. I think that if President Hoover had incorporated the referendum into his platform, he would have carried quite a few states.

Hoover was not a good politician and hadn't had much experience in politics. Perhaps if he had, it would have been a different story. He wasn't a great speaker, either, and he wasn't able to appeal to the people. They knew that he was honest, that he was trying to do the right thing; but he was just a difficult man to elect.

I knew that we'd probably be defeated, but we did the best we could and put up a good fight. Hoover had the right ideas, but the Democrats just wouldn't accept them to prevent the closing of the banks, which was a big issue. The Reconstruction-Finance bill was another of Hoover's ideas, but it wasn't adopted until after the Democrats came in, and they took the bill and used it.

What is interesting is that people don't know that FDR, when he ran for president in '32, ran on the most conservative platform ever issued by any party in the history of the country. It was much more conservative than any the Republican party ever had, unbelievably so. He accused Hoover of wild spending, of extravagance, and said he was going to cut 25 percent of the budget and 25 percent of the people employed.

My wife voted for him in '32. *I* would have voted for him if I hadn't been running for Congress. After all, I thought Hoover was somewhat to blame, that some mistakes had been made and therefore we should have a change. And running on a very conservative platform and coming from a good background, Roosevelt ought to have made a good president. But instead, when he got into power, he changed: first to a left-wing liberal, then to a radical and finally to a socialist.

A few weeks after he was elected, Roosevelt repudiated almost every item in the Democratic platform. That's why Al Smith said he had betrayed the Democratic party and turned it into a socialist party. FDR brought down to Washington a host of radical extremists, pro-Communists and socialists who tried to create a welfare state. And that's where inflation started, right then. Even Republicans today don't know that.

Now, during the first Hundred Days I supported Roosevelt in every policy. The situation in the country was very difficult. I thought the Republicans should go along with Roosevelt on everything he suggested in order to open the banks, restore confidence and put people to work. After all, he had been elected by an overwhelming majority, and I thought that was common sense.

We were very friendly at that time. Then I opposed him on the National Recovery Act and the Agricultural Adjustment Act (both were declared unconstitutional by the Supreme Court), and he hated opposition, so we split. He had a very vindictive character. He tried to defeat me for re-election, but it didn't make any difference.

Roosevelt's "Martin, Barton and Fish" refrain? It didn't do me any harm at all. In fact, it gave me a lot of publicity. actually prestige, in that Martin was the Speaker of the House and Barton was a senator. Besides, I was glad to have people know my ideas: I was against Roosevelt and I wanted everybody to know it. And I never lost Duchess County, Roosevelt's county, ever.

In '36, we never thought Landon had a chance. Nobody was optimistic. Landon carried two states; I didn't think he could carry any. It was utterly ridiculous. They nominated him because they wanted someone from the Midwest. Now, you ask me what I did about it. I did a lot, but it didn't work out. A group of about 20-30 congressmen came to me and asked *me* to be a candidate. Some top leaders were there, including the ranking member of the Ways and Means Committee. And, of course, I was far better qualified than Landon would ever have been; there's no question about that. I knew it and my friends in Congress knew it, but I had no money and I told them that. I said, "I have no money to go out there and make this campaign, but would you go along with me if I got Senator Borah to run?" And they said, "Yes, we'll support Borah if you say so." So Senator Borah agreed to run, even though we had no money and *he* had no money. I campaigned for him in Illinois, with no money and a lot of radio speeches. We carried Illinois and Wisconsin in the primaries; but the obligation was so strong (and still we had no money) that by the time we got to the convention, it was hopeless.

So I went to Borah and said, "We have no chance. Landon can't possibly win the election, but you can't get the nomination. You should. You could win, I think. You're a great orator, a liberal within the limits of the Constitution, and you ought to get an enormous vote, but you haven't got it within this convention." Then I asked him, "Would you support a man named Senator Steiwer who is a veteran from Oregon and introduced veterans' legislation? He could get the veterans' vote in the convention. I think we can nominate him. He's supposed to give the keynote address." Borah said, "Yes. You can tell him that if he makes a strong American appeal and takes the nationalistic side on the issues, I'll support him. But I don't thing he can do it."

Well, I went to see Steiwer and he was thrilled. He said, "What have I got to do?" I said, "You've got to make a strongly nationalistic speech, bring them to their feet, and *you'll be nominated!* The word's already gone out to all the vets and they'll be for you." Well, he got up and made one of the weakest speeches I've ever heard. Then we knew it was over, and that's how Landon got nominated.

The third term? The reaction was absolutely unanimous. We thought we could win with the war issue and the third term. I think if Taft had been nominated, he would have won easily. What happened in that campaign is that 25,000 people in Illinois, without my consent, signed petitions to have me run for president in the Republican primary and filed them with the secretary of state. The secretary of state called me and asked what he should do with the petitions. I said, "Don't accept them. I haven't got enough money to come out and make even one speech." That night I went to the Women's Colony Club, a very fine organization made up of wealthy women, and I told one of them, Mrs. Crane, about the petitions. She said, "Mr. Fish, I will give you a check right now for $10,000 if you'll call the secretary of state and tell him that you'll accept." So I called the secretary of state and he said, "I'm sorry, Congressman, but there's nothing I can do about it now. It's gone to the printing press."

I would have won the primary in Illinois and might have won it in Wisconsin, Oklahoma and two or three other states. I would have beaten Willkie out there; I would have gone after him and said, "Here was a man who once was a noninterventionist and now he's changed. If you want to keep out of this war, you have only one thing to do, and that's vote for me. I have led this fight and that's all there is to it. There's no other issue and I'm not going to have anybody change issues. It's up to you people. I know how you feel." Then I would have given all my votes to Taft. He would have been nominated, would have won the election, probably would have made me vice-president, but I didn't give a damn about that; I wanted to keep us out of war.

You see, when the war issue came up, I was for keeping out of war unless attacked, and so were 85 percent of the American people. (When the Polish war began in '39, it was 93 percent, but due to the enormous propaganda of the New Deal administration and FDR to get us into the war, it was reduced to 85 percent.) And that's where we really split, because I was working as ranking member of the Rules Committee and of the Foreign Affairs Committee to keep the country out of war unless we were attacked.

You ask me what I did. I was actually the leader in the House of Representatives of what they called the "noninterventionists." Some people called us "isolationists," but that was a misnomer. There was no isolationism in America; an isolationist is a person who doesn't want to do business with any foreign government at all. We were noninterventionists from war unless attacked, simple as that. And that was 85 percent of the people. The eastern press and the radio were against us, Roosevelt and the whole cabinet were against us, but the people were sound; they couldn't be budged by all the massive propaganda that went on day in and day out.

In Congress, 85 percent of the Republicans followed me on

every vote, and often I had a number of northern Democrats supporting me. The southern Democrats were entirely different; they had all this money, but Roosevelt could defeat any one of them and they knew that, so they went along with him. I don't think they liked it, but they had no choice.

I think the most important thing I've ever done or ever will do was fight continually on the war issue. I was on the radio every week, talking about keeping out of war. I said we had been in one world war and weren't even thanked and we ought to keep out of the other war, because if we got into it, it would mean we would be in the blood feuds of Europe forever. My idea was to let Hitler and Stalin fight it out, kill each other off, and let the other people sit on the sidelines and damnation to both sides. We tried to bring that about, but Roosevelt wouldn't let us. So it was a terrible ordeal. Every American family owes those noninterventionists who kept us out of war before Pearl Harbor a debt of gratitude. If Roosevelt had got us into the war before June 22, 1941, when Hitler attacked Russia, Hitler never would have made that attack. See, Hitler lost 3,000,000 men and all those guns, airplanes and munitions fighting in Russia. Instead *we* would have lost the millions and had more millions wounded and hundreds of billions of dollars in expenditures, with it all ending in a stalemate.

The destroyers-for-bases deal? That was one of the first steps to get us into war. It was totally unconstitutional; Roosevelt had no authority to do it. I led the fight against it. When it came up to Congress, Roosevelt brought tremendous pressure to bear. He had every cabinet member seeing every southern Democrat, threatening them and everything else. Oh, they did everything in the world to get votes. A lot of Democrats came to me and said they were willing to vote with us; but the pressure was just too great. We got only 20 votes.

When I saw we were defeated, we offered an amendment to show where we stood, to give the British $2 billion to buy anything they wanted in this country in the way of arms, munitions or food. And I said if that wasn't enough, we'd increase it. But they wouldn't accept that. And that's typical of the way Roosevelt took us step by step into war. He knew public opinion was against him, so he had to manipulate it and deceive the people.

And then came the tragic events the American people don't know about even today. On November 25 Roosevelt called his war cabinet together in the White House. That cabinet was composed of himself, Secretary Hull, Secretary Stimson, Secretary Knox, General Marshall and Admiral Stark—just those six. All they discussed was how to force, goad, compel Japan to get into war—nothing else; nothing about Germany or anything. And the next day they sent a war ultimatum to Japan to get out of China and Manchuria immediately, with all their armed forces. Nobody in America knew about that. Nobody in Congress knew about it except those six men. Of course, the Japanese had no alternative but to fight. They couldn't surrender and get out of Manchuria and China. Two days later, because the Japanese hadn't attacked yet, Roosevelt said to Stimson, "Should we send a stronger ultimatum, since they haven't attacked?" It's not Fish who made up the word "ultimatum"; that was Roosevelt's word.

I have a moral right to speak out on that, as does any living man, because I got up on the floor of Congress and made the first speech for war, upholding Roosevelt's "Day of Infamy" speech, the day after Pearl Harbor. My speech was broadcast and was listened to by 25 million people. In it, I denounced the Japanese for attacking us. Now I have to repudiate every word I said.

The nation is entitled to know how it was tricked into war. There were investigations, but they all covered up the story of the sending of the ultimatum to Japan. And it's been covered up by the Democrats to this day, because it would hurt them.

There were reasons for Roosevelt's wanting to get into war. First, he was an internationalist. Second, there were about 13 million people unemployed, according to the AFL, which showed that the whole New Deal policy, and all its divisions and subdivisions, had completely failed; the people had lost confidence in it. Roosevelt knew that and he knew that war was the one way out. Then there was his lust for power. He knew that in war he'd be commander-in-chief and would have power over the whole country. He would have stayed in for a fourth, fifth and sixth term if his health had permitted.

The New York *Herald Tribune* was for war, the *Times* was for war, the big Wall Street interests were for war. (Wall Street had lent England $6 billion before we went to war, and, as soon as we got into it, they were paid back.) Armament people were for war. These groups were very strong; they controlled radio, newspapers in the East—and they didn't like me at all. A lot of them were Jews, whom I don't blame. They hated Hitler and all they cared about was killing him. If I had been a Jew, I probably would have been for war myself.

The other thing I'm very proud of, along with keeping us out of war, is that I was chairman of the first committee to investigate communism in '30. The Communists were quite active then; they controlled the CIO—nine out of 14 members of the executive committee controlled it—and the American Labor Party had 500,000 votes in New York, but that's all gone. It's all gone because of my committee. We didn't persecute individuals; we didn't arrest anybody, send anyone to jail. All we did, as ordered by Congress, was to find out what were the aims, purposes and policies of the Communist Party. We'd call in their leaders and ask them, "Are you for our form of government?" They'd answer, "No, we're not for your form of government; we're for the Communist form of government." "Are you for the American flag?" "No, we're not for the American flag; we're for the red flag." I got this out in a report and sent it to labor all over the country, and when labor found out that the Communists were against freedom, against democracy, against religion, against our form of government, that's what did the trick. Later, McCarthy and others went after individuals and, of course, got into trouble with the liberals and other people. But that was the beginning, way back in 1930, and that's the biggest thing I've ever done, except for keeping us out of war.

Of course, I should tell you that as a member of the Rules Committee, I organized the Dies Committee. It was a Democratic committee; they went after individuals. And these congressmen, you know, are prima donnas; they like to claim credit for everything. But Dies told me, "You deserve the credit. You saw the danger coming and you did something about it." It's all in black and white; I have it in a letter from him.

Many people will be surprised to know that for the first 15 years I was in Congress, I was known as a progressive Republican. I always believed in social-industrial justice and a square deal for labor. Because I led the fight against Roosevelt and communism, many people thought I must be a reactionary; but I have always been a middle-of-the-road Republican. The reason I dropped saying that I was a progressive Republican was that when Roosevelt came into power, he used the word "liberal," and liberalism immediately became extreme radicalism. But I've always been for a fair deal for all elements of our population. You can call it what you like, but that's my whole life. My record is there in Congress and hasn't changed. True I made some enemies in those days, but the rank and file of Congress, 90 percent of them, followed me all the time.

> Much has been written about the growth of presidential power that occurred during and since the New Deal era. However, it was not just the executive branch that expanded, as Senator Jennings Randolph (D-W. Va.) observes; it was the Congress, too.
>
> In the early thirties, Congress had a much more personal, deliberative character; it was not yet affected by its own expansion "into so many fields," as Senator Randolph puts it, or by the technological revolution.

JENNINGS RANDOLPH

Back in '30 I was a candidate for Congress. I had won the nomination but lost the election, though not by a large number of votes. At the time, I was a member of a college faculty and had a political background; my grandfather and then my father had run for Congress.

I felt that we were approaching a period in which the conditions of the country were in such distress and even tragedy that the executive-branch leadership and Congress would be Democratic in '32. So when I ran for Congress that year, I ran on my own candidacy, although I was supportive of Franklin D. Roosevelt.

There were 13 counties in the Second District of West Virginia, where I ran. They were counties that had varying interests—mining, farming and horticulture—atmospheres and attitudes ("northern" versus "southern" thinking).

I took office in March, '33, the same day President Roosevelt did. I never considered myself either a northern or a southern Democrat. I have always been a realist, not a liberal or a conservative. But in Congress, we were almost unified on the Roosevelt proposals. The situation called for action across a broad front. Twenty-five percent of the labor force was unemployed; business had generally collapsed; there were the runs on banks; bankruptcies and foreclosures were at an all-time high.

West Virginia itself was very hard hit. Our mining industry was at a very low level, the farmer was having a difficult time selling his produce, and the lumber industry, a very important part of the area, had fallen off, because people were not building houses.

I think we were near disaster. The president knew that mistakes were bound to be made but felt that if he as president and we as Congress did not act immediately, we might not even have the opportunity later to make mistakes, let alone take positive action.

The House of Representatives took only 38 minutes to pass Roosevelt's emergency-banking bill, and the Senate only three hours. We were stamping approval on FDR measures almost at the pace of a bill a week. I think we may have passed 15 measures that became law in the first Hundred Days. Of course, these were rather new and innovative fields that were being tapped, so all of these legislative enactments were racked with some question marks. You understand, they had to be.

There was a tremendous feeling in Congress that something was happening. You sensed it. But with it all was a somberness, a wondering if we could and would do it, and if we did, what the result would be. How would the legislation that plowed new fields serve people? Could the nation do the job?

People still wonder about the New Deal. They realize it took care of an immediate situation, but they wonder whether, on the whole, it was worthwhile. I think it was not only necessary but also highly worthwhile. We brought electricity to rural sections of this country that had never had it before and, by so doing, gave the farmer better living conditions. All across the board, I think the quality of life was improved. I served with eight presidents, all of whom had their strengths and weaknesses, as I have mine, but I look upon FDR as the one I would place above the others.

Yes, we voted a $500 pay reduction in '33. Just recently, in the Senate, I said that members should vote directly on the matter of raising or lowering their pay, and a member asked me, "When did Congress ever lower its pay?" I said, "Well, we did in

'33." And, as I recall, it was at the initiative, not of the president but of House members. We wanted people to know that we were trying to participate in the application of discipline, and that was a way we could show it.

Yes, I knew Huey Long. I used to come over to the Senate chamber expecially to hear him. His very manner of speaking fascinated me. He might not have been the most eloquent senator, but he had a charisma that caused me to listen and to watch him. I can't describe it to someone who wasn't a part of it, but I remember a book about him in which he was called "a lion in the Senate," and that's what he was, in a sense: He usually roared, but there were times when he was a little subdued and strolled around, just as a lion would.

He was a man interested in redistribution of wealth, and this was a new idea, in a sense, a populist thought. But then the Senate and the House were filled with men who seemed to be crusaders. They were part of a movement to build an America that would respond to the changes.

I think some members of Congress thought that Senator Long was an opportunist, that he was grabbing hold of a popular idea. They weren't sure how sincere he was. All I can say regarding the general feeling about him is that he had very vigorous opponents and very active supporters. In addition, he was certainly a man to be reckoned with. Even Roosevelt was worried about him at times, because he saw the great support Long had. But I do not believe that he could have defeated Roosevelt.

Then there was Father Coughlin, who was thinking in terms of possible dangers to our society. He also had a tremendous following, as did the Townsendites. I was not for their programs as they were presenting them, but they were highlighting problems in our country. In West Virginia, in my district, there were thousands of Townsendites. I don't remember the exact number, but their meetings were well attended.

Congress? Well, even though we were working long hours then, there were not the pressures that come today—the pressures of an increased population, the creation of so many programs, the changes in transportation and communication.

Today people can move into Washington in a matter of minutes. In the thirties that was not possible, so we relied not so much on quickness of response, as on letters. Since correspondence was mainly by mail, a congressman's life was somewhat well ordered from the standpoint of consideration. I know I did much more reading in those days.

During my first term as Representative, I had an office, and my staff—two people—and that was it—two rooms. Today, I imagine, a member has three or four rooms and eight or ten on his staff. That's just one indication of how the work load's increased.

It was a more personalized Congress back then: There was more contact, more rapport between members. They were not shuttling back and forth on aircraft in a few hours; they had to stay in Washington. They were not here as long as now, but it was more leisurely, a slower-paced effort. I think they gave far more time to what were called "substantive matters." Today they have to put those matters on the shoulders of the staff. In the old days, you went to the Library of Congress for your reading matter more often. Today the lobbyists give you a dozen books. The trade groups, for instance, are also here. I expect they all moved out of New York and Chicago and into Washington. They're here by the thousands. One trade group alone will have about 600 people working here.

Also, Congress has gone into so many fields. Some were fields that were introduced by Roosevelt's actions. We began to think in terms of the federal government's being involved in certain issues, such as wages, hours, working conditions. It's the governmental structure with so many layers that we didn't have back then. And with it has come increased personnel and often a lessening of the Representative's *personal* attention to the solution of a problem. This was just a change that had to come, but sometimes I feel at a loss not knowing quite what to do, so sometimes I vote with a feeling that I'm just not as certain as I'd like to be of my own position. There used to be more careful consideration of bills. It wasn't a matter of wait, wait, wait but a very deliberate manner of doing business and one that gave me the opportunity to really feel that I was convinced of a certain bill.

Today, I think it's just the amount of subject matter and the whole process of more bills being considered, more roll calls. A member now offers an amendment, and even if he knows the amendment's going to be accepted by the committee, he wants a roll call just the same, to show that the vote was 85-6 or whatnot. In the old days, you just didn't have the roll calls, except in matters of extreme importance. It all just shows the heavy hand of input into the legislative life of America. No, it wasn't that way before.

The New Deal, the threat of fascism, the question of isolationism, the Democrats as the new majority party—these were all issues Democratic congressmen wrestled with in the thirties. And for his part, former Representative John McCormack was deeply involved in many of them, as he recalls in this memoir.

Mr. McCormack was first elected to Congress in 1928 and served until 1971. Upon the death of Sam Rayburn in 1962, he was elected Speaker of the House of Representatives, a position he held until his retirement in 1971.

JOHN McCORMACK

When I was elected in '28, I was elected to both an unexpired term and a regular term. So I was elected in November and took office in December, because of the lame-duck session, instead of waiting until the following March, when Congress normally started. At that time Coolidge was president, and I served during the last three months of his administration.

With the exception of those three months, the first four years of my service in Washington were under President Hoover, and that's when the Great Depression developed. I always thought that President Hoover was well intentioned, a good man, but he failed to understand and grasp the leadership necessary in a great crisis. I was talking about conditions in the country, as were a few others in the House and Senate, trying to get through legislation that would help the sick, the poor, the afflicted. But it was fruitless under Hoover, because he was of a mind where such legislation was foreign to him. And with the Republicans being in control, we didn't have much chance of getting any legislation through until Roosevelt came in.

As I remember, we took control of the House two years after I was elected, in '30, and Jack Garner was elected by a small vote after that. You see, the Republicans claimed a majority in the House, but between the election and the time the new Congress met, about 13 months later, there were several deaths among the Republicans and they were succeeded by Democrats, which allowed us to gain control of the House by a few votes.

Yes, I was a delegate to the '32 convention. It was felt that with the dire situation existing throughout the country, as well as the lack of leadership in the White House, almost any Democrat could get elected. The rivalry between Al Smith and Roosevelt, both coming from the same state, was intense, there's no question about that. As I remember, a two-thirds vote was required to be the nominee. Roosevelt had the majority, but he didn't have the two thirds, while Garner furnished the rest of the necessary votes. Now, I don't say there was a deal made, but common sense would have told FDR that if he had a majority and couldn't get two thirds, then the practical thing to do, besides being consistent with the interest of our country, was to ask Garner if he'd be interested in the second place. Of course, it was a trying position for me and other progressives, because Garner was not a progressive. But he was a fair man and very well liked and I had great respect for him.

I was for Smith at the time. Our delegation had pledged itself to him in the campaign. I thought that he was entitled to the nomination because of the great record he had made as governor of New York and because he had run four years before and had had the religious question raised against him. And when he didn't get it and Roosevelt did, I was disappointed. But I enthusiastically supported Roosevelt and the Democratic party, because they were the only ones who fought for the people.

You have to realize that when Roosevelt took over, there was still quite a division in the country. Most of the members from the South were opposed to Roosevelt's programs—honestly so but, in my opinion, mistakenly so. We had some very hard fights, with 95 percent of the Republicans and 35-40 Democrats, principally from the Deep South, voting against the programs, making it very difficult to get some of the legislation through.

We'd pick up some votes from the Deep South, but not many. There was a political environment there that they responded to because it meant their political future. So although they were good party men, when it came to progressive government, they were more or less wedded in those years to the status quo. They were afraid of change.

Yes, it was generally known that the Supreme Court was against Roosevelt's programs. The members are like anybody else, human beings, and some talked a little bit too much, indicating that they were just waiting for the constitutionality of a bill to come before them. Roosevelt knew he had the Court stacked against him, so he tried to do something to unstack it. I favored his proposal. If it would have come to a vote in the House, I would have voted for it. I favored increasing the number of members from 9 to 11, as he wanted to; but I felt he would have been in a stronger position to get support for the bill if he had recommended that, as a member died or retired, the vacancy not be filled. But that really didn't mean an awful lot in my considerations at the time, because I knew what he was up against. There was nothing else he could do.

Yes, in '34 I was on the committee that was investigating communism, Nazism, fascism and all forms of bigotry, including the Klan, which still had a big carryover. The committee was established as a result of a few members of the House demanding investigations of the German Bund, principally in New York. There was a very fine German-American press there, and this goose-stepping Bund had taken it over, intimidating the owners by threatening that their relatives in Germany would be punished, imprisoned, probably killed. Who knew what would have happened under a regime such as Hitler's? Of course, now, looking back, we know what would have happened.

I was drafted chairman of the subcommittee, and we uncovered some amazing things. For example, one of the biggest public-relations firms in America, on a contractual basis, was advising Hitler on speeches that could be made by members of the German ministry that would be favorably received in America. Yes, they had this contract, but instead of making it with the Nazi government, the firm made it through the German Dye Trust, one of the big corporations in Germany.

Then there was the fellow who represented the railroads on

tourism and who had a similar position with another company in Germany, which indirectly but in fact was with the German ministry. We uncovered that, and as a result came the Foreign Agents Registration Act. I was the author of that bill. It was a very effective piece of legislation.

The reason these incidents didn't provoke so much of a reaction in '34 was that the country was intensely isolationist up to and including Pearl Harbor. I had a firm opinion then, not just a reaction, that Hitler was a menace to the world. As a matter of fact, I was one of those who opposed him during that period as a matter of conscience. I felt the national interest of my country called for it. The came the war, and those of us who recognized the danger of Hitler and Nazism couldn't do a thing.

When Roosevelt wanted to introduce the Lend-Lease Bill in '40, he had some problems about who would introduce it in the House. It was a bill considered by most Irish-Americans as a bill to save England. Well, I'm an American of Irish blood, but I *wanted* England saved at the time—not for England's sake, but for the interest of my own country. I felt it was against the interest of the United States to have England and France defeated. France was practically out of the war and DeGaulle was in exile. So if England were defeated, it would be very harmful to the interests of our country. And I had a feeling that, sooner or later, we were going to get drawn into the war, though I didn't then know how.

We had two or three discussions about it, and finally I suggested that the majority leadership in both houses introduce the bill at the same time. (That's how I got to introduce it.) There was a lot of work done on it, because at that time the country was still intensely isolationist. We were fortunate in getting it through. That was on January 10, 1941. And Pearl Harbor happened on December 7, 1941!

That was on a Sunday. I was in Boston at the time, and Roosevelt telephoned to say that he wanted me back in Washington immediately. He said, "I need you, John." I said, "I'll be there, Mr. President, I'll be there on Monday."

It was very tense. The attack on Pearl Harbor showed the sinister intent of the coalition of Germany under Hitler, and Italy under Mussolini and the tie-up with Japan. The transformation was complete. Isolationism vanished. Pearl Harbor was war itself, without a declaration. Our declaring war was a formality.

One of my fundamental guidelines where defense of my country is concerned is that it may be every other American's country, but it is *my* country, too, John McCormack's country, so that if I am going to err in judgment, I prefer to err on the side of strength rather than on the side of weakness. And I always followed that guideline.

Was Roosevelt the force of the New Deal—or the coward of the "Jew Deal?" Did he do all he could, or were millions of Jewish lives lost because of American inaction? The debate continues to this day, and as one of the participants in that prewar drama, former Congressman Emanuel Celler believes neither FDR nor the State Department did all they might have to save "many thousands of Jews from Hitler's Holocaust."

Mr. Celler, now a lawyer in private practice in New York, was a Democratic Representative from 1922 to 1972. Prior to his retirement he was chairman of the House Judiciary Committee.

EMANUEL CELLER

I was with Roosevelt from the very beginning and I remained steadfastly with him. My difference with him was over the Court-packing bill. I was a member of the House Judiciary Committee, the committee to which the bill had been referred. Roosevelt sent all kinds of emissaries to me so I would change my mind, but I wouldn't, because I felt he was dead wrong trying to pack the Court. He was trying to control the judiciary.

After that, he did everything in his power to hurt me. For example, he never again invited me to the White House. But, while I was stricken off the list, things like that, he didn't try to stop my bills. The views that I reflected were more or less like his own, so he couldn't very well object to those.

I also quarreled with him over his refusal to arrange for the admission of German Jews to this country, from '36 on. He could have saved many thousands of Jews from Hitler's holocaust, but he refused to do it. He was afraid of what was called the "Jew Deal." Also, he didn't want to oppose Churchill, who didn't want Jews coming into Palestine.

We sought to amend the Malcolm-McDonald White Paper, which admitted 75,000 Jews into Palestine for a period of five years, at 15,000 a year, so as to have unlimited emigration to Palestine. But Churchill didn't want any changes, and Roosevelt sided with him. We fought against that and incurred Roosevelt's disfavor because of it.

I went to see Roosevelt at the White House once to get more help for displaced German Jews, and he said, in effect, "Stop making waves. I have an agreement with Churchill that we will surreptitiously allow Jews to enter into Palestine unlimitedly. So forget about stirring up trouble. This will be taken care of." Well, there wasn't a bit of truth that an arrangement had been made with Churchill, because it never developed along those lines. Palestine's gates were closed except for the 15,000 a year, and the few Jews who could get out of Germany perished on rotten hulks of ships.

Cordell Hull also offered no help at all. As a matter of fact, he followed the temper of the State Department, which was anti-Jewish; it was always pro-Arab and anti-Jewish and still is. Breckinridge Long, undersecretary of state, did all he could to prevent the immigration of the limited number of Jews from Germany who would have been allowed into this country under the immigration statutes. His argument was that they were likely to become public charges. According to the immigration statutes, nobody could come into this country if he was likely to become a public charge. Hull used that clause to keep the Jews out. Of course, I fought him on that. They were displaced persons and I didn't think that that particular provision should apply.

No, I didn't object when Roosevelt ran for a third term. I had some misgivings, but I wasn't vocal on them. I was a good Democrat and I wanted him to win, though inwardly I felt it was wrong. But I didn't express myself. Perhaps I should have.

Whatever I say now about Roosevelt is in no sense meant to denigrate his greatness. He was a great man. Of course he had his faults, and I'm just pointing them out; but that doesn't detract from his place in history, which is a very great one.

As for me, I simply feel that I did the best I could. As representative of the people in my district, I felt that I should use the power given me judiciously. I think I did a conscientious job.

Many of the far-reaching reforms and legislation enacted during the New Deal era are considered as having originated in the White House, which they did. However, some of them came from men like Senator Robert Wagner (D-N.Y.) and, as his former aide, Leon Keyserling points out, were actually opposed by President Roosevelt.

Dr. Keyserling was himself in good part responsible for much of the legislation—e.g., the National Labor Relations Act—and was as deeply involved in promoting presidential measures and drafting party platforms as well.

After the Roosevelt era, Dr. Keyserling went on to serve under President Truman as chairman of the Council of Economic Advisors, becoming the only person to hold that position at a cabinet level. Dr. Keyserling lives in Washington, where he is still involved in the political-economic scene.

LEON KEYSERLING

I came down to Washington with Rex Tugwell at the start of the first Roosevelt administration. I had been teaching at Columbia and knew him rather well. In fact, we had written and published a book together. He was slated to be assistant secretary of agriculture (and later became under secretary), so naturally I came down with him. But within about two weeks, through my work on the drafting of the National Industrial Recovery Act [NIRA], I got to know Senator Wagner and went over to his office.

What happened was that we had a meeting in Senator Wagner's office. The NIRA had originally been drafted as an act to suspend the antitrust laws. I was insistent that it was not a sufficient approach to the problem and talked about writing into it provisions relating to wages and hours (which provisions were the forerunner of the Wages and Hours Law of '38) and also of writing in section 7a—the collective-bargaining provisions—which led in 1935 to the Wagner (National Labor Relations) Act. Senator Wagner was so impressed with me that he asked me not only to write these provisions but also to be his legislative assistant. I was with him until '37. After that, I was called in by him whenever there was anything important until he left the Senate in 1946.

I was the principal draftsman of the National Labor Relations Act, more commonly known as the Wagner Act, which was introduced at the beginning of '34 and enacted in '35. It was in response to Senator Wagner's feeling that the carrying out of the NIRA was one-sided; business was getting everything. It wasn't his view that the NIRA itself was one-sided, but that the administration of it was one-sided and inadequate.

The NIRA was ruled unconstitutional in '35, as were certain other acts, which decreased the pressure against the passage of the Wagner Act. Still, the opposition to the act was greater than to any other legislation, owing to anti-union sentiment, and even after it was enacted in '35, it was not observed, because after the Schechter decision and the Triple A [Agricultural Adjustment Act] decision, nobody thought it would be held constitutional. Not until '37 was the Wagner Act held constitutional by the Supreme Court; so it was only after that year that it really became a practice.

Another thing that isn't generally known is that the Wagner Act was not supported by the president—that it was in fact hampered by his actions—until it passed the Senate and went over to the House. I don't know why; I'm not a psychiatrist. I'm just reporting what happened. In '34 Congress passed a joint resolution, #44, to sidetrack the bill; but that's what FDR wanted. Very little of this is in the history books. You read them now and think that all this legislation came from the White House. But it was not a Roosevelt measure; it was a Wagner measure, a congressional measure.

Yes, the administration of the National Labor Relations Act was a very controversial issue. But Senator Wagner never interfered with it. He could have appointed a lot of people to the top jobs over there, but he kept out of that. He believed that after the law was passed, it was the business of the executive branch to handle the administration.

I was very active in helping Senator Wagner steer social security through Congress. He made more speeches, wrote more articles, was on more radio programs than anybody else in connection with all of these programs, and I prepared all of this work. And when you come to the U.S. Housing Act of 1937, which was the first slum-clearance and low-rent-housing act, I actually drafted that one.

Opposition to the New Deal became greater as the years went by, and by '37, as a result of the reaction to the Court-packing plan, Roosevelt couldn't get anything through Congress. The Wages and Hours Law squeaked through in '38, but the New Deal was practically over after '37.

You know, the opposition to the Court-packing plan, on the surface, looked ideological. In other words, a lot of the senators who opposed it said they did so on grounds that it would interfere with the courts. But the fact that there was so much opposition was a sign that the New Deal had politically worn out. If the plan had come up in '33, the opposition wouldn't have been so strong.

For that matter, Roosevelt couldn't have beaten Willkie in '40 without the international situation. Of course, it may be that the international situation saved Roosevelt, but Roosevelt saved the world.

My other work for Senator Wagner? There was a lot. In '36, toward the end of the campaign between Roosevelt and Landon, Landon claimed that the Social Security Administration would never make any payments, that it was a fraud. And Wagner was designated by the president to go on a nationwide radio program to answer Landon's accusation. I prepared that talk. Then, in '40, when John L. Lewis came out for Willkie and Wagner was designated to comment on that on nationwide radio, I handled that, too. And in '36, '40 and '44, we didn't have nationwide committees drafting convention platforms, and I drafted the platforms Roosevelt ran on those three times. Wagner, as chairman of the Platform Committee, took those drafts to the convention, where the Resolutions Committee made very few changes.

No, as far as detracting any credit from Senator Wagner, he was the one who stood for these things, he was the one who took the pounding; and he was the one who had the power to get legislation enacted. I can't detract from what he did. I remember one year in the '30s, when he was doing all this work, the Washington press voted him the ablest, hardest-working, most popular and best-dressed senator. He was the greatest senator we had. I couldn't have done it without him, and he couldn't have done it without me.

Most of these things, you see, don't get into the history books. The reason is that most of the historians look at the written records, while most of the history is made orally. It's made by conversations and discussion and by decision.

In 1977 Jacob Arvey, one of the last of the great political bosses, died. In this interview, made a few months before his death, he relates his experiences as alderman and committeeman of Chicago's largely Jewish Twenty-fourth Ward. As he says, his efforts were as much for the benefit of the Democratic party and the ward organization as they were for his people and their institutions. And it was by fulfilling the benefactor's role that he was able to help build one of the most powerful political machines in twentieth-century history.

A lawyer, Jacob Arvey served as chairman of the Cook County Democratic Central Committee and was a member of the Democratic National Committee.

JACOB ARVEY

In '32 part of our party, especially the Irish part, wanted Al Smith again. But Smith was a loser; he had lost to Hoover. Congressman A. J. Sabath, of Chicago, had known Franklin Roosevelt when he was assistant secretary of the navy. He kept talking up Roosevelt's qualities and the potential he had to be a great president. He said that Roosevelt had had a good record as governor of New York, was a new face on the national scene, and looked like he would make a good candidate. He convinced me, he convinced Mayor Cermak, and we wound up being for Roosevelt. Of course, I think Al Smith would've won, too, because it was an anti-Hoover vote.

One of the greatest thrills of my life was to see Roosevelt at the convention, crippled, draw up to the podium, and refuse to have any help. He had to hold on to the podium while he spoke. The courage he displayed! We had no television then. If we had, he'd have won by much more, because people would have seen a man whom they could respect and in whom they could place their faith and trust. I used to speak of him as the Moses who would lead us out of the wilderness.

I think the Jewish vote for Roosevelt in '32 was the biggest Democratic vote up to that point. He transformed the national thinking of the Jewish electorate from Republican to Democrat. Our ward, the Twenty-fourth, had always voted Republican, although in '28 we carried it for Smith, because the Jews resented the religious bigotry manifested in that election. But we seldom won in national elections. Then in '32, when Roosevelt won, the ward became Democratic from top to bottom. In '36, when Roosevelt ran again, he got 2,800 or 2,900 votes to Landon's 700 or 800 without any effort. All we had to say was, "I'm the Roosevelt precinct captain," and people'd say, "We'll come out to vote."

In the first Hundred Days, Roosevelt had passed all this legislation that helped the little guy to work. I used to make speeches in the ward in which I would tell my precinct captains, "You're responsible for social security. You may not think so, but you in your precinct delivered the winning precinct for Roosevelt, for a senator, for a congressman. They in turn formed legislation, including social security. Without you and thousands like you, they wouldn't have been in office to do that."

All this time I was committeeman and alderman of the Twenty-fourth Ward, which felt the impact of the depression more than most wards in Chicago. So every year I had an affair at the Chez Paree, a leading Chicago night club, to raise money. I raised about $50,000. Nobody in our ward contributed; it was all from people outside the ward. And we used that money to pay doctor bills, medicine, gas, rent. We used to brag that in our ward no one spent Passover without having Passover food.

I used to hold court, receiving visitors in my ward headquarters every night, excluding the Sabbath, from 7:00 to 10:00 P.M. On Sunday morning, from 9:00 to 12:00, there'd be an endless parade of men and women coming in to ask for things. If they wanted advice, I'd send them to one of the lawyers in our office. If they wanted help, we had a woman who was a social worker. Most of them asked for jobs and financial help. But I tell you,

90 percent of the people walked away empty-handed. We had to go out and plead with people in industry to give our citizens jobs. We had no jobs, since this was in the height of the depression. The city was laying off men; the county was laying off men. But people did come away with two things: hope and a feeling of consolation. There was somebody in authority to whom they could speak, to whom they could go, who would listen to them.

Our ward organization was like a philanthropic organization. No man could be a precinct captain of mine unless he belonged to a synagogue, a church, the B'nai B'rith, the Knights of Columbus, the Masons, the Elks or the Odd Fellows. He had to participate in the affairs of the community. One of our men was an Exalted Ruler of the Elks, and we had two or three who were Worshipful Masters of the Masonic Lodges.

I did all this deliberately, because it would help politically too. If you were my precinct captain and you belonged to Temple Judea, I knew you'd have to meet people from Temple Judea, so your influence would be expanded. The more customers my salesmen knew, the greater the opportunity of selling my goods. There was nothing remarkable about it; it was just a case of plain common sense, good salesmanship.

I also cultivated sports activities in my ward. I sponsored a basketball team and a softball team, and we used to have amateur prize fights. We had picnics at which we had sporting events and marathon races. We had so many affairs. We even had a Yiddish theater. At the request of the rabbis and leaders of the Yiddish-speaking community, especially the *Jewish Daily Forward,* we looked around for a place where we could subsidize the Yiddish theater. We organized a B'nai B'rith Lodge in the ward. The Talmud Torahs [private religious schools] were partly organized in the basement of my home. The Twenty-fourth Ward was really a community.

Yes, the Bund was spreading Nazi propaganda. But there were people who would fan out when the Bund was having a meeting and they'd break them up. We had a member of the Police Department who was Jewish, a German emigrant, who infiltrated their ranks, so he got to know where they were going to meet. There were people who cultivated pool halls and restaurants, Zucky's on the West Side and Tuchman's on the North Side. I knew that Zucky and Tuchman were recruiting university people who were leaders to go out there. Did I organize them? I did not. Aid them? Yes, I admit that quite frankly.

Hitler was saying that Jews were a curse, they had to be blotted out, some way must be found to erase Jewish influence. In a crude way, it was like what Agnew was saying. But few dreamed that Hitler would finally enter upon a final solution that was extermination. Some people, though, did pay attention to it. Let me recite a little incident to you. In '39 I attended a meeting in the home of Rabbi Solomon Goldman, where Chaim Weizmann, then the president of the World Zionist Organization, later the first president of Israel, spoke. He was trying to get money to aid the Jewish victims of Nazi oppression and he said, "If the Allies win this war—pardon me, gentlemen, *when* the Allies win this war. For if they do not win this war, we will have no Jewish problem. There will be no Jews." So he had an awareness of the implications of Hitler's program. But most people never dreamed of the ultimate conclusions.

In the years prior to the depression, a black Democrat was as rare as a southern Republican. But by 1936, because of the New Deal's impact and because of the efforts of such political leaders as Earl Dickerson, black voters were making a historic shift in their political alliances; the Democratic party, once the political symbol of white supremacy, was becoming biracial.

Mr. Dickerson, a retired Chicago alderman, is a director of the National Urban League and of the NAACP and a founder of the American Legion. He is also the former president of the Supreme Life Insurance Company of America.

EARL DICKERSON

I had something to do with the building of the two-party system for the colored people. It was my activity that did that. When Al Smith ran for the presidency, I was in charge of seven states— Illinois, Ohio, Michigan, Indiana, West Virginia, Wisconsin and Missouri—in an organization that was known as the Smith for President Colored League. I had a budget that was $50,000. For the first time, we got as much as a third of the black vote in the communities where we worked.

In '32 I was a northern delegate to the convention that nominated Mr. Roosevelt. I was present when Roosevelt flew in and came to the floor of the Chicago Coliseum to make his acceptance speech.

There were no black delegates, but I was an alternate. I think there may have been another black, I don't recall. No, I didn't notice any mistreatment. We had no real following; we were just like the white delegates and alternates, dominated by the heads of the delegations. But we were enthusiastic about it, because we knew about Roosevelt's record as governor of the state of New York, and for the first time we knew that the Democratic party was not just ancillary to the Republican party. Up to that time, the two parties stood for the same thing, the dominance of the rich at the expense of the poor and underprivileged.

I spoke in Chicago, in Philadelphia, in Los Angeles in fact, wherever we were trying to convince the people that there was need for a change. But even then the majority of the blacks voted Republican. It was only in '36 that they began to come in as a majority.

I was then assistant attorney general of the state of Illinois and active in the political arena, pleading the case of black people as participants in the democratic process. You'd go to the political organization, to where they were making decisions, and you'd see the chairman. The chairman at that time was a man named Nash; later it was Kelly. And you'd make a plea for jobs for blacks. That was a big important thing, political jobs: jobs as lawyers in the city council, in the corporation counsel's office, in the attorney general's office, for instance, and sure, working as a precinct captain was part of holding a political job.

You see, the Democrats had been coming into office over the years, but it was only now that they began to give recognition to blacks—though never in line with the contributions we made. And that's true today.

Nash and Kelly were always polite. I remember, on certain days I'd go to their office to ask them to give certain jobs, and there'd be a line of about ten people standing there. Say I was the fifth person in that line and the people behind me were white. When I'd get to the top to go in, well, many times I was asked to step aside until the whites went in.

Later, because of my activities in the campaign to elect Governor Horner and Roosevelt in '32, Cermak, then mayor of Chicago and the boss of the Democratic party, asked me if I wanted a job. I said, "Yes, but only if you give me a job in the attorney general's office and let me participate in the legal affairs, as you do the whites." (Prior to that time, Negroes were appointed by the Republicans and just sat there and collected money.) "If you let me argue cases and participate to the extent of my ability, I'll take it." So he called up the newly elected

Illinois attorney general, Otto Kerner, and said, "I've got a young man here in my office who has helped us all the time and has never asked for anything, and I want you to appoint him as assistant attorney general," and a few days later I was appointed.

I identified myself then with the black organization in the Second Ward. I participated in various public matters. I spoke wherever there was an opportunity for me to speak, at public meetings, in churches. Sometimes the minister was tired and wanted me to give the Sunday-morning address. I remember one address I gave from the Book of Esther—"Who know but that thou art coming unto the kingdom . . ."—Mordecai and Esther and all that, trying to get the blacks to come over to the Democratic party and saying that the two-party system is better than one. It was on that basis that I made my case.

It was very difficult to get blacks to become Democrats, because the Democrats had done nothing more for the blacks than the Republicans had. And, in addition, blacks identified Democrats with the lynching and persecution the people in the South had heaped on them.

Hard it was, difficult it was. They called me traitor because I was leaving the party of Lincoln. One who made much of that was William Dawson, who later became a Democrat. Dawson was a Republican in this ward at that time. He ran for Congress as a Republican, and he started this rumor that all blacks who espoused the cause of Democrats were traitors to their race. Dawson used to have cartoons of me as a light person having an office downtown, slamming the door to black people who came there, saying I didn't like black people, trying to compare me with Democrats in the South, saying that I was joining the white forces to subdue blacks.

In '39 I was elected alderman. When I was called to speak (I had been the most popular fellow in the organization that whole period in the formation of Democratic strength in that ward), I said, "Now that we have a black Democratic ward committeeman [chairman], and the majority of the people are independents and lean toward the Democrats, we should be able to build a black political force in this community to demand recognition in all phases of political life in Chicago, instead of getting on our knees." The people went wild.

I was a gadfly who would disturb the peace and tranquility of those who wanted to make America separate, black and white. And being so, naturally, I was not accepted as a sane, safe person. However, the opposition gave me strength to continue the battle, even to this day—and I'm 84. There's never been any stopping, any peace or tranquility, either in my actions or in my mind.

Between 1935 and 1937 the Supreme Court invalidated more federal legislation than it had during the first 35 years of the twentieth century. Responding to the Court's opposition to the New Deal, President Roosevelt tried to expand the number of justices on the bench through his Court-packing plan, his intention being to create a majority favorable to the New Deal. However, in so doing, he nearly precipitated a constitutional crisis, and finally backed off from his proposal.

Joe Rauh, now a Washington attorney, president of the Americans for Democratic Action and a director of the NAACP, was a witness to the Court-packing controversy, as indeed, as Justice Cardozo's law clerk, he was witness to many of the judicial controversies of that era. In this interview, he recalls some of those controversies and the personalities behind them.

JOE RAUH

I came to Washington in September of '35 after I graduated from law school. I was one of the breed known as the "Frankfurter Hot Dogs," because Felix Frankfurter had been my professor. It was he who sent me to Washington, where I had a job with Ben Cohen and Tom Corcoran as a glorified messenger and law clerk. I worked for Ben and Tom for a year and in September, '36, became Justice Cardozo's law clerk by virtue of Professor Frankfurter's recommendation.

When I got there, the Court was on the verge of making its shift. Up until that time, a lot of the New Deal legislation had been knocked out, so in '37 Roosevelt sent up the Court-packing plan. The result was that Roberts and, to a lesser extent, Hughes made some important shifts. As a matter of fact, they reversed themselves on so many of their previous decisions that Drew

Pearson and Bob Allen, in a book they wrote, referred to them as "the men on the flying trapeze."

Without any question, four justices (Sutherland, Reynolds, Vandevanter and Butler) were out to do Roosevelt and the New Deal in. They were openly hostile and voted against everything. Plus there was Roberts, who went with them very often. Then there were the three (Cardozo, Stone and Brandeis) who were always with Roosevelt and were liberals. In self-defense, these three held meetings the day before the weekly Court conferences in order to have a joint position. Now, Hughes often voted with the liberals, but he couldn't make a majority.

So it came down to three liberals who felt that Congress should have the right to do what it wanted and that, further, it wasn't up to the Court to tell Congress it couldn't pass the statutes Roosevelt asked for. Then, on the other side, were the four Neanderthals, who would hold everything unconstitutional, whether it was regulating business or helping poor people. And in the middle were the two on the flying trapeze.

What was the Courts' reaction to the Court-packing plan? Everybody was vicious but Cardozo, who I think mildly enjoyed the discomfiture of his colleagues. He'd say, "Well, you know, Mr. Rauh"—he was very formal—"it's a little hard for a man who's been on the bench this long to be very objective about the idea of putting some people here to make us do things we should do anyway." He was opposed to the plan, but he was also very critical of Brandeis, who had supported Hughes. Hughes had written a letter to the Senate Judiciary Committee attacking the plan and saying that he had cleared the letter with Brandeis, a clever stunt he'd devised to show that while the conservatives were obviously with him, he had cleared his position with this great historic liberal. Well, Cardozo thought that was an absolute outrage.

Cardozo was a very interesting man. He lived only for his work; he had no family and he didn't go out much. After he died, I wrote a review of a book about him in which I pointed out that he had no friends. I got a letter from Justice Stone denouncing that point, saying that *he* was a friend. I didn't respond, but I could have said, "Yes, it was a very close relationship. He went to your house once a year for dinner, and you went to his house once a year for dinner. A very close relationship."

Cardozo was really never happy in Washington. His friends were in New York, and when he got here at 62 with angina, he never could make good friends. As for his law clerks, how often did he see us outside work? He came to our houses once for dinner, we went to his house once for dinner. He was unhappy, so he lived for his work.

To show you how important his work was to him, Hughes would assign the opinions on Saturday night after the cases were decided at the weekly conference. The messenger would take them around, and Cardozo would get his case assignment about 6:00 or 7:00 that night. Well, we'd walk in on Monday morning and he had the opinion all written out. On Sunday he had done the whole thing.

As far as Roosevelt went, Cardozo absolutely loved him. They knew each other from New York State when Cardozo was the chief justice, and occasionally Roosevelt would call up to say hello. I remember the morning of the '36 election; when I walked in, Cardozo said, "Oh, wasn't it wonderful?" I mean he really loved Roosevelt.

After Cardozo died, Frankfurter was appointed to succeed him in '38, and I became his law clerk. I loved him very much. He had more effect on my life than anybody else. He talked me out of being a Cincinnati lawyer and coming down here. He had taken a shine to me in my third year of law school and diverted me from a more normal course of going to a big Jewish law firm.

He was almost indescribable. He was the biggest man I ever met, in the sense that he knew more people, knew more things and did more things than anyone I'd ever known. He was a one-man liberal movement.

He staffed the New Deal. Tom Corcoran, Ben Cohen, Jim Landis, Charlie Wyzanski—none of them would have been here if it weren't for Frankfurter. He was a one-man recruitment agency for the New Deal. Roosevelt and others were always asking him for people. Hugh Johnson, the head of the National Recovery Administration [NRA], referred to him as either "the most single influential man in the United States" or "the single most influential man in the United States." He wasn't quite clear which way he meant it, but either way, there was a little anti-Semitism in Johnson's statement. He felt that Frankfurter, a Jew, was running the Roosevelt administration.

Once a group of rich, conservative Jews went to see him to complain that there were too many Jews in this radical New Deal and these Jews were creating anti-Semitism. I'll never forget his reply. Felix listened to them and then, after a while, said, "So you would build your *own* ghetto." It was beautiful. And he was beautiful, an absolutely beautiful man.

Brandeis was also very influential. Every Sunday afternoon there was a tea at his house, and it was a big deal to be one of the 20 or 30 people invited. He would talk to each person to try to get information, but he also tried to influence them. We once got invited because we were Cardozo's law clerks and Brandeis particularly tried to influence young people, though by this time I think he was a little less liberal. He was quite states'-rights-minded and very hostile to the NRA. But I don't mean to suggest that, though less enthusiastic, he was less pro-New Deal than Cardozo. After all, Roosevelt did centralize the government, and Brandeis had great reservations about the centralization of the government. But remember, Wilson appointed him in '16, and we're talking about '36; that's 20 years later.

As far as his Jewishness went, I don't think there were many instances in which it affected his decisions—or, for that matter, in which Frankfurter's or Cardozo's affected theirs. I don't think the right wing ever beat them down, because it couldn't. They were giants. I can't picture that a lousy right wing could have had much effect on them. The only time there was any discussion of that problem was when Frankfurter upheld the constitutionality of the flag salute in the case involving the Jehovah's Witnesses. Some people argued that that was his way of showing he was a loyal American. But that's the only time I ever remember its really coming to the fore.

It's hard to say who, among the justices, had the most effect. I think the greatest effect came from the political climate, the totality of the New Deal period. It was a wonderful time.

Today the Washington media not only reports the news; it often *makes* it. This involvement of the working press with the workings of government is not a post-Watergate development but has, in fact, been going on for decades. However, as Marquis Childs notes, when he came to Washington in the early thirties the press was still limited in its role and function. But as Childs suggests, it was in the thirties that some journalists (including himself) began to have extra-journalistic impacts, thus making the decade a time of transition for both the government and the media.

Mr. Childs is a leading syndicated columnist and commentator for the St. Louis *Post-Dispatch* in Washington. In addition to his newspaper writing, he is also the author of a number of books on the American contemporary scene.

MARQUIS CHILDS

Washington was where the action was, and I was very glad that the St. Louis *Post-Dispatch* transferred me here in '34. There was an atmosphere of continuing excitement and exhilaration. FDR was not a very orderly president. He had a lot of temperamental people in his administration, and they sounded off very often without any regard to what he might want or say. Take Harold Ickes: He was going to the press all the time with one complaint after another, one story after another. These people weren't as adept as Roosevelt in dealing with the press, but they were just as aggressive. So you had a continuous flap of news about the Civilian Conservation Corps, about the gold standard, about Huey Long. It was a time that, well, makes the present seem very dull.

Roosevelt was a master of public relations; it's just as simple as that. With the "fireside chats," he had a mastery of reaching out and giving the sense that he was talking to three or four people in somebody's house. It was part of his strength that he was a kind of *paterfamilias* to whom the American people looked up and whom they respected.

And, of course, the contrast with Hoover was so great. Hoover had been so distant, so removed and so hurt. During the last couple of years of his administration, he had insisted that there could only be written questions at his press conferences. He would stand up before the press with these cards and thumb over them and answer only the ones he chose to answer. Well, Roosevelt knew exactly how wrong that was from the point of view of public relations. But, of course, he was also very careful; you couldn't press a question with him. I remember his saying once, when somebody tried to ask a second question, "Remember, now, no cross-examination." Oh, he was a master of public relations.

The difference between press conferences then and now is that then they were so much smaller. I don't suppose there were more than 100 or 150 reporters who were eligible to come to a Roosevelt press conference. We were not then such a world power, so there were very few foreign correspondents who came.

The conferences were held in the Oval Office, with the press reporters gathered around the president's desk, so the mechanics of the thing were entirely different. Now you have that room over in the Executive Office Building with something like 400 to 500 people crowded in.

The requirements to attend a press conference then were the same as they are today: You must be a reporter for a newspaper or a magazine. Now, of course, the security is so intense you have to have a security card to get in. You never did then; it was so informal.

Stephen Early? He was an extremely able press secretary. He had the complete confidence of Roosevelt and sort of a good relationship with the working press. He also had a rather low boiling point, but that was rather understandable in that office. It's an impossible office.

No, I don't think the press was as influential as it is now. You certainly didn't have the role of the investigative reporter then.

Today, it's the desire of every young reporter to do another Watergate and bring somebody down, which I don't think prevailed in the times we're talking about.

You see, the whole thing has changed completely. At the time of Roosevelt's press conferences, you could not quote him directly out of the White House. That was the rule. You couldn't quote Hoover directly, either. You could only say, "The president believes, the president said" and so on. It had been that way all along. Perhaps the press was too kind to Roosevelt, I don't know. There was a kind of standing agreement I think we worked out with Early that Roosevelt was never to be photographed in his wheelchair. He was photographed walking in his braces on the arm of his son James, but never in his wheelchair.

Roosevelt's campaign style? There again, it was that sense of reaching out, of talking. I remember in '36 there was a crowd of about 25,000 packed into the Chicago Coliseum, making an incredible clamor. It was one of the few times I ever saw Roosevelt slightly deterred by the intensity of it all. Yet he quieted them and talked to them as if, again, he was talking to just a few people. His use of pronouns was very important: "What *we* believe," not "What *they*" or "What *I*," but "What *you* and *I* . . ." As I say, he was a master at creating a great sense of intimacy. He could do it with a large crowd, he could do it with people assembled at the back of his train; he could do it anywhere.

As far as developing sources, that's what every reporter who comes here does. My wife and I met a lot of these people when we began going out to dinner parties and receptions, and I very soon made some very good friends. One of them was Justice Brandeis. He gave me one of the real insights into the Roosevelt Court-packing plan, and I think I had some responsibility for helping to block that.

Yes, I was quite involved in that situation, because, besides Brandeis, I was close to Senator Wheeler, who was one of those instrumental in blocking the plan. I brought Brandeis together with Wheeler, and out of that came the letter from Chief Justice Hughes, which was in a way, the *coup de grace* for the plan. I would say that "go-between" is a little bit of a pejorative term; rather, I was developing a story and so wrote about a lot of this just about all the time it was going on. I was also the first who was able to write that two of the senior justices would retire, which was the key business in the plan.

Yes, I was also very close to Justice Stone. We got in the habit one winter of going on late-afternoon walks, and he talked about his deep concern for the Court. He felt that at least one or two of the men Roosevelt was appointing, such as Justice Black, were not equipped with the proper background to be able to carry their weight in the Court.

So I wrote an article for the *Post-Dispatch,* and Justice Stone said, "Well, this is fine, but if you could put the whole thing in a national magazine, with a national audience, I think it would be even more helpful." Whereupon I then wrote the same thing for *Harper's,* and at that point a lot of Black's friends in the press rushed in and took after me and Stone. It was a very unfortunate thing. I should have had better sense, but I didn't. What happened was that an individual in the bureau—I won't mention his name—stationed himself in the lobby of the press club, to say that I had received the material from Stone. Why did he do it? Well, this was a very unfortunate man. He was a brilliant reporter, but his trouble was drink, and I think that had something to do with it.

Yes, that ended my relationship with Stone, because he was terribly embarrassed. His secretary called me two or three days after the incident with, "There are twelve reporters in the judge's office and I'm calling from a pay station. What do you think he should tell them?" I said to her, "Tell him to deny the whole thing, that he had nothing to do with any of it. That's the only option he has." Which I guess he did, I don't know. By that time I wanted to do anything I could to help him. I'll never forget a comment his wonderful secretary made the last time I saw him after the whole thing had broken open and he had suffered a lot from it. She was sitting there and said, "Well, I always told the judge he talks too much."

Yes, I was quite close to Harry Hopkins. I was a reporter trying to get news from him, and developed a sympathetic interest in his plight. It was manifested by his efforts to make this damn system work and then by the terrible pressures and strains he was under, which, I suppose, were the causes for the terrible illnesses he had. I used to see him when he lived in the White House and spent most of his time in bed in the Lincoln Bedroom. Here was a great big bed all strewn with papers, and the whole thing was a bit, well, on the disorderly side.

Hopkins was an extraordinary man, curiously ambivalent. He was supposedly the champion of the downtrodden and the unemployed; yet he had a great penchant for the rich and for people who lived high on the hog. During the '30s he worked tremendously hard setting up all these programs for the unemployed. Of course, we know now that while this was reform, it was not recovery, and I think that later Hopkins began to realize that; because it was perfectly obvious that until the war orders began to come from Britain and France in '39 or '40, you still had this great mass of the unemployed.

3
MOVEMENTS AND MINORITIES

> The thirties were the years the American Civil Liberties Union began to have a major impact on the American scene. Whether it was owing to an increase in its membership and activity, or to the economic, political and social upheaval in that decade, the ACLU became one of the country's most active organizations in protecting basic American liberties.
>
> Roger Baldwin, whose name has been almost synonymous with the ACLU, joined the organization in 1917 and served as executive director from 1950 to 1955. Born in 1884, Mr. Baldwin lives and works in New York City.

ROGER BALDWIN

My recollection is that by '30 people who responded in public affairs were stunned, not knowing what to do. At first there was no protest movement from labor, from the farmers or from the middle class. It was a time of trying to adjust. People weren't sure that the collapse was complete. It wasn't until '31, when the banks began to fail, that the protests began.

I think the first sign of real resistance was the first dollar-mortgage sale, which became epidemic throughout the West. Farmers would appear at a mortgage sale when a bank foreclosed and they would be so completely united that nobody would offer more than a dollar. So these farms were sold for a dollar and the mortgages were wiped out.

Generally, however, we were all in a state of depression over the forces of resistance in this country. There was nothing to take hold of. And I think that was in large part responsible for the hope that greeted Mr. Roosevelt's nomination and the kind of program he announced when the campaign got under way in '32. Of course, when he came to Washington, everything changed. He and his advisors represented an entirely different attitude toward the function of government. They insisted from the very beginning that the federal government had a responsibility for all parts of the country superior to any states-rights or local claims. Therefore, all that legislation the New Deal advocated was based upon humanitarian concepts, not upon a property concept. It reversed the tendencies of the previous administration to emphasize the necessity of maintaining the business community without intervention or interference. The Roosevelt administration began to interfere and to regulate and assist, and I think all of us in the ACLU thought this was perhaps the greatest change we had had since the early reformist days under Teddy Roosevelt and Woodrow Wilson before the war.

The old Progressive party under Teddy Roosevelt had the same idea about government; but it took the New Deal to enact it into statutes and make it a solid body of law. Now, Woodrow Wilson, it's true, was not for the welfare state. After all, he and Teddy Roosevelt were opponents in the 1912 election. Wilson was for taming the trusts and the big boys. But FDR's administration did that, too, through the Court-packing plan. You remember, the Supreme Court was sticking with its property notions, and Roosevelt threatened to appoint new justices and to overcome this majority that would not accept his humanitarian ideas. But then Chief Justice Hughes saw the light and got his own majority of the Court to accept these ideas, and they validated most of the New Deal legislation.

How did we make our contacts in Washington? A lot of our people were right there in the government. We had people who were very close friends. For example, Mr. Ickes had been one of our people in Chicago, and he became a member of the cabinet. As soon as the cabinet appointments were made, it turned out that we knew half of them. Also, we had a small office in Washington, and I went down almost every week.

When we couldn't get what we wanted out of the government, we had to resort to some sort of legal proceedings. There were a number of cases. The National Labor Relations Board case was the most important of them. Now, the reason our board took a long time coming around to the National Labor Relations Act was that in our experience in government intervention between capital and labor, government would always be on the side of capital. We had no conception that the government could become the friend or the defender of trade unions. We also had a case against post-office censorship, and some cases involving the deportation of aliens. A little later we had an extradition case, which became a *cause célèbre* and was the basis for the movie *I was a Fugitive from a Chain Gang*. We got former Supreme Court Judge Harry Osborne to take it. He argued it out with the governor of New Jersey, and the governor said he wouldn't return a man to that kind of punishment. We had a number of those extradition cases at different times.

The 30s were also the years of the united fronts, organizations created by the Communists. I think the party strength was probably greater in those years than at any time before or after. They recruited a large number of members, as a result of the threats of war in Europe, through the League Against War and Fascism (later called the League for Peace and Democracy). They also had their organization to defend the Spanish Loyalist government and, in the early 30s, another organization, the League Against Imperialism. I had gone to Brussels in '27, when it was founded, and was chairman of the American section until the Communists threw me out because I was supporting Mr.

Gandhi in India, whom they regarded as a bourgeois reactionary.

Yes, I was active in all of them; it was rather natural that I should be, since these were all civil-liberties issues. The Communists supported practically everything we were doing, and we supported individually the united fronts. But the ACLU was never officially involved in any united front at all. It worked with the Communist defense organizations the way it did with the socialist defense organizations, the American Bar Association and various other organizations that went into court.

Of course, we've always been suspect as sympathizers with the causes we defended. People cannot distinguish between defending a right and defending a person. If you defend a person, they forget the fact that you're really defending a right all people have together.

And because the major part of our clientele, the people we defend, are bound to be disturbers of the peace, we've always been attacked. These are people who are unhappy, dissatisfied. The conformists don't need our help; nobody troubles them. It's the nonconformists who need our help. And therefore we've always been looked upon—by large sections of the public, anyway—as subversives, in that we are not considered part of the mainstream. But we *are* part of the mainstream; we are something a democracy has to tolerate.

When you ask me to evaluate what I've done, I'm not one to think much in terms of an individual's importance. Nobody knows what he contributes. You make your best effort, you hope for results, and I happen to be one of those who never predicated my activity on success. I didn't care much about success. If I won, so much the better; if I failed, after all, I'd tried. I took more satisfaction in trying and doing my best than I did in the results.

Although white and black America still lived under the "separate-but-equal" doctrine of the 1894 Supreme Court decision *Plessy* v. *Ferguson,* by the thirties organizations like the National Association for the Advancement of Colored People were laying the foundation for legal changes—and in some cases winning landmark Supreme Court decisions. But, as NAACP Washington Bureau director Clarence Mitchell observes, the black man's rights were still far from guaranteed by law. For many blacks, while they were winning their rights under constitutional law, lynch law remained the reality of their status.

Mr. Mitchell has been associated with the NAACP for almost half a century. In 1945 he became the organization's labor secretary, and in 1960 he was named to his present position.

CLARENCE MITCHELL

I first became associated with the National Association for the Advancement of Colored People as a volunteer in the Baltimore Branch in '32. At that time I had just finished college and was full of idealism. Because I was working as a newspaper reporter, the NAACP put me in charge of public relations. But the title I held was really somewhat misleading, because once you were a member of the local board or in touch with the national officials of the organization, you might be asked to do almost anything: write a useful story or, as in my case, go to public officials to ask their aid in changing conditions. I was asked to participate in efforts to end exclusion of blacks from the police force in Baltimore and to get people into institutions from which they had been excluded on the basis of race. So, while I had the title of public relations director, as a matter of fact I was also involved in the day-to-day operations of the organization.

Fortunately, at that time Walter White, the national executive secretary of the NAACP, struck up a relationship with me and therefore I had an opportunity to have some insight into and impact on the national operations of the organization. It worked this way. Walter would get an idea and he'd want to bounce it off people who were in tune with his approach to things. So he'd ask you to a meeting or, on the other hand, ask you to present some kind of testimony before a legislative body. As a reporter, I had covered a lynching that occurred in Princess Anne, Maryland, in '33, and Walter made sure that I had an opportunity to present that testimony to the Senate Judiciary Committee, which was then holding hearings on an antilynching bill. That was the way he operated; and there were other people in the NAACP, too, who were on the lookout for the young and volatile who might have something to contribute to the organization.

As to the lynching, it was something that was well publicized in advance. The victim had been charged with doing something to a white woman. It was never clear what he was charged with, but it turned out it couldn't have been rape. He was arrested on a simple charge of assault and sent from Princess Anne to the Baltimore city jail, where, supposedly, he would be safe from any mob attack. However, local people on the eastern shore of Maryland who were politically powerful insisted that he be brought back to their jurisdiction, and the governor of the state, who was politically beholden to that group, agreed. It's hard to know why he agreed, since only two years before in Salisbury, in the same area of the state, there had been a lynching, and common sense would have indicated that if there had been a lynching in a larger, hopefully more enlightened community in '31, there was no reason to think there would not be one in '33 in Princess Anne. Nevertheless, the man was brought back and there was a lot of publicity, including indications that he would be lynched. Accordingly, a number of reporters from various papers went to Princess Anne.

No, I wasn't fearful, not because I was brave, but because when you're young you have a lot of illusions, and I had the illusion that the status of a newspaperman was such that it conferred a kind of immunity on me. When I got to the town of

Princess Anne, I discovered there had in fact been a lynching. The man had been strung up, his body drenched with gasoline and thrown into the middle of the street. The people standing around professed not to know how it had happened. They indicated that a lot of people from Virginia had come and perpetrated this crime, and nobody knew who was responsible. Of course, it later turned out that some of those who were standing around were actually mob members, and there had been a total breakdown of law enforcement. These were the facts I stated in my testimony before the Senate Judiciary Committee.

All I had to do was tell what happened; the events were so horrible in themselves I didn't have to editorialize. When you see a fellow human with a rope around his neck and skin coming off his body, you don't need to add any touches of horror.

The most vivid recollection I have of that experience is that while I was waiting to testify, Senator Huey Long, Sr., came to me, and in my dual role as newspaper reporter and witness, it occurred to me that it would be a good story if I could get his opinion of the antilynching legislation. He stood in the doorway of the Senate Caucus Room and, in a loud voice, said, "I don't think much of this bill, but I think some of those senators in there conducting the hearing should be lynched." And he said that at least three times to make sure they would hear.

I think the attitude of the opposition was that whether or not this lynching was the work of people acting outside the law, you couldn't invade the rights of states in order to do anything about it. And, of course, there were others who had stories just as gruesome, so by that time, I think, the country had become a little hardened to what took place in lynchings. People were revolted by it and wanted to do something about it, but the full horror didn't come through, because it wasn't portrayed as atrocities would later be on the television screen. We had some horrible pictures of lynchings and yet they could reach only a limited audience, because you had to see them in the papers (and many wouldn't even print them) or at a meeting, where the whole terrible part wouldn't really come through. Still a considerable part of the public was determined to control such things by having a law by which lynchers could be brought to justice.

Unfortunately, there was an equally strong group that felt that lynching was a means of keeping blacks in their place—that if they didn't have such a weapon, blacks, particularly in areas where they were numerically strong, would take over—and therefore they were attacking the bill. The antilynching law was never passed as a national statute; but the objectives have since been realized in separate statutes. For example, in '60, when we got the Fair Housing Law passed, the Workers' Protection Statute was also passed. But this was really a series of amendments to Title 18 of the criminal code, which gives the government authority to bring criminal prosecutions in almost every conceivable situation where individuals would otherwise have been lynched—for example, if it was a case where a person moved into a neighborhood and the neighbors decided to burn his home and, if he resisted, to lynch him. That is now a criminal offense that can be punished by imprisonment, even life imprisonment, if the victim dies as a result of the crime. So, while the antilynching statute as such was never passed, the basic tools enabling the government to act in these situations did become part of the law.

I think that in some communities where people were comfortable with segregation, some of us were considered radicals. I lived in Atlanta for a year during the '30s when I was studying at the School of Social Work. During my stay there, I refused to ride on streetcars and buses because they were segregated, so I walked everywhere. And once, when the oppressive elements in Atlanta attempted to invade an NAACP meeting at which I was present, I verbally attacked them and they finally became disconcerted and left. It was such behavior that caused people to think I was a radical.

However, those people were not numerous, because not that many people were well off. I'm pleased to say also that some who *were* well off but had come out of oppressive backgrounds and seen raw violence now wanted to help others. Indeed, a large part of our organization's leadership was made up of people from humble beginnings who had achieved status in business, medicine, and other fields and now were so concerned about segregation that they were willing to lay their lives and properties on the line.

We never had any problems in terms of credibility. It's true that during the depression we were under heavy attack from the Communists; but it was their strategy to discredit everybody. They described us as tools of Wall Street, saying that we were not militant enough; but I don't think anybody paid much attention to it. They made several efforts to start organizations to do essentially what the NAACP was doing. They held mass meetings, issued statements and generally beat the drums. But when their ideological and political objectives were found out, they quickly fell apart. So while they got a lot of publicity, they never were a real threat to our organization.

Perhaps the most dramatic illustration of the situation with them was the fight we were making against imposed segregation. Those other groups would have a big demonstration over a statute requiring segregation on intrastate or interstate travel, but they wouldn't raise the money to go to court or get the legislature to change it. By the same token, if a person was charged with a crime and was the source of much newspaper publicity, the group was happy to be involved in it. But once the publicity died down and was no longer suitable for fund-raising, they would bow out. The classic example was the Scottsboro case in '31. Some groups saw a lot of financial possibilities, plus a lot of ideological opportunities to exploit, and used it accordingly. And when those opportunities were exhausted and other issues became more attractive as moneymakers, they got out of the case, whereas the NAACP continued right up to 1977, when we were active trying to get a pardon for the last of the Scottsboro boys. Throughout the years, we had a fund that was used for some of the necessities of the people who had managed to escape or had gotten out of jail and were living in other places. It was discontinued only very recently, and only then because most of the defendants had died or disappeared.

Regarding our efforts against segregation, our strategy was to work under then accepted principles of law to make the separate-but-equal doctrine so obviously incapable of realization that it would fall of its own weight. As a matter of legal requirements, the first and most difficult hurdle was to find a legal theory that would make it clear to the Court that the question raised was not one on which the Court had already made a decision, but on points not ruled on before. Therefore, when we got into the field of eduction, the point was at the college and professional-school level. We had clear examples of total disregard for the rights of blacks, even with the separate-but-equal theory.

The states' efforts to counter us took various forms. One was that funds were established for blacks to be educated outside the state. Another was to set up regional schools that were segregated. In other words, if you were in Tuskegee, you could set up a school of veterinary training that would be available to blacks in Georgia, Alabama, Tennessee, or wherever. This would mean that blacks who tried to get into a similar school within their own state would be met with the argument that there weren't enough blacks to be in a separate school and therefore they would have to go to the regional school. This effort got as far as Congress sanctioning such agreements between the states. In our office, we were able to defeat these resolutions in Congress by showing that the intention was to establish a way of getting around the duty of the state to provide within its borders education to blacks that was equal to that available to whites. And, of course, all the while we knew that there was no way in the world for blacks to be accorded equal education if there were separate institutions. It seemed obvious to us that all we'd have to do is find that there was a certain course in the separate schools, and you were face to face with the conflict of the separate-but-equal doctrine. I remember some humorous observations about very exotic scientific equipment, costing maybe $100,000, being available in one of the white schools. Since obviously they couldn't have two of those, they'd have to admit the blacks.

It wasn't only the colleges where we focused our efforts, but also high schools and other state institutions where blacks were not admitted. There was a public library in Baltimore, for instance, that gave courses to whites in library training. The NAACP challenged successfully, and blacks were admitted to this training program. But our really concentrated, long-term efforts were made at the graduate and professional-school level, because it was believed that this area would be the hardest to even give a semblance of equality on a separate basis. It turned out that this was exactly the case. There was just no way for the states and local political entities to set up anything that was equal, and even when they tried, the courts said they couldn't be equal. This was particularly true in the field of law the courts said, because an important part of the educational process was the interaction between classmates who later would become the prosecutors and judges.

So I would say that as far as state institutions were concerned, our first objective was to get them open. The trend was based on the Donald Murray case, which challenged the University of Maryland Law School in '35. It was the first case in which a state court struck down the practice of barring blacks on the basis of race. Around '39 there were similar cases in Missouri, Oklahoma and Texas. Later other schools were opened, but even now there is still much to be desired in terms of black enrollment.

I think a by-product of the depression and the suffering in the black community was a greater awareness of what could be done to correct some of the conditions. For example, for years in cities like Chicago, Cleveland and Washington, white owners would open businesses in black neighborhoods with only white people working there. I'm sure had it not been for the depression, people might not have paid much attention to that. But because it was the depression and it was a scramble for jobs, a "buy-where-you-can-work" movement developed in this country, which caused blacks to picket for jobs. And, indeed, one of the famous cases arose in Washington between the New Negro Alliance and the Sanitary Grocery Company. In '38, the Supreme Court upheld the right of blacks to picket in that kind of dispute. Up to that time, a restraining order was issued if blacks picketed in a quest for jobs. Picketing became a very effective movement in almost every community where it was used. It resulted in blacks getting jobs, and in a new look at municipal employment. I remember in Baltimore somebody suddenly realized that blacks couldn't get jobs as street cleaners and as social workers in welfare programs. These also became targets.

Looking back, I feel very encouraged by the fact that it was possible to surmount what at that time seemed insurmountable. I do know that what has been accomplished is permanent only if we fight to preserve it and continue to work to move it forward. It's not the kind of thing that is likely to lull me into a false sense of security. Rather, I think of it as a challenge to know that if one tries, one can succeed.

The collapse of the American economy in the early thirties produced a multiformity of responses and movements. One of the most powerful and far-reaching of such movements was the Old Age Revolving Pensions, Limited, of California, popularly called the Townsend Plan.

The originator of the plan, retired physician Francis E. Townsend, proposed the establishment of a monthly government revolving fund for the purpose of both supporting retired persons and stimulating the economy. While the plan was never put into effect, it *did* have an influence on social security legislation and carried considerable political clout, while receiving widespread support.

Today, the Townsend movement is still promoting its philosophy through the person of its last living member and Washington representative, John D. Elliott.

JOHN D. ELLIOTT

Dr. Townsend believed that money is the main commodity in the consciousness of mankind, when, in reality, it represents only three things: goods, commodities and services. Money is only a common denominator of value. Thus, in a free-enterprise system, we should never subsidize a competitor (as Hoover, Roosevelt and the Reconstruction Finance Corporation did with what amounted to public-paid loans to business) but rather the flesh-and-blood, heart-and-soul human beings who are noncompetitive for various reasons: old age, infirmity, disability, etc. That way, instead of stockholders, investors and so forth subsidizing competitors, the public would subsidize noncompetitive people, people who are in a position to pay for being subsidized.

But what was publicized when Dr. Townsend's letter to a California newspaper editor was put on the wires was the idea of a $200-a-month giveaway. Now, what the Townsend Plan actually proposed was this: On a revolving fund based on a tax of the monetary authority and issue, money would be collected and distributed. In the meantime, until this fund could be set up, $200 a month would be given to every person over 60 who would agree to spend it on nothing other than goods, commodities and services, the idea being to fill the gap created by the depression, to separate human beings from the dollar, which had become the license to live. By the way, the legislation for the '36 veterans' bonus demonstrated the validity of all this. It was a $2 billion proposition that temporarily created buying power, and when it ran out, we had the recession.

Now, that letter of September 30, 1933, to the editor that the wire service picked up went everywhere. And some people sat down and thought it over and what the hell, it worked. I mean, here all the brains in the world were stumped, and this guy comes out with this goddamned idiocy that was actually the reverse of the depression!

You know, people were terribly hard up. They were asking what was to be done. As for me, after *I* thought it over, the first thing I did was talk things over with some neighbors. Then, on November 7, 1934, we organized what became the first Townsend Club east of the Mississippi River, in Waltham, Massachusetts. We organized the second one on March 17, 1935, and I was its president. In Massachusetts at one time we had over 400 organized committees. Next, as the clubs began to form, we organized a speakers' bureau, traveling around the state, calling meetings for the newspapers, etc. I remember organizing, in '36-'37, as many as 30 clubs in a month. See, when you had about 25 people, you applied to the Old Age Revolving Pension Limited of California for a charter.

There were two kinds of responses to us. There were a lot of snotty people, people who were, what shall I say, prideful in the wrong way, conceited—people who had something and wouldn't concede anybody else's getting anything unless it was at their own expense. Then there were the ones—200-300—who made up caravans of automobiles that would go to a town where we had a committee of willing people, just to show the people on the committee that they weren't alone in the community.

Our following began to be significant, and it started to become a balance of power in statewide elections and then throughout New England. Elsewhere it was the same picture in various ways, except in the Deep South.

The first national convention of Townsend committees took place late in '35 in Chicago's Stevens Hotel, and the second in the Cleveland Auditorium in '36. In terms of actual elected delegates from community memberships, there hasn't yet been a convention to equal that second one. Father Coughlin was there. Huey Long was invited, but he didn't come, although about 20 people representing him were there. Norman Thomas was there, and so were innumerable members of Congress, senators and governors.

The '36 convention was the signal to all political entities that this thing had to be stopped or, at the very least, contained. It represented an element of people who weren't compromising. The first measure taken was the enactment of the social security amendment. Remember, the Brain Trust originally forecast social security legislation by the year 1950, but it came in August of '35. It was to head off, in the words of Franklin Roosevelt, "the rising sentiment of the Townsendites." Now, when Roosevelt said that, it was at a press conference in '39 pertaining to his first amendments. When asked the reason for those amendments, he said in effect that his program was a very far-reaching one and had a lot of unfolding to do in the future, and that it was enacted in haste in order to head off "the rising sentiment of Townsendism."

Dr. Townsend reacted to social security in terms of reality, as the biggest payoff any public element had yet achieved in terms of humanitarian freedom and justice.

Ultimately, it was World War II that disintegrated the Townsend movement. Yet, at the same time, the war demonstrated the movement nationally, because we retired 15 million men into war work. We undertook to support them in that effort and ended unemployment in a period of a year. After that, everybody forgot.

The movement was an extraordinary thing. It may well be

that since the founding fathers, this has been the only political phenomenon that can be defined as a genuinely national organization for people. What people learned in the movement, that's the real meaning, and it isn't going to be made available to anybody else. To replace these people as they die off is an impossibility.

The Townsend Plan could've meant so much more if we had had it. It could have been a different country, let alone a different world, and in a better way. But now the movement is an enigma. Because when you speak of this organization, you're talking to it. So I don't know how long all our platforms can be kept in the record. Certainly it will be as long as the Lord allows me to live with my faculties, that much I guarantee. Beyond that, I have no way of knowing.

> They marched off to war to fight for democracy and stop the Fascists. They fought; they suffered; they bled; they died. And when it was over, they came home—the soldiers of a defeated cause. Such was the odyssey of the members of the Abraham Lincoln Brigade. The idealistic youth who fought would then wait nearly 40 years for the vindication of their cause.
>
> Milton Cohen, a member of the brigade, has been involved with liberal and civil-rights causes since his involvement in the Spanish civil war. In the late sixties he won a landmark nine-year legal battle against the House Un-American Activities Committee. Mr. Cohen is currently the executive director of the Jewish Council on Urban Affairs in Chicago.

MILTON COHEN

I was in my last year in college in '36 when the war broke out. The army, the Fascists, revolted against the elected Republican government, and the government was not getting all the help it had a right to get. Of course, Hitler and Mussolini were sending in all sorts of materiel and men.

We were having some anti-Fascist meetings on campus, and the issue of aid to Spain was raised. First, there was a Committee to Aid Democratic Spain, to collect money and to get medical volunteers. Then, when the International Brigade, the Veterans' Brigade, the Abraham Lincoln Brigade were formed, the question was raised: Were there any volunteers? I guess it became in my mind a testing ground: Was fascism going to win or could it be stopped? I looked at it as something very, very important. And if you had a belief, a commitment, the next steps were easy. To me, it was natural. I was involved, I was committed, I felt it was important. There wasn't any deep probing, any intellectual agonizing, anything like that.

Sure, I suppose there was fear, but the conviction and commitment overcame that. You became submerged beyond your personal thoughts, your personal ego, being part of something in history. Maybe it sounds a little abstract, obtuse, but as I look back, that's the way I really felt.

I left New York on a ship on May 1, 1937. The trip over was very nice. I had never lived in such luxury, going over on an ocean liner. Of course, we had to be careful, because we were doing something illegal. Your passport was stamped "Nonvalid for Spain," so you had to act as if you were a tourist. The whole feeling was that you were going into something very exciting, important, that you were doing something way beyond yourself. It was a powerful feeling. I think you've had it, under different circumstances with Jewish people who went to Israel. Maybe different motives, different ideas, but the same feeling of commitment.

Even going through France, we had to be careful; it wasn't legal to be there, either, because France had closed its borders with Spain. Most of the soldiers got there by crossing the Pyrenees at night. They actually had to do about 15 ot 20 hours of very difficult walking. I didn't do that. They took a few hundred of us, internationals from all over the world, and secretly loaded us on a ship called *The City of Barcelona.* I guess it was a new method to get people into Spain.

Early the next morning, while the ship was on its way from Marseilles to Barcelona, an Italian submarine hit us and we went down in a matter of minutes. It was a disaster; about 50 people lost their lives. I was lucky; I wasn't a swimmer and got on the only lifeboat that worked. We weren't far from shore when a fisherman from a Spanish village came out and helped us. That was our welcome into Spain.

I joined the American section of the International Brigade but wound up being part of the Canadian battalion. I had a little training, not too much; the armaments and military equipment were very inadequate. We went through the simple military fundamentals, learning how to shoot and take care of a gun, how to conduct ourselves under fire. It was hard getting used to a new country, new life, new food, new circumstances, but we did it; we were committed.

The first battle, no matter how you thought about it, how you prepared for it, you weren't ready for it. It was in the Aragon area, east of Barcelona. September of '37, I think. There was an offensive to try to crack the Fascist lines. It was very difficult. We were on a plane and they had us covered with gunfire. We couldn't move for maybe ten hours. No drink in the hot sun, no food.

We didn't succeed and we had a lot of losses. A close buddy of mine was killed in that action. I began to taste and see death and understand what it meant. It was very hard. But, as I say, you kept going because you were fighting for a cause you felt was important.

Next we were sent over to the Madrid front for some reserve action. Then we were involved in some heavy fighting in an important battle that winter. I recall living outside in zero-degree weather. Again, that was an offensive action, trying to break through the line. But we always faced overwhelming superiority in planes, in artillery, in ammunition, and guns that Hitler and Mussolini were throwing in. The Republican side just couldn't get anything. The Western democracies had adopted a neutral position that wasn't neutral. So it was always a very uneven battle: democracy versus fascism.

This superiority of arms led to the Fascists' breaking through and cutting Spain in half. We were surrounded and had to retreat with terrible losses. I remember getting wounded, but I was lucky; I was in the last ambulance that got out of the area, across the bridge at Candessa. After that, the bridge was blown up. Two guys I was with I never heard from again.

It was hard; it was rough. You longed for home, missed your country, but you kept going. I remember once we were lying out in the fields in a barn, cold and hungry, and we got a paper from the United States. Roosevelt had just given a famous speech in Chicago—I think it was the fall of '38—in which he spoke out against aggression. I was so stirred; we all were. We thought that here, maybe . . . But it wasn't followed through. It was one of the things that led to Munich and appeasement.

Time never hung on your hands. You had to keep alert, keep your equipment clean, take care of a lot of chores. And there was always a lot of discussion, political discussion. That was very important as a morale factor.

You got used to the difficulties. I remember the first time I found that my body and clothes were full of lice. It was a terrible feeling. But, you know, after a while you almost had to live that way. You were hungry most of the time, and a little piece of bread became so meaningful. But you fought it. You learned to adjust by getting outside yourself.

As to the enemy, I don't know. Sure, they were going to kill you. But it was more that you didn't personalize it or individualize it. The Fascists were the enemy, and if they won, the world was going to suffer. That was it.

Of course, the war, the issue, was being decided outside Spain, in the League of Nations. The Western democracies were putting up a sham of nonintervention; but it wasn't nonintervention. Hitler and Mussolini poured in unlimited arms, men, materiel. I remember being bombed by big German junkers. It was the first big saturation bombing that took place in the world. Then, as a last effort, they removed the International Brigade to show there was no intervention on our side. But it didn't mean anything.

I remember so clearly that day, waiting to leave. I was in a town in northern Spain, and we got word of Munich and the Nazi army marching into Czechoslovakia. That had a profound effect on me. But I guess as a young person I didn't get depressed too much.

When we came back, we got a tremendous welcome from the American people, a very positive welcome. But then, later, anti-Communist feelings became very strong in the country. The veterans of the Abraham Lincoln Brigade were placed on the attorney general's list for many years. We were treated as outcasts.

Personally, it didn't bother me. I never had time for bitterness, I guess because I think I understood what it meant. The powers that be had their motives for wanting to castigate us. They wanted to whip up a hysteria. It wasn't that they were bad people and didn't appreciate what we did. Maybe they were defending what they had, their well-being. It just made me work harder to try and make the changes necessary for our country, for justice, humanity, peace, whatever you want to call it.

In this last period of time, I didn't forget Spain. I got involved in other things, but Spain was there. Recently, as the effort for democratic Spain intensified, I really became excited. It had a special meaning to me. I directed a lot of my time and energy to it and still do. It was a question of fulfilling my action of 40 years ago.

In fact, I visited Spain in '70. A couple of us veterans went. We rented a car and traced our steps, every place we fought. It was one of the greatest emotional experiences of my life. We went into little towns, little villages, saw big changes in Spain, sensed the democratic feeling. We talked to people. We told them who we were, and we were received in a very positive way. It was a tremendous experience, going back.

I feel very good about what I did. I've been involved in social struggles, political struggles, ever since then. You may have done the right thing, sometimes the wrong thing. But this thing, there was no question about it; it was the right thing. Would I do it again? I sure would. It helped make my life meaningful. It gave me the basis of continuing the struggle for social change. My feeling is that that's what life, what Judaism, is all about, struggling and fighting for the betterment of mankind. It may sound like words, but to me it has a lot of meaning.

The war in Spain had its impact on world history. It makes me feel good that I had a little part in it. And, eventually, history is made because of ordinary people like me.

Students dropping out of school to work for radical causes was a common phenomenon of the sixties political scene. But, despite their "Don't-trust-anyone-over-30" slogan, those students could have learned much from a generation that, 40 years ago, also dropped out to work for the causes of *its* day—perhaps, as Richard Criley suggests, with a deeper understanding of the nature of that commitment.

For many years, Mr. Criley was the executive director of the Chicago Committee to Defend the Bill of Rights. He is now retired and lives in California.

RICHARD CRILEY

It was a period when factories were shut down and everyone was unemployed, and you faced this weird contradiction: Factories were shut down because people had no income to buy their products, and people couldn't buy their products because they were unemployed. So you went around in this vicious circle.

It hadn't affected me that much personally, although students were encountering increasing economic difficulties. The longer we stayed in school, the more apparent it became that there were no jobs available; so we really had nowhere to go. We stayed in school, taking graduate courses, because there were no jobs available except administering relief. We all felt the pinch, renting cheap apartments, organizing our own kitchens to live on a minimum. There was quite a militant spirit, particularly characteristic of universities that had a rather large working-class student body, like the University of California.

I had transferred to Berkeley from Stanford, and when I got there I joined the Student League for Industrial Democracy, a Socialist Labor group. When the student leadership at Berkeley was expelled for asking for an open forum to which Upton Sinclair would be invited, we called a sympathy strike to get them reinstated. At that point, I got more education when a fellow student with whom I had gone through school almost from kindergarten, being somewhat ambitious and opportunistic, told the university I was a dangerous radical because of my involvement with the forums in sympathy with the San Francisco waterfront strike. So when our strike committee went to bargain with the president of the university, the committee was told that I was on the verge of expulsion because I was this dangerous agitator (even though I'd been a Phi Beta Kappa, captain of the fencing team, all those things that a 100 percent red-blooded American student does for his alma mater). I was told by the administration I would never get a job because of my nonconformity. So I thought, shoot, since I'm never going to get a job as a teacher, rather than teach history, maybe the important thing is to try to make history. From then on, I became rather consistently a rebel.

I was getting a very small stipend from my family, about $25 a month, and in the depression days you could live on that. It was a little bit like the concept of living as the farm workers did, on a subsistence level. And because I felt very keenly the contrast between the rich and the poor, I felt that I was doing something wrong if I had a different standard of living from that of the poor people I was struggling for. So if I had more money than I needed, I gave it away to the cause.

It never occurred to me that I was depriving myself of something. On the contrary, I was doing the things that seemed most rewarding, most important. This was combined with a great deal of warmth, of love, that was generated between people. It was an association with a very diversified and sort of rich area of fellowship.

I had a profound experience when there was a very bitter coal strike in the mines in the Sierras where vigilantes were breaking up the union. I went with a student delegation to make an investigation of the suppressions of the rights of the strikers. There was a lot of silicosis in the mine, so that the older miners had hunched backs and were showing the effects of the bad lungs you get from breathing in powder from hard rock. They were just damn poor and were being pushed around by sheriffs at the same time they were being sold out by the leadership of the union.

I was also a part-time volunteer organizer for the cannery and field workers in the Santa Clara Valley, where we were trying to organize the CIO union. We organized something like 10,000 workers, but we were unable to sustain it; we had a great deal of enthusiasm but darn little knowledge. We tried to bring cases under the National Labor Relations Act, but it was a slow process. And even though the National Labor Relations Board was very good in terms of personnel, when you lost a few weeks, you lost the ball game, because the season was so short.

The ethnic background of the workers was very important. In the Santa Clara Valley, there were the little towns of Sunnyvale and Mountainview, which provided the major part of the agricultural workers, who were Spanish. We went door to door, house to house, canvassing. Problem was, whenever you went into the kitchen, they'd bring out the wine bottle (they made their own wine), and by the time you'd made a three-house visit, you didn't know whether you were walking or flying.

We also organized the young people at that time in support of the Spanish Republic. Those towns were totally committed to the Republic. There was almost a state of civil war in Santa Clara between the Jesuit priests in Santa Clara College, who supported the position taken by the Catholic hierarchy for Franco, and the Spanish residents, who were ready to lynch the priests. Then you had Franco sympathizers, like the rich Spaniards who ran the movie theaters, who were faced with a boycott unless they came up with a weekly contribution of $100 for Loyalist Spain.

We had mass meetings every Saturday night in Sunnyvale and Mountainview, and 500 people would turn out. The Society of Isabella the Catholic and other Catholic agencies would come in with $50, $25 and so on. The poor agricultural and cannery workers would come in with not less than $10 apiece, and $10 was a whole lot of money at that time.

We organized youth groups around the idea of supporting both democracy and unionism at home and the Loyalists in Spain. Ultimately, however, the Spanish Republic was defeated, these groups disappeared, and I moved elsewhere.

As industrial unions swept the country with the organizing days of the CIO, to those of us who were middle-class intellectuals, this became a powerful, creative, even romantic force. It had a mass base and was determining in which directions society was moving and was a force to which we could attach ourselves. There were aspects of the civil-rights struggle there, particularly as represented by the struggle to unionize. There were situations in which the unity of black and white workers was paramount, because without it, unionism was impossible. And I was involved in that, of course. It was no more unusual than the involvement of white workers at a later stage in Mississippi.

I was lucky enough to get a job on the waterfront; college graduate or not, you were lucky to get a job as a dishwasher in those days. As a matter of fact, the dishwashers' union in San Francisco became a place where a lot of college and graduate students got jobs. They were ultimately elected to the leadership of the union, and it became a very radical, very creative union! They undertook a pretty creative campaign against discrimination and won the right to dispatch workers. Under the contract, the employers could not hire workers off the street. Whenever they'd call the union hiring hall and say, "I want a white worker," the dispatcher would say, "Is there a black worker in the hall?" If there was, it was common agreement that you didn't rotate on the basis of how long you'd been waiting for a job but on whatever minority worker was first in line. Oh, yeah, they shut down restaurants right and left. The result was that they made a total breakthrough; no employers discriminated anymore among the dishwashers.

Another very major influence on us was the coming to power of Hitlerism in Germany, the horror of anti-Semitism, and the total wiping out of all freedom. And then our greater awareness of fascism in Italy, the threat of war as it became manifest in the total national chauvinism of the Fascist movement. The fact that there were obvious American parallels, people like Reverend Winrod, Huey Long, Father Coughlin. So one could sense an Americanized version of the Hitler package being thrown into the confusion and the suffering and the dire needs of American lives, which could lead in one of two directions: either toward a rational and progressive solution of the problem, or a pursuit of the simplistic answers that composed a large part of the demagogy of the Fascist movement.

All these things meshed in a way that has striking parallels to the meshing of the same kinds of elements that went into the creation of the youth movement of the sixties. But we were not involved in civil disobedience as a major thing; it had not become a mass technique.

I've always tried to maintain an understanding and knowledge, because I think that is the key to effectiveness as a social activist. If you don't have a social perspective, you're going to be counterproductive, as some of the young people in the sixties were. Groups such as the SDS and the Weatherpeople represented middle-class, idealistic young people who were eager for change but, unfortunately, lacked the experience I got in the depression years of being part of the working class. They had a detachment from people. When you work in industry, you find that you've got to be darn patient with people. They're not suddenly sold on rhetoric; you've got to know the nuts and bolts of the problems they're dealing with and be patient.

No, I haven't experienced any generation gap. The fact that I'm almost 65 does not cut me off from young people. The problem arises only when a person, *regardless* of his age, becomes irrelevant in the social process. If you have, then there's a generation gap.

In recent years, young people who are social activists are taking a second and much deeper look at the social process. They're finding, I think, that those of us who have been through 40-50 years of struggle in this social process are worth listening to.

In "the world of our fathers," the *Jewish Daily Forward* was more than a newspaper; it was an institution. Its pages were a virtual mirror reflecting the spirit of the American Jewish community. In this reminiscence, the *Forward*'s editor, Simon Weber, speaks about both the newspaper and the community it served.

Mr. Weber joined the *Forward* staff in 1939, after writing for other Yiddish newspapers in New York and Philadelphia.

SIMON WEBER

I came to New York and I got work at the *Jewish Daily Forward* in '39 and have been here ever since. Abraham Cahan, the editor at the time, was one of the most able editors in the sense of inventiveness, a man who could almost look out the window at any time and think of an idea to write about. A fantastic man, a great individual. He was also a strong man, strong-willed; some called him tyrannical. When he set upon his course, nobody could deter him.

The *Forward* is published by an association that decides policy. The association very often had hot debates with Cahan, who nevertheless always prevailed by winning their votes. They had confidence in him. His course was completely vindicated.

It was very difficult to work for him, difficult in that you had to prove; you couldn't just put things down on paper and present them in an article. When I came to him with articles against the Communists, I had to justify and prove every point I made in every article, which taught me a lesson in responsible journalism, and I do exactly the same thing now.

He was also difficult because he was insistent on style. It had to be simple without any hyphenated, seventy-five-cent words. We were told to write in a way that everybody could understand. You must remember that when he started out, he had a mass of completely illiterate immigrants he had to teach first *how* to read before they would buy the paper, then bring them to read the paper, and then develop their taste in reading better literature.

And while developing a reader, he also developed a reader for the classic Yiddish literature. Thus he brought in I. L. Peretz; he brought in Sholem Asch; he brought in all the great Yiddish writers, including Isaac Bashevis Singer, who came to work when Cahan was editor and is still with us. There were others: I. J. Singer, for instance, the brother of Bashevis. He was a man who, when you saw him in the editorial office of the *Forward* and when he talked to us, made us feel like schoolchildren standing before a giant. But he did not behave at all like one; he talked to us as an equal. He shared with us; he came to meetings of the staff and he told stories. When you heard him tell a story, you realized why his fiction was so great, because he was a fantastic storyteller and so was his brother.

Abraham Reisen, the poet and short-story writer, was also here when I came to the *Forward*. Reisen was a very fine man and also a very good colleague. If somebody felt that an injustice had been done him in one way or another, Reisen would say, "All right, let's fight for it!" He was always ready to go fight for a colleague.

Sholem Asch? Yes, he was still here. I met him quite a few times. I knew him when he was a man already up in years, a very handsome person, a strong figure and personality. He thought of himself in a way like a Jewish king. He felt that he was *the* Yiddish writer and all the others were just the periphery. So when he came into the Café Royal, where all the writers and actors gathered, he wore a European coat with the cloth outside and the fur inside with a big fur shawl collar. He'd come in with some people and there would be the king who has taken the table, and all the other writers would come over. He knew their names well, but he pretended as if he didn't.

Asch as a writer was great, but he did not know Yiddish grammar and syntax too well, so there was a poet at the *Forward* who would correct the copy, a fact very few people knew.

Asch had a dramatic struggle with Cahan that finally led to their severing relations. He brought *The Nazarene* in Yiddish to the *Forward,* and Cahan read a few chapters and then refused to publish it. "The *Forward,*" he said, "won't publish it because it's a missionary work." Well, Asch didn't listen to Cahan. He went to the association and fought Cahan, but Cahan prevailed, and Asch published the book in English.

Asch had a kind of dream that these books would bring him the Nobel Prize, that the only reason he hadn't already won it was because he wrote about Jews, like the *Tehillim Yid* [*Salvation*]. Well, he made a lot of money; he wrote one book after another; *The Apostle, Mary,* and others, and they didn't bring him the Nobel Prize, either. As a matter of fact, that prize was ultimately given to a Jew named Agnon, who wrote only Jewish stories. After his break with the *Forward,* he later published some stories in the Communist paper, which was nothing. He was actually kind of wiped out as a Yiddish great.

Of course, there were also writers on the other papers at the time who were among the giants in Yiddish journalism, literature and literary criticism, like Samuel Niger, whose real name was Charney. He had two brothers: B. Charney Vladeck, was a manager of the *Forward,* onetime minority leader of the New York City Council and also somewhat of a writer; and Daniel Charney, a poet. Another giant was Joseph Opatashu, who used to come to the writers' meetings on the *Forward.*

Yiddish literature was very much richer in those days than it is now. There were three large daily newspapers—the *Forward,* the *Morning Journal,* and the *Tog*—plus the *Freiheit,* and they all employed large staffs. The largest staff was at the *Forward.* In New York, we had a full-time staff of approximately 60-70 people, and there must have been another 50 or 60 who were scattered throughout the world as correspondents. It was almost a case of waiting in line to get an article with your byline in the paper, because there were so many correspondents.

There was no real distinction between Yiddish journalists and writers, because on the newspaper staffs were fiction writers, poets and journalists, and all made a living. For instance, Jacob

Glatstein made a living as a journalist for the *Morning Journal* and wrote poetry on his own time.

Then there were, of course, many cultural activities. There were about 12 or 13 Yiddish theaters functioning on Second Avenue and others in Brooklyn and in the Bronx. When you went to a premiere of a Yiddish play, it was like Yontiv [a Jewish holiday], really. Nowadays, it is a vanishing world. But they're not all gone; there are others here. We may not be Singers or Aschs, but we speak with the voices of the present.

Let me give you the economic side. In '34 and '35, the Newspaper Guild, the union of newspaper people employed in the editorial and business offices of the newspapers, was founded by Heywood Broun, one of the outstanding columnists at the time. The Peretz Verein, the union of Yiddish writers, which had been established in '15 after the death of Peretz, did not want to join the guild for a very simple reason: the guild established a minimum wage of $45 a week for editorial employees, while the Yiddish journalists had a minimum wage of $70 a week and most of them were getting $90 and up. It was economically a very good position at the time, especially during the very lean years of the '30s.

Then it was more or less an easier life. You didn't have to produce as much as you have to produce now, since the staff has shrunk a great deal. So a lot of people had it quite easy. They came into work for half a day at most. Some of them didn't have to come in at all; they just sent or brought in their one or two pieces a week. You take people like Zalman Schneour and Sholem Asch, who were writing novels. The novel would run for six months, the salary would run for a full year, and so the second six months they had time to think and prepare another novel. So it was a pretty good life.

Nazism? There were front-page articles, editorials, appeals, written by men like Chaim Lieberman, who poured his heart out every day. We were crying! Yes, we organized a few demonstrations in Madison Square Garden, boycotts and so on. But to say that 200,000 came out to demonstrate, like for Soviet Jewry, there was not any such thing.

The Jewish organization response cannot be called a response, because the Jewish establishment was captivated by Roosevelt's charm. Who could doubt anything about Roosevelt? When Rabbi Stephen Wise went in to see Roosevelt as a spokesman of the Jewish community, Roosevelt would say something like, "Don't you know, Steve, that I'm doing everything I can?" or "Well, what do you want us to do?" When the *St. Louis* was swimming around in the waters near Cuba with 900 Jews on board, Roosevelt wouldn't let them in; the ship floundered, turned back, and nothing was done.

Members of the Yiddish-speaking Left were an integral part of American social, political and cultural movements in the thirties. As Paul Novick, editor of the leftist *Freiheit* observes, they were active in protests, demonstrations, and conferences, and thus played a significant role on both the international and the national scene.

One of the founders of the *Freiheit*, Mr. Novick is still an active member and leader of the Yiddish Left in the United States.

PAUL NOVICK

Generally, as a socialist paper during the Hoover period, we had no confidence in the government. On the contrary, we tried to combat all kinds of administration measures and kept telling our readers that no good would come out of the administration. Of course, we couldn't foresee the Crash; but when it did come, we interpreted it as a result of capitalism in its reactionary and most rapacious form, although we didn't say "I told you so." After the Crash, our business became not only to criticize the Hoover administration, which we did, but to mobilize the masses.

I would say that the turbulent '30s really began at the end of the '20s. There were already evictions, and we mobilized people to fight them forcefully by putting furniture back into the apartments and by demonstrating against the landlords. We were also already demonstrating for social security in those days, for unemployment insurance, for relief.

There was a very active relief organization then—the Women's Councils. They played *the* role in strikes, in picketing stores, butcher shops, in demonstrating against the high cost of living, and, in particular, in demonstrating against landlords who were raising rents or making evictions. The fraternal organization we had at that time established a special women's division, which was called the Emma Lazarus Federation of Jewish Women, which still exists. They helped, to a great extent, the Women's Councils to conduct their struggles.

Regarding Roosevelt, we had a wrong position in those days, which we later recognized. We recently had the celebration of the 55th anniversary of the *Freiheit* at the Americana Hotel—and also of my 85th birthday, believe it or not! I spoke at length of our mistakes, said that our approach to Roosevelt had been seriously mistaken. At that time, we held to the position of the Communist party that Roosevelt was no good, that the NRA was kind of fascistic, things like that. In my speech, I referred to the historic speech given by Dimitrov at the Seventh Congress of the Communist International in August, '35, for the People's Front, in which he mentioned Roosevelt over and over and cited the mistakes committed in the Third Period. I recalled the shock as this speech came over the ticker. An extremist position had been taken by the Communists and it was a pretty sad chapter. So, during the '36 election, we were all for Roosevelt, even if indirectly. At that time the slogan of the Communist party was "Defeat Landon by all means," which meant, of course, by working for Roosevelt. And that was really the beginning of a broad front, which was a reflection of the People's Fighting Front, which in '36 was quite influential.

At that time in our movement we had our fraternal organization, called the International Workers Order, one component of which was the Jewish People's Fraternal Order. It was a big organization, with about 50,000 members, and was quite a powerful factor in helping to mobilize the masses. In addition, we had a Jewish People's Committee, which was devoted solely to the struggle against fascism, Nazism, anti-Semitism, anti-Jewish pogroms in Poland, and to building the People's Front. We worked with Rabbi Stephen S. Wise and Rabbi Abba Hillel Silver, among others. Those were the days of mass demonstrations and mass meetings in Madison Square Garden. Our own jubilee celebration of the *Freiheit* was held there, with 18,000 to 20,000 people attending.

We also started, in '36, a broad front for the building of Jewish culture, and in September, '37, we held the first World Congress for Jewish Culture in Paris, with representatives from 23 countries. That was a very important period in the struggle of the *Freiheit*. On the subject of Jewish culture, we succeeded in mobilizing a majority of the Jewish intelligentsia. The head of the delegation that was sent to Paris was our editor, M. Olgin, a leading spirit of the congress, who read the most important paper there; but there were also writers and poets from other newspapers, such as the *Jewish Morning Journal* and the *Jewish Day* (later the *Day-Morning Journal*). Among those writers were Alexander Mukdoni, B. Z. Goldberg, the son-in-law of Sholom Aleichem, H. Leivick, the poet and playwright, and Joseph Opatashu, the novelist.

About the same time, prior to the Paris conference, we had here a national Conference for Jewish Culture, attended by 800 delegates of various organizations in New York and other parts of the country. And, again, there were those people from the other newspapers, in addition to people who didn't go to Paris, like the playwright Peretz Hirshbein, and a number of others, including people not in the Communist movement, even anti-Communist. Oh, that was truly a glorious period, the struggle of the *Freiheit* for unity, for the preservation of Jewish culture, for the survival of the Jewish people.

Of course, there was opposition to us. At the time we were trying to mobilize people for the congress, there was a group, the "Group of 36," connected with other newspapers, like the *Jewish Day,* the *Forward* and the *Morning Journal,* who were influenced by virulent anti-communism or reactionary Zionism. (When I say Zionists, I always differentiate between reactionary Zionists and socialist Zionists.) They mobilized themselves and came out with a call against the Paris congress. We conducted a struggle against that committee and we had the masses on our side. You see, our struggle for Jewish culture, as the Paris manifesto pointed out, was combined with the struggle against fascism. So it was not just the building of Jewish culture *per se,* but the building of Jewish culture for the continued existence of the Jewish people.

As to Nazism, we were the only newspaper that was warning against it and, particularly after the Dimitrov speech, the only one fighting for the People's Front. Unfortunately, other Jewish papers didn't participate at all in the mobilization of the people. Prior to the rise of Hitler, the *Forward,* the biggest Jewish newspaper in those days, was negating the whole thing. They were saying, "It's not serious; we can rely on Hindenburg. Hitler is just a madman, you know, and he should not be taken seriously. It's not so dangerous as things are portrayed." They were demobilizing the masses. So in those days we really played quite an essential and honorable role.

Yes, we participated in the struggle to mobilize the Abraham Lincoln Brigade in the Spanish civil war. It was to a considerable extent Jewish and its leadership was also Jewish. We were all for it. This was one of the great, glorious periods here on the paper. We featured the struggle in Spain in our news—front-page headlines, editorials, various articles. We also had our own correspondents in Spain to send us their impressions. So, on the one hand, we kept the struggle before the eyes of our readers and the general masses; on the other, we called for people to enlist in the brigade. Later on, when news came of casualties, particularly when the person was Jewish or was a leader in one of the branches of the International Workers Order, then, of course, we wrote about it and organized memorial meetings. We also had quite a number of poets whose poems for the struggle in Spain, for the people who sacrificed themselves, we published.

In various ways, through the *Freiheit* and through the organizations assisted by the paper, we developed this mass struggle that encompassed hundreds of thousands of Jewish people in the United States and through them hundreds of thousands of other Americans.

We had an organization called the Jewish Music Alliance, which is still in existence. This was, and still is, the center of the Jewish People's Choruses. We also had the Jewish Philharmonic Chorus and the People's Chorus in New York. The choruses produced a poem by our own Yuri Suhl, with music by Max Helfan, as well as other poems and cantatas. And these choruses were instrumental in mobilizing the masses through songs, cantatas, oratorios. In addition, there were dancers and dance groups.

We also had an organization of Jewish writers and poets who would organize their own meetings, mobilize others, march in May Day demonstrations with their slogans. In '36 we had an enormous May Day demonstration. I remember, the whole section of writers and artists marched with their slogan: "Culture against fascism."

So, as you can see, there were various aspects of this struggle—cultural meetings, songs, poems, meetings, lectures on the meaning of the struggle against fascism, on the meaning of Nazism, on the meaning of Jewish culture. Many of us would go out lecturing every Friday evening to various organizations, mostly to branches of the Jewish People's Order. Fifty, 100, 150 people would come to the lectures. There was a beehive of activity all over New York and around the rest of the country.

No, we had no conflict with the Communist party in those days. They recognized that we in the Jewish movement, that the *Freiheit,* had to have more leeway than, for instance, the *Daily Worker.* And inasmuch, in the latter part of the '30s, we became more and more engaged in People's Front activities, we removed ourselves from narrow, sectarian political activities, though not completely. So there was a period when officially the party recognized that since the *Freiheit* was a different paper, a broader type of paper, it had to have a different approach to issues than the official organ of the Communist party. In those days, then, there was a separation in actual fact, even if not officially proclaimed.

My contribution? I will leave it to others to evaluate. I'm still living the life I have since I helped establish the *Freiheit* on April 2, 1922. This is the proper way, I think, for a Jewish Socialist, without separating the Jew from the Socialist, the socialism from the Jew. I live the life of a progressive, having at heart the interests of the Jewish people, of the American people generally, without separating the Jewish people from American problems.

Of course, it would sound nice to say that if I could live my life again, I would do the same things. But one cannot say that because human beings commit mistakes and I realize some mistakes were made. And if I had not made those mistakes, I probably would have made different mistakes. You can never tell: It's all dialectics and all is in flux, according to some wise men. "Everything in society and nature is movable and conditional." So that's the way it is, always conditional, always in movement.

The depression era was many things to many people. To Rabbi David Graubart, it was a time of economic crisis and social upheaval, much of it fraught with significance and foreboding for his people, as he remembers here.

Dr. Graubart is the presiding rabbi of the Bet Din ("religious court") of the Rabbinical Assembly of Chicago. He is also a widely published writer and lecturer and contributes a weekly column to the *Jewish Daily Forward*.

DAVID GRAUBART

My first pulpit was in Rock Island, Illinois. I was in pretty bad shape. I negotiated the post for $2,500, very soon I didn't get that; it became $2,000, then $1,500, then almost nothing. They settled with me once for $300 for the whole year; and the third year I was there without any salary whatsoever.

But even in the midst of the depression, there was fun. I had wonderful friendships. I met my future wife. I was popular with the Jewish community and non-Jewish community alike. I spoke in all the schools and clubs and was friendly with the ministers and the Orthodox and Reform rabbis in town.

Then they heard about me in Des Moines. It was a very prestigious pulpit—one of the outstanding Conservative synagogues in that area and a forerunner of Conservative Judaism in the whole Midwest—and I was elected to it. But again, there were problems financially. The salary was first $2,000, then $1,800, then $1,500. It was a miserable salary, and to get it, you had to go to the treasurer of the synagogue, who worked in a shoe store. So the cantor and I would walk over there to collect our salaries. They had a lovely building, lovely facilities, but no money.

I was offered a Chicago post and came to the Humboldt Boulevard Temple in 1935. There were many poor people in the area who came to me for money, and, of course, I didn't have much to give; but small amounts we always gave. I gave of my own money and whatever others would give me for these people. A dollar was a lot. I'm embarrassed now to say this: The widow of one of the greatest Hebrew writers of all time, David Frishman, came to the United States for money, poor thing, and I gave her a dollar. A dollar! For the widow of one of the most brilliant Jews of all time, who translated the most magnificent works into English, Hebrew . . . So that shows you. They came to me—important scholars, distinguished European rabbis, the chief rabbi of Budapest, the chief rabbi of Kazan, Russia. I was always able to get them some money through colleagues who had funds and large congregations. I remember I would call Rabbi Gerson Levi, the father of former U.S. Attorney General Ed Levi, and say, "This poor scholar, a great scholar, is a good lecturer. Why don't you have him for your synagogue Friday night for $25?" It was terrible—I mean, it sounds frightful today.

That was a whole period in my life when I was involved with radical movements. And since I was pretty radical as a Zionist, these people became my clients, so to speak. I soon became the rabbi of radical and unaffiliated Jews. All kinds of people would come to my study, people who were not too popular, but they knew that here they would get a hearing.

Soon I became quite well known in Chicago and made a living, but there were problems. The establishment could not stomach my kind of political and economic radicalism. The time I reviewed *The Grapes of Wrath,* by John Steinbeck, I never saw such an uproar. My congregants acted as though I'd done something so radical that I had to be a Communist. I didn't quote Karl Marx or Friedrich Engels or Clara Leibknecht or Lassalle; I quoted the Prophets to support my views. I talked about the Okies who were uprooted from the soil. My congregation complained, "Why the Prophets all the time?" Whenever I spoke in Chicago and referred to the Prophets, people would say, "Why do you always talk about the Prophets?" I knew these people were like red-baiters; to them it was communism.

So much went on politically in those days. I was one of the pioneers among Jews and non-Jews to fight for civil rights for the oppressed. I didn't do it with the Jewish establishment but with leftist groups. I was involved with all leftist groups—Jewish, not Jewish, it didn't matter. I knew that was what I wanted to do. I was a progressive. One of those groups was the Jewish People's Fraternal Order. They were considered unkosher, *treyfe*. It was funny: The Labor Zionist movement, such a kosher movement, was on the attorney general's list; so was the Labor Zionist order Farband, because it was socialistic. Funny too that at the same time I was a leading rabbi, one of the leaders of Conservative Judaism, but I wasn't kosher enough for some. A newspaper for which I now write, the *Jewish Daily Forward,* refused to mention my name.

I was very active in the boycott against Japan. The Japanese were going to be on the side of the Nazis, so I spoke against Japan. And in the early Hitler days, I was shouting from the pulpit, "This man is a menace!" And people said, "What do you mean? You talk nonsense. He's not a menace."

In Des Moines, I recall, to the shame of those people and of the rabbinate of that city, they brought a Nazi, Hjalmar Schacht, to speak, and I said, "What are you doing? You are smuggling in a Nazi!" But they couldn't see it. They said, "What do you mean? He's not a Nazi. It's not going to be so bad." So at a meeting of the governing body of the community, of which I was a member, they took me to task: "This young rabbi," they said (I was only in my 20s), "has the *chutzpah* to speak out against the elders! What kind of nonsense is he talking about?" I quoted a Hebrew poet: "The Middle Ages are upon us. This is going to be a horrible thing." Not that I had facts. I just intuitively felt that something horrible was going to happen to our people. And they said, "No, you're naive. What are you talking about? It's your naiveté." Well, it wasn't pleasant.

I also spoke out against Mussolini one Friday night, and they said to me, "What do you want from Mussolini? As long as Mussolini lets Jews alone, we have no quarrel with him." But I said the following Friday night, "I don't care if Mussolini loves the Jews. He is a menace to the world, and Jews are human beings."

I felt very strongly about the Spanish civil war. When a boy who joined the Abraham Lincoln Brigade was married by me I wouldn't take a fee. They knew I was their friend.

A favorite sermon of mine was on Elijah and Elisha. I saw a great dialog between them—that we must be involved in the world, that we must care for Jews, and that our inspiration must be the Torah, and Jewish tradition, not Marx, Liebknecht and Lassalle. Friends used to ask me. "Aren't you afraid to walk home from the synagogue at night? You'll be attacked. You should have a bodyguard." But my inspiration wasn't socialist doctrine; it was good old Jewish religion. I loved my people.

The depression didn't do anything to me that was wrong. I went through it, and by and large, I didn't suffer. Sure, when you come home and someone calls to let you know that you lost your job because of a meeting, sure, it's unpleasant. But you get over it. The last words my father said to me when I left to study at the Hebrew Theological College in Chicago were from Deuteronomy: "Fear no man." And I always remembered that.

4
THE UNION MAKES US STRONG

One of the untold stories of the American labor movement is that of the black worker and the unions. According to A. Philip Randolph, black workers were reluctant to join white unions, because of anti-black prejudice. Hence they formed their own unions and became a powerful labor force.

Randolph was for many years the president of the Brotherhood of Sleeping Car Porters, one of the nation's largest unions. He is now retired and living in New York.

A. PHILIP RANDOLPH

In '29 I wanted a meeting with the leaders of the AFL in order to have our organization become a part of it. I felt that to be effective, every union needed the support and cooperation of powerful mechanisms, especially ones like the American Federation of Labor. I knew Bill Green [president of the AFL] quite well and talked with him frankly about the problem of racial discrimination in various unions, adding that the AFL, as a broad labor mechanism, had a responsibility for bringing various groups of workers into its fold.

Bill knew that racial discrimination existed in some of the unions and felt that it was not only unfair to the black workers but also unfavorable to the labor movement itself. I thought that was a splendid position to take.

Some of the leaders of the international unions were not friendly, I suppose because the general racial temper of the country was such that they didn't feel they would be condemned if they were prejudicial to black workers.

As to the local unions, they were not interested in having any of the black workers taken in, because they felt they would be taking jobs away from the white workers. We carried on a campaign in various areas to show that a black worker was no different from a white worker in his ability to carry out a job, that he needed the same opportunities as the white worker, that he had the same responsibilities to maintain toward his wife and family.

I attended the various conventions from time to time and expressed my views on discrimination against workers of different races, religions, nationalities and so forth. I felt it was the responsibility of the labor movement to change this situation. This, of course, was a little new to some of the labor leaders, but I found that there was in general a growing interest within the labor movement in bringing black workers into the fold. I won't say that we made any phenomenal progress during that period, but we moved forward.

We moved forward not only with the labor unions but also with black workers themselves. The black workers felt that it was useless to join a union that had no respect for a person because of his race. A good number of them felt that the labor movement was not their friend, that they were not wanted in some of the unions, and they had no desire to bow and scrape and stoop to get into one. But I pointed out to them that both their interest and that of the labor movement would be greatly served if they became union members.

The Brotherhood of Sleeping Car Porters was quite effective in carrying out educational programs in the interests of workers, regardless of race. They felt that they were in the same position as the white worker: They had a job to maintain, and it was not going to be on the basis of race but of ability.

So it was a great struggle we had to carry on, not a racial struggle, but a labor struggle. I considered myself part of the labor movement, working for the advancement of the movement as a whole, which meant that the black workers would advance, too.

It was a great period and it was a great struggle. I was elated over the fact that the black leadership all over the country supported my position and spirit, although some of them didn't want to have anything to do with my kind of trade unionism. They felt that the unions were against the black worker.

Union battles for the right to organize were usually bitter and bloody. But, as Patrick Gorman, one of America's pioneer twentieth-century labor leaders points out, they weren't always so. Indeed, there were times when agreements were concluded under amicable, if slightly unusual, circumstances.

Mr. Gorman, a lawyer, joined the Amalgamated Meat Cutters and Butcher Workmen of North America in 1911. He was recently elected to the position of chairman of the board, his present position.

PATRICK GORMAN

In the early years, I remember I seized an opportunity to organize the chain stores. I was a pretty young delegate at the AFL convention at which the federation was going to go on record as favoring the Patman bill, which would have taxed chain stores out of business. So I took the floor to oppose adoption of that resolution, saying, "Now you're taxing chain stores out of business. The largest chain-store organization in the world is the American Federation of Labor. You have all these affiliated unions, 200 in ours, 500 in the Teamsters, and altogether there are thousands. And so the same boomerang you throw legally at the chains can be thrown at us to tax us out of business if we have so many unions in our international organization." The bill was defeated, and believe it or not, the chain stores invited us to come in and organize their people. They gave us supervisors to acquaint us with their people in the stores. And that's how we got the chain stores organized.

I won Safeway stores by playing a game of horseshoes. I got into the offices through a powerful political fellow who believed in unions. I met the president and talked with him for three days. One day he called me over to the window and said, "What do you see down there, Mr. Gorman?" I said, "Looks like somebody's been playing horseshoes." He said, "Do you play horseshoes?" I said, "Yes." He said, "I'll tell you what I'll do. I'll play you three games of horseshoes. If I beat you two, you'll forget about the contract. If you beat me two, I'll sign that contract." I don't think I had had a horseshoe in my hand three times before that, and I don't think he had had one in his hand too many times before, either. But he won one, I won one, and then I beat him on the third game. He said, "My word is as good as my bond," and we signed the contract.

Yes, I was among the founders, with John L. Lewis and others, of the CIO. We felt it was idiotic to hold down craft unionism any longer. That age was as dead as a dodo bird.

At one point, John L. Lewis sent me a picture of himself on which he had written, "To my very dear friend, Pat Gorman— John L. Lewis." Not many such pictures can be found, because John L. Lewis was not a dear friend to anyone who was not a dear friend to John L. Lewis and his thinking. He was a man who was capable of ruling the world. On the other hand, he was also a man who was capable of destroying the world he himself had created. He could not stand opposition, and when he decided to secede from the AFL, he took a plain piece of paper and wrote to chairman Bill Green, "Green, we disaffiliate—John L. Lewis." That's all there was to it.

I had stayed with the CIO until they decided to secede. I could never see that we were going to make the labor movement any stronger by seceding. We'd only cut it in half. So although I had more differences with the leadership of the AFL on economic thinking then perhaps anyone else in the labor movement, I could not see deserting.

They call organizing a genius sometimes, but it's just the tricks you use to accomplish it. It's just taking advantage of a time, hitting it when it pops up. In all my years, I found none of the employers bullies. They were always polite in their negotiations, and yet I could tell whether that politeness carried with it the sting of the wasp.

Although today labor unions are almost America's third party, from the twenties through the early forties they were literally fighting for survival. The part Abe Feinglass played in that struggle as a union leader was a major one, and it was dedication like his that sustained organized labor during "its lowest ebb."

Mr. Feinglass's labor career began in 1925 with the now-defunct Needle Trades Industrial Workers Union. Since then he has been active in many labor-related causes, including serving as international president of the Fur and Leather Workers' Union. Mr. Feinglass is currently the director of the Fur and Leather Workers' Department of the Amalgamated Meat Cutters and Butcher Men of North America.

ABE FEINGLASS

The '30s were very difficult years, years in which there was a lot of unemployment and we came up against many terrible situations. People were breadless and jobless and almost hopeless, and there was very little we could do for them.

The fur industry was especially hard hit; many workers worked only two or three months and for the rest of the year were jobless and had nowhere to go. I recall an elderly woman coming into my office one day and saying, "I've been coming here every day asking you for a job and you won't give me one." Then she took out a gun and said, "I'm gonna blow my brains out, and I have a note here saying you're responsible, because you won't give me a job." My reaction to her was a very sharp one. I said, "You've got a daughter. You don't care about your daughter? Well, go ahead and shoot yourself." She dropped the gun and began to cry hysterically. This was the kind of emotional experience you had. Day after day you had people coming to the office looking for work and finding none.

I was determined to do the best I could. My wages were very low. During the early '30s I worked for next to nothing in the union, but I was dedicated to my job, and even if I couldn't give everybody help, I could help many. And I did. I got people jobs; helped them to get a few days' work at a critical moment; helped them get to a doctor, a lawyer; helped them find a way out of a difficult situation.

We were trying to improve wages, hours, working conditions, which at that time were terrible. In '31 we organized a large shop on the South Side of Chicago called the Hopkins Shop. There were 1,500 black workers working in that shop, getting $3.50 a week for a 54-hour week. We declared the employer, a man named Hopkins, on strike. The police were murderous in that strike, using violence against the picketers, all women. They beat them and arrested 85; they kept them in jail, gave them Wasserman tests, as though they were prostitutes. I had to go out and beg and borrow bail in order to get those people out.

They tried to break the strike, but couldn't, because even though the women weren't organized, they got so little, they had nothing to lose. We simply set up a soup kitchen, and they got out of that almost as much as they got out of wages. After about three and a half weeks, we won the strike. We got a ten-cent-an-hour raise, which was a *big* increase!

But after a few months the situation changed. What Hopkins did was lay off the shop, close it for two months. Then, when they reopened it with the help of the pastors, the churches and the congressman at that time, Oscar De Priest, they were able to bust the union and again create an open shop. They weren't organized until after the ILGWU came in '37, when we organized that shop and Hopkins left Chicago.

We had many conflicts with management, of course, and because of the nature of the union in those days, whenever we organized a shop, management very often turned to hoodlums, so we had strike struggles and we took beatings. Well, I don't know how you describe a beating, but I'd be warned that if I spoke at a meeting, I might not get out alive. The threat would be very direct! You'd be killed or put in the hospital crippled. We used to have our meetings in halls downtown, and sometimes they'd pull the main fuse and it would become dark. If you weren't careful, you found a knife in your back. I've got a scar from that period. I just barely pulled away from a knife that would have taken my eye out. I still have bruises all over my body from those days. So we fought and we didn't use hoodlums. We used to get together ourselves with guns and knives to fight against the hoodlums. We met them and we gave a good account of ourselves.

Those were very rough days; but it was part of the struggle of building a union. On the one hand, you were, well, not afraid but uneasy; on the other, you felt the job had to be done; somebody had to stick his neck out. That's true with workers even today. In any union, if you take a position against the leadership, you face very grave dangers. But people are doing it all the time, just as they did in the peace demonstrations, just as they did in other demonstrations, just as my son did when he went to Mississippi to be a Freedom Rider. He was afraid, but still he faced the danger of that kind of thing.

There are people who have will, who have strength of character, and we had a lot of those people, dedicated workers, in the fur union. Many of them were European immigrants who were determined not to allow hoodlums to take over their union and their livelihood, so they fought back. We were able to organize a broad coalition of people to defend the union, people of diverse nationalities, people young and old. They fought on picket lines, attended meetings, contributed money, and gradually we achieved the kind of union we wanted.

Ours was a forerunner in many ways for other unions in the fight for better conditions. We worked a 35-hour week. Wages were $4, $5 an hour, with time and a half after seven hours and on Saturdays and Sundays, at a time when $1.50, $2.00 was considered a big wage. We were one of the first unions to have eight, then ten holidays with pay, and to develop education and health-insurance programs. We were the highest-paid union in the country in those days—and we're still here to talk about the union.

> For decades one of the largest and most active unions has been the International Ladies Garment Workers Union. In this memoir, Hannah Haskell Kreindler, who has been former President David Dubinsky's secretary for more than 50 years, shares her recollections of the union's leaner years, years when the ILGWU was struggling for higher wages and, at the same time, building a broad political base.
>
> Mrs. Kreindler lives in New York City.

HANNAH HASKELL KREINDLER

I came from a socialist background. My father was with the *Jewish Daily Forward* for 40 years and was very active with the Workmen's Circle. As a matter of fact, he and I organized the first English-speaking branch of the Workmen's Circle, and my three brothers and I are still members of it. When I left high school, there was no Workmen's Circle school to study typing and stenography in Yiddish, but I worked with Abraham Cahan, editor of the *Forward,* on his memoirs, and with Vladeck, the great Yiddish writer, taking dictation; so when I came into the union, it was as a Yiddish stenographer, typist and translator.

In '29, with the Crash, the cloak-and-dress contracts had to be renegotiated, and the negotiations were not very easy. Our workers in the cloak industry had been on a wage system of work, and their employers demanded that piecework be brought back into the industry and the union. The workers always felt that piecework was more like slave work, pressuring them to get out more and more, and they were afraid that they might feel impelled to work longer in order to make an additional buck. But the employers insisted that that was the only remedy for the chaotic conditions in the industry, about which the union had consistently complained.

The union argued that the employers ought to limit contractors, the ones who did all the cutting of the material and then sent the cutwork to the jobber or the manufacturer, so as to do away with the cutthroat competition among them. At that time, the union was preparing to strike. Roosevelt was governor of New York, Lehman was lieutenant governor, and it was Lehman who intervened in the deadlock between the union and the three employer groups by offering his personal services as mediator.

Lehman had been very helpful to us in many situations, but I think this was the first time the industry had contacted him during his term as lieutenant governor. He wasn't partial to labor, but he was sympathetic to the struggles of the workers. It was his intelligent and skillful direction that brought about an understanding between the two parties. He was a wonderful human being, very philanthropic. He never acted like the millionaire he was, just like a decent man.

Roosevelt? Well, when he was governor, the union didn't have much contact with him, and frankly, we didn't consider him anything extraordinary at the time. After he became president and came out with the New Deal legislation, we felt he was terrific, since the New Deal did wonders for us.

We had been starved for activity. Our workers were just down and out, and we were down to between 24,000 and 29,000 members. This was in '32, when Benjamin Schlessinger, who was our president, died, and Mr. Dubinsky, who had been our secretary-treasurer, succeeded him. Mr. Dubinsky was very astute politically and had written a wonderful pamphlet for our organizers down south telling them to be prepared for the New Deal. So when it was enacted, our organizing efforts were successful, not only in the South, but in every other part of the country. During the Roosevelt administration, we reached about 500,000 members. We had our organizers; we had stories in the press; we used just about all kinds of ways of getting to the workers, even personally. And Mr. Dubinsky was the man who really did it.

Working conditions were very bad. In the nonunion shops the hours were endless. And every time we got to a nonunion shop, the employer would organize what was called a "company union" in an attempt to ward our union off, then deny that it was a company union.

Then too, there were the gangsters the employers paid to keep the union away. Many of them were Jewish, like Rothstein and Little Augie. But there were enough workers who had the courage to go from house to house to persuade the workers to stay with the union.

The ILGWU wasn't interested only in wages and hours. Our people came from the socialist movement, and so, from its very beginning, the union felt that politics were important in the life of the individual. Because of that, the ILGWU was one of the founders of the American Labor party in the '30s. We were also active in the statewide Labor Nonpartisan League. When the Communists took over the American Labor party, we left it and became a moving spirit in organizing the Liberal party of New York, which is still operating and is still a good influence in state politics.

Yes, we supported Fiorello LaGuardia throughout his term as mayor of New York. We sometimes had our differences with him, but he was one of the best mayors we ever had. LaGuardia was very sympathetic to the needs of workers—even though he was a Republican, he was a very progressive Republican—and he helped us out in the few strikes we had when we needed arbitrators.

We even had an International Affairs Department in the union, and through Mr. Dubinsky's efforts, the AFL got very interested in international affairs. One year, because of the rise of Nazism in Germany, Mr. Dubinsky, B. Charney Vladeck (general manager of the *Jewish Daily Forward*) and some others went to the AFL meeting in San Francisco to appeal for a boycott against Germany. The boycott was adopted and was very effective. There was a boycott on everything: buying goods, traveling to Germany, anything German. And it was not only a Jewish boycott, because the AFL was primarily non-Jewish.

The Labor Chest? That had to do with Spain and the anti-Fascist, anti-Nazi underground. It was separate from our International Affairs Department. It raised money and distributed it abroad.

Yes, we were a very progressive union. I remember, at our '34 convention in Chicago the Medinah Club refused to permit our

Negro members to go into the elevator or come up to the convention. So Mr. Dubinsky sent one of our officers to find another place to house the convention, and he found the Morrison Hotel. Well, instead of only the Negro members going there, the *whole convention* marched to that hotel, which really publicized the incident. It was a terrific thing for the union and for the issue of civil rights.

Looking back, I feel very good about it all. I feel that even though I came in as a stenographer-secretary, I was part of this union and made a contribution here. I've loved every day; it seems the harder I worked, the more I loved it.

Over the years, the image of the union organizer being the blue-collar, front-line risk taker has become almost stereotypical. We tend to think of the union struggles in terms of auto makers, steel plants and coal mines. But, as Morris Yanoff recalls, there was also the matter of organizing the *white-collar* worker, a matter that, as with blue-collar trades, called for dedication not only on the organizer's part but also on the part of the worker. And, as we also read in this interview, it called for a certain creativity and resourcefulness as well.

Today Mr. Yanoff, a retired business executive, lives in Chicago, where he is active in community affairs.

MORRIS YANOFF

I came out of a Jewish tradition. There were people in Brownsville, N.Y., who had belonged to trade unions for many years. Brownsville had a labor lyceum and housed the Workmen's Circle [Yiddish-speaking Socialists] and labor forums. As a matter of fact, Brownsville was one of the few districts that elected a Socialist to the state assembly. And because it had a tradition of militancy, the children shared in that.

In '29, '30, I was 22 and I was aware, involved. We had a club called the American Youth Club, made up of young people who were interested in social and economic problems of the day. We participated in the activities that were organized by the various left-wing organizations that proliferated in Brownsville. We even had a march against Hitler, which attracted hundreds and hundreds of people.

Then, when I got to be an office worker, because of the background I spoke of, I joined the trade union. Now, I didn't join the AFL union, because it was a very small, inactive union, made up mostly of office workers who worked for the large trade unions, like the International Ladies Garment Workers Union or the Amalgamated Clothing Workers. I joined one of the left-wing unions, the Office Workers Union, because it was active in trying to promote organization among office workers, since they were not organized in those days.

Then the CIO was formed in '35, and all organizing took a spurt. There was a movement to bring the existing AFL union of office workers into the CIO. Their main base was called the Bookkeepers, Accountants, and Stenographers Union (BASU for short). When our office workers began to move in and the BASU saw the CIO coming up, they thought in terms of forming a national union. So there was a merger of the Office Workers Union and the BASU, and in '37 we formed a national union called the United Professional Workers Union of America. UPWUA became part of the CIO organizing committee and stayed in the CIO with the Mine Workers and all the other unions.

At that time I was a member of the union's general board and of the national union. I was already working in an office, but they invited me to become an organizer and I accepted, going from a job that paid $75 a week to one that paid $25 (the minimum was $21). But my idealism motivated me to do this.

There were usually a few ways of organizing, because, you see, in those days it was a hazardous business. The methods of organizing were underground, secret, because the National Labor Relations Board was in its early stages. If an employer found that someone had joined a union, he'd fire the employee. That is what organization meant. You took your job in your hands. And to take your job in your hands when your whole family was unemployed was a dangerous thing.

Sometimes we distributed leaflets that said: "This is the Union of Office Workers. We have organized the —— Company at a minimum salary of $21 a week. Are you making $21 a week as a minimum? If you're a secretary, you should be making $25 a week. If you're not making these kinds of wages, if your hours are longer than 40 a week, if you can be fired at any time at the whim of the employer, then you need a union. The union address is here, and the telephone number is, too. Come down and talk to us. If you do, it will be in confidence." You had to put that in because many a person feared that it would come back to the boss and he would be out of a job. This was one method of securing contact.

The second method was one I used in the case of one of the large, well-known, old-line book-shipping companies. I would go to the cafeteria there and mingle with the workers. I'd introduce myself and eventually find one or two people willing to talk about trade-union organization. You had to get the right person, a natural leader, one who was willing to speak up and whom other people would follow.

In this particular case, organization was consummated in a couple of weeks. They signed cards; the cards were taken to the National Labor Relations Board to certify our majority, and then we were entitled to collective bargaining. Another way was simply to go to the employer and say, "We have a majority—negotiate." If he refused to negotiate, we could prove we had a majority either by having an election ordered by the board or just by taking them out on strike. In that case, you'd say to the employer, "If you want to see our majority, look out the window. They're out in front."

A third method was what we called "colonizing." A young, enthusiastic person would want to help build a union, and we'd say, "Okay, you take a job where we send you." And we'd send him to a place to get a job. Then, once having gotten the job, he'd get to know the people and see if he could get a union group started. There were many, many people who colonized—people who had had good jobs but who were dedicated to the cause of the working class. There was this feeling that to become a member of the working class was the right thing to do.

We had some interesting strikes. For example, there was a strike at the Credit Clearing House, a company that gave out credit information. In other words, when a business had a sale and it wanted to know whether it could give credit to the buyer of the merchandise, the Credit Clearing House served as a credit department for the smaller companies. We organized about 200 people there. The company was located in a large office building, which posed a problem: How do you picket such a building to keep the strike breakers out? There are hundreds of people going in. You don't know if they're going to the tenth floor, where the Credit Clearing House is located, or another floor. So we had to develop a new tactic.

The telephone was the main avenue of business in this company. When people wanted to know if the credit was okay, they'd use the phone. So what we did was to give the strikers nickels to go into a pay station and jam the telephones. The company had only a certain number of lines and it couldn't get new lines that quickly. So our strikers would call up and they knew exactly what to say. Well, the credit company couldn't call back and check each telephone, so after about four or five weeks, we finally won the strike because of this nickel-in-the-slot tactic.

In those days, too, began the struggle for certain social insurance. Remember, in the '30s there was no unemployment compensation. I can remember marching down the street with others, shouting in cadence, "We demand unemployment insurance, we demand unemployment insurance!" The cry was taken up by hundreds of people who were marching down the street toward a particular government agency, demanding that it be put on the books. Today people take it for granted, unaware that there was a great struggle around that issue. But this was one of the things we asked for, and, of course, later each state enacted its own unemployment-compensation bill.

Another thing was social security, or retirement, pay. At that time it was called a Communist measure and took longer to get than unemployment compensation. But I remember the first time I had to pay: It was one percent of the first $2,500. I paid only $25. This was one of the great measures promoted by the trade unions. I remember feeling that it was a great thing.

5
THE SPORTING LIFE

In the early thirties the fledgling sport of professional football was a game, according to the grand old man of the gridiron, George Halas, in which players made $125 per outing, box seats were $2.20, and a T-formation had something to do with a hot drink in a cup. Now, of course, all that has changed—in great part because of the Halas influence on the game.

Mr. Halas first joined the gridiron scene in 1919, and in 1920 he began an intermittent career as owner-coach that would extend until 1967, when he retired from the playing field.

GEORGE HALAS

During the '29 season we didn't do very well at coaching the Bears, so Dutch Sternman [then co-owner] and I decided to get another coach. We got Ralph Jones, who was at that time coaching the Lake Forest Academy, which was having an excellent season in all sports—baseball, basketball, football. I don't remember the amount of his salary, but at that time we had to come across pretty well to get him.

He was an excellent detail man, which was so necessary in using the T-formation properly. He improved it by putting a man in motion, which was the thing that really made it a great step forward. It changed the entire concept as far as defense was concerned. And being the only team in the league having a T-formation with a man in motion, we were able to take advantage of it. It was a big success in '32, '33 and '34.

Jones had predicted that in three years we would win the championship, and we did that in '32. But it was a disastrous year financially; we lost $18,000. There was no way to turn, because there was a big depression at that time. So I gave $1,000 notes to some of the guys—Ralph, Bronco Nagurski, Jack Manners—and was able to pay them off in a year.

In '33 the economy improved, and that, plus the fact that we had established ourselves as a winning team in '32 increased the attendance. Reserved seats were $2.20. Still, I don't think we paid the players more than $125 per game, so some of them had jobs on the side. But they had to practice every morning; that's one thing we insisted on. Then they'd have jobs in the afternoon. During the off season they would get regular jobs.

The first playoff? George Marshall made a fine suggestion that we split the league into two divisions and have this championship game at the end of the season. So we played the Giants at the Polo Grounds. We practiced in the mud on Saturday, and during the night a northeast wind came in and froze the field solid, making it very difficult to get good footing. The Giants had their equipment man go out for rubber-soled shoes, and they put them on between halves. They got excellent footing, whereas we got no footing, and so they went ahead and won the game. That was the lowest ebb in my career as a football coach. Everybody knew we had a great team. We had great spirit and the play was exceptional. We had defeated the Giants earlier that year and had won 18 in a row. But that frozen field, it had to be an act of God.

We installed the draft in '36 when Birch Bell, of the Philadelphia Eagles, proposed that to give the lower teams a chance to improve, we permit the last team to select first, and so forth.

That was an excellent rule, and it did a lot in showing that the low teams were able to improve substantially.

We were very fortunate with the draft because we had Frank Korch, who had the ability to look at all these newspapers, magazines and weeklies and also had a very canny perception of football players. So he would be in touch either with the players themselves or the coaches. He did a splendid job for us, and because of our ability to find the players in smaller colleges, we had the advantage over other teams in our league.

Sid Luckman? In '38 Pittsburgh wanted "Eggs" Manski, so we said we'd be glad to trade him for the first-draft choice. That's where we were again very fortunate. Luckman was one of the greatest halfbacks in the nation on the football field. He had played with Columbia and was an excellent passer from the single wing, but he'd never played on the center of the T-formation. So, for the first five games, we put him at quarterback, and he was never replaced.

Dan Fortmann was just the luck of the game. He was about the last man left on the board, and we were just fortunate that he turned out to be a great guard, an all-pro guard. The only reason I selected him was that there were a couple of names left and he had the prettiest one.

At that time the game was becoming a combination of running and passing. We had been playing the college rules that the passer had to be five yards behind the line of scrimmage. Then, in a game against Portsmouth, Bronco Nagurski faked into the line and threw a swing pass to Grange for a touchdown. Coach "Potsie" Clark raised a hue and cry, stating that Nagurski was not five yards behind the line of scrimmage; but the officials indicated that he was, and the touchdown counted. We scored a safety after that, which made the score 9-0.

Due to that ruling, I saw no reason why there shouldn't be a pass from anywhere behind the scrimmage. And that was the rule I installed in February, '33. It had a profound effect as far as tie games were concerned. We had six tie games in '32 and only one in '33.

As I said, passing was becoming a favorable part of football.

Wilson Sporting Goods Company was very interested in it, so I got together with Dan O'Brien to see if he could come up with a ball that would make for better passing. They made a beautiful football, without any laces, symetrically shaped. There was only one thing wrong with it: When you attempted to pass or punt it, you could not get a spiral. I told O'Brien that the reason for no spiral was that Wilson had discarded the laces. To retain the spiral, the football had to be overweighted in one part, and that's what finally happened. It had a profound effect on passing and punting.

Baseball in the thirties was a far cry from what it would be in the seventies. Today, baseball news concentrates as much on player drafts and multi-million-dollar contracts as it does on game scores and home runs. Forty years ago it was quite the opposite: The emphasis was far more on team pride than dollar prize, though, as former Detroit Tiger star Charlie Gehringer points out, not exclusively so. Here, he recalls his experiences with some of the leading players of that decade.

Mr. Gehringer is now a retired businessman and lives in the Detroit area.

CHARLES GEHRINGER

Yeah, '33 was the first All-Star Game that was scheduled, and it was a tremendous thrill being in it. I played in six games and was picked for the seventh, but I had an injury. In fact, I played every inning of all six games, which is a rarity today, because now it's more or less just a show-off of all the players that get picked by the fans. Back then, managers really wanted to prove the supremacy of their league. The All-Star Game was a one-game World Series, and we were very serious about it.

The American League was younger than the National by only two or three years, and we felt that it was a better league and we were going to prove it. At that time we had quite an edge: We had won eight of the first 12 games and the cycle was strictly in our favor. Then it switched over to where the National League has been very prominent ever since the '40s.

Carl Hubbell's strike-outs? Yeah, that was in '34. I led off the second All-Star Game and got a base hit, and Hymie Manush followed me and got a base on balls. Then Gehrig came to bat, and on the 3-2 pitch, we stole second and third and he struck out. Of course, we thought we were in a pretty good position with Ruth and Simmons coming up next, but then Hubbell struck those two out, too. Then he struck out three more in the next inning with a walk to Bill Dickey somewhere in there.

Generally, I tried to hit the ball where it was pitched; I didn't go for any distance. We had fellas like Greenberg, York and Goslin, a lot of guys that could hit the long ball. But guys like me and Mickey Cochrane, we more or less just tried to get on. I did hit 20 home runs one year, but that turned out to be one of the worst batting years I had, so that more or less proved you can't do both.

As far as the toughest pitchers go, when you're not hitting well, they're all tough. I think Lefty Grove was without a doubt the toughest I ever faced. And although I came at the tail end of Walter Johnson's career, he could still throw rather hard when I was playing. Of course, Feller was a tremendous pitcher, Ruffing, Gomez, there were any number of them. Then, when you got in the World Series, there were people like the Deans, who were tremendous pitchers. In '34, I think that between them they won 50 games. In the World Series we played against the Cardinals, they each won two games.

I think we got $4,000 or $5,000 for the Series that year. The next year we got what was at that time the largest World Series check, about $7,000, when we beat the Cubs. Half the ball park seemed to be box seats, which gave 'em a good price. Of course, Detroit had a good-sized stadium with a lot of box seats, and that's what made it count. Nowadays you've got television rights and everything.

Generally, in the off-season in the early years, I'd go on barnstorming tours. (Remember, there was no television then and a lot of places didn't even get very good radio.) We'd go out through the West and up through Canada and to places where they had never seen a baseball game but only read about it. We'd get some guy to pick an All-Star team from all the clubs in the American League. There were always guys around that could get a schedule going, and all these little towns had teams in those days that would challenge us. I don't think we ever lost a game, except once in a while when we'd bump into one of those Negro all-star teams. They were tough.

As a matter of fact, we scheduled two Negro teams that sort of traveled with us on a couple of occasions: the Chicago American Giants and Satchel Paige's team. We played against Satchel practically every night for two weeks. He pitched each night and he was tough. He always said that I gave him a lot of trouble, but I wasn't happy hitting against him, I'll tell you that. He was a great pitcher.

There were some great hitters, too. I remember one big first baseman called Mule Suttles, who played with Chicago. He used the heaviest bat I'd ever seen in baseball; it was 50 ounces, and man, he could swing that thing. He was a tremendous hitter. We had a good pitcher named Earl Whitehall, and this Suttles would kill everything he threw. They were all good ball players, and a lot of them would've been big leaguers without a doubt had they broken the color line.

Otherwise, most of the little town teams couldn't give us much of a tussle. They enjoyed seeing us and they didn't care whether they beat us or not. The fans just wanted to see the guys they'd read about. It was just a show, I guess.

We used to try to get the guys that either were colorful or hit the long ball, guys who were outstanding. I went most of the time with guys like Lefty Grove. He always liked to go where he'd pitch only two or three innings, but he was like old Satchel Paige. Everybody knew him and wanted to at least see how hard he threw. Then we'd usually clown it up a little. We'd make a double play where there weren't any, and the fans got a kick out of that, too. We'd be gone three weeks or a month and make $1,500 to $2,500 per man, so it was worthwhile, besides being a lot of fun.

When we traveled, it was always by train. The first few years it wasn't so great, but after they got air conditioning, I thought they were very enjoyable. Our trips during the season weren't long. We'd go from Boston to New York to Washington to Philadelphia, making them all in three or four hours. They had great food and we always had a private car with lower berths, so we were comfortable. If we got caught in St. Louis and had to go to Boston, then we had a two-day ride, which was kind of boring, but ordinarily I didn't mind the train travel.

The hotels were always great; they gave us the best. Everything was good then. We didn't get terrific salaries, but we got enough and we were well taken care of. Now everybody's looking at the material side of it. But me, I played in a few series and I played in a great town. I don't know that I'd change anything if I had it to do over again.

They were the hero-victims of depression-era sports—heroes because as stars of the Negro leagues, black baseball players felt the same kinds of thrills and won the same kinds of glories that white players did in the major leagues; victims because as blacks playing out their dreams against a segregated backdrop, they could never achieve the major-league status they deserved. And so it was the destiny of stars like John "Jimmy" Crutchfield not to make it on their own but to pave the way for black greats of a later generation.

During his professional athletic career, Jimmy Crutchfield was an outfielder for the Birmingham Black Barons, the Indianapolis ABCs, the Chicago American Giants and what was perhaps the greatest team in Negro baseball, the 1932 Pittsburgh Crawfords, five of whose members are now in the Baseball Hall of Fame in Cooperstown, N.Y. Mr. Crutchfield was elected to five All Star teams and retired in 1945 with a .325 lifetime batting average. He now lives in Chicago.

JOHN "JIMMIE" CRUTCHFIELD

I always had a love for baseball. Back when I was a kid, I played on the local team in my home town, Moberly, Missouri. About '28 we had an old-time player from Chicago by the name of Bill Gatewood. He was well known in the black leagues; he was a great pitcher. Naturally, with his ability, we made him the manager of the team. I played two years under Gatewood, '28 and '29. Well, he told me during the winter of '29 that he was going to send me to Birmingham the next spring. Most of the people didn't approve of that, because they didn't think I was that good. I was a good local ballplayer, but to go into the big leagues with all those big guys, well, I weighed only 138 pounds and looked younger than I was. But I believed I could make it, I had faith, and that next spring I was sent to Birmingham.

How they laughed when they first saw me. They didn't think I could make it. I was just too small, they said. We were training in Fort Bennings, Georgia. They had a peacetime army there. The guys had nothing to do but get up in the morning and report; then they had the whole day to spend doing anything they wanted to do. Most of them spent their time watching the Birmingham team train, and I could hear them laughing at me, saying I didn't have a chance, I was too small. But after only seven days our manager, Clarence Smith, called me over and said, "When the season starts, you're going to be my center fielder and leadoff man."

We started the season in late April of that year. It's hard to tell you how I felt being in that line-up and knowing I was going to be playing in Kansas City, Chicago, Detroit, all those big cities, against well-known baseball players. There were the Monarchs, one heck of a ball club, and the St. Louis Stars, equally famous, equally great.

No, I wasn't scared. That's the difference between some rookies making it and some failing; they just don't have that confidence, and that's all it takes sometimes, belief in yourself. Well, I knew what I could do and I was anxious to get out and show people.

In the first game I was a little shaky and got one out of three. We were playing the Cubans from Havana, it was the first inning and our pitcher, one of the ace pitchers on the team, had the bases full and two out. The hitter hit a line drive to me in center field. I started in but stopped just in time, reached up to make the catch, and retired the side. From then on, that was it. I was just hoping that they would hit the ball to me, because I was anxious to show the manager and the players what I could do.

I was being paid $90 a month. It was pretty rough, but I didn't worry about the money. I loved baseball. Besides, I hadn't had any money, so $90 looked kind of big. But once you spend a little for clothes and send a little home, you've got nothing. And before the season was over, you had missed a payment. It was right in the midst of the depression.

We finished out the season in Birmingham, but the team broke up in the winter—most of the southern teams broke up then—and I was sent to the Indianapolis ABCs and stayed there half a season. Then we heard that there was a fellow in Pittsburgh named Gus Greenlee who had money to throw away. He was starting the Pittsburgh Crawfords baseball team, and they sent for me. I got $125 to go out there, with an advance of $50. I thought that advance was really something.

Gus Greenlee loved baseball, and being a big man around there in politics and in the rackets, he wanted a great baseball club. The only known players on the team then were Pickens, Sam Streeter and Satchel Paige. That winter he signed Josh Gibson and Oscar Charleston. Well, that was almost half the ball club right there, those two. As the years went on, we added a player here and there: Judy Johnson, Cool Papa Bell, both of whom were elected to the Hall of Fame. In fact, I played with five Hall of Fame players on that team: Johnson, Bell, Paige, Charleston and Gibson.

Gibson was just a big, overgrown boy, 6'2", with broad shoulders, but he was powerful and he was fast. A swell guy. I never heard Josh brag about his ability. He could hit three home runs during a game and the fans would be out and he'd say, "Ah, get away." It wasn't that he didn't want to be bothered with the fans; he just didn't want his teammates to feel that everyone was hanging around him, so he would run the other way.

Satchel? A good guy, comical, full of fun all the time and a great pitcher. He was something else. He pitched games the average person never heard about. I remember a time when we had 47,000 people and they all came to see Satchel. We were playing the Philadelphia Stars, and they had a pitcher named Slim Jones. He and Satchel hooked up in a pitcher's duel in Yankee Stadium and the score was 1-1, going into the last of the ninth inning. Well, I've seen it happen time and time again. To make a long story short, Satchel struck out the side. No one scored. That was in '36.

Charleston was of the old-school type of baseball player, the Ty Cobb type, rough and tough. He was fat and he was slow, but he was one of the best base runners in our league, because he knew how and when to steal. I saw him get a 10- to 15-foot lead off first base and the pitchers just couldn't pick him off. He just had that baseball knack.

Cool Papa Bell was the gentleman of gentlemen. I think he was one of the best liked of all the baseball players. He, Josh, a fella by the name of Matlock, a really great left-handed pitcher, Sam Bankhead, an infielder, and I were called the "jug buddies." After the games, we hung out together, and we never talked about our baseball ability. It was just one of those things; to be in that club, you had to be good.

We felt we could win whenever we wanted to, and we got to a point where if the crowd was big, well, nobody could beat us; so, naturally, we would be the strongest on Sundays and holidays.

Yes, there were a lot of black fans, but I'd say with the exception of Cleveland, most of the fans were white; they had the money to spend, and admission to the games was 50¢.

In those days, crowds were usually 5,000, though we moved up to 10,000, and once, when we played in Yankee Stadium, we had 47,000. In Chicago, for our East-West game, we had 12,000 the first year, '34, 25,000 the second and on up to 51,000 in '41 and they had to turn people away.

I was on the team in '34, '35, '36, starting in right field, and played again in '41. [He was elected to the '39 All-Star game but broke his arm before the game.] It was a great feeling. In some of the games, players were elected by the fans. The Pittsburgh *Courier* conducted the voting in the East and, I think, the Chicago *Defender* in the West. And there were others, the managers who selected the players they wanted for their teams.

I got a kick out of the '34 East-West game. Along with Satchel, I was one of the stars of that game, 1-0. I threw out Mule Suttles at home plate. And in the '35 game, they said I made one of the greatest catches ever made at White Sox Park. Well, it was just a catch, a bare-handed catch, a line drive with two men on base, two out. At the last moment, after making a long run, I just leaped into the air and, with a bit of luck, made the catch.

Traveling conditions then were bad. There was a lot of

discrimination, mostly in hotels. We'd run into nice hotels in New York, Philadelphia, Washington, Chicago, but when we hit the smaller towns, it was really rough. I remember one in Nashville, Tennessee, where I could lie in my bed and look out through the ceiling!

That same year we played a doubleheader in Chicago, beat the American Giants 1-0. It was 105 degrees. Well, when we finished the game and came out of the dressing room, it was just like you had taken a shower with your clothes on. But we got in the bus and headed for Philadelphia, because we had a doubleheader scheduled there for Tuesday. Since that was before they had the turnpike, we had to go up over the mountains, and it was a long, tiresome ride. When we arrived in Phildelphia, about nine in the morning, my ankles were swollen. We got there but there was no time for rest or anything. After our meal, the first one since we had left Chicago, we went out and split a doubleheader. We lost the second game 5-4 and almost had a fight—because we lost it after riding all that distance!

We had some bad baseball parks, but most of the time we played in good ones: Connie Mack Stadium in Philadelphia; Yankee Stadium and the Polo Grounds in New York; Forbes Field in Pittsburgh; Ebbets Field in Brooklyn; Sportsman's Park in St. Louis; and the Municipal Stadium in Cleveland—all major-league parks.

Usually we'd play the farm teams of some of the major-league clubs. Once we played the Boston Braves, a farm team in Canton, Ohio. They all came out one night to watch us play, especially to see Gibson and Paige. Well, Gibson didn't disappoint them: He hit one of the longest home runs they'd ever seen. We won the game 2-1: Cool Papa Bell doubled, I singled, and Gibson hit the home run.

We played in Newark, too, against the Newark Bears [a New York Yankees farm team], at that time one of the most powerful teams in the minor leagues. They had Buddy Rosar, Pinky May, Charlie Keller, McQuinn, Hershberger—all those guys went into the major leagues.

We always played the white teams—it was always white against colored—and they made more; sometimes their guarantee was twice as much as ours. They were always surprised by the ability of our players. They just thought they could go out there and beat us any way they wanted to. Well, we had guys that could play the infield, the outfield, pitch, throw and hit as well as anybody, but they didn't believe it.

You see, in our league, a pitcher was subject to pitch the first game and maybe play the second game because of his hitting ability. Our infielder might play third base in one game and then play the outfield in another in order to put another guy in the line-up. And most every team had two or three players who were real base stealers.

I remember one night we played against this exhibition team that had Denny Doyle, John Frederick of the Dodgers, Rabbit Walshler from the Red Sox, Chuck Fuller and Conway English from the Giants, Larry French, Earl Patton and Bill Swift from the Pirates, and Hack Wilson, who was the most dangerous hitter on this team. Well, Wilson had a habit of stepping way back in the batter's box and then stepping forth. We had a very smart pitcher, W. Bell; he had perfect control and a good screwball. He would throw the ball on the outside and just barely nip the corner with it. Well, he struck Wilson out about four times.

Once in Denver, Colorado, in '36, we played a team that had Jimmy Foxx, Johnny Mize, Rogers Hornsby, Pinky Higgins and other great players, and they were betting that day 2-1 that the major leaguers would just run us out of the ball park. As a matter of fact, we had heard around town that we wouldn't show up for the game that day. Well, we beat them in a doubleheader.

Still, you'd pick up the papers and read about the major leagues, about a guy in your position, and you'd wonder if you could play out there, too. But there was nobody around to rock the boat then. We just accepted it. So we would go out to the major-league ball parks and watch the guys and it was just . . . well, tears would be in our eyes because we couldn't be out there. Connie Mack watched our team play, and Cal Griffith always said that he wished some of our ballplayers could be out there; but nobody had the guts enough to make the attempt to sign any of us.

The most frustrating part about the whole thing would come

at the end of the season, when you had nothing to show for your season's work. They called me the black Lloyd Waner; but in '32 he was making $12,000 and I was getting $125 a month. It was rough, but I don't know, I always figured conditions would get better next year. So here I went through the whole depression and then, at the time black ballplayers began to make a halfway decent salary, about '45, well, I was at the end of the line.

But I look back and I have no regrets. I'm thankful for baseball. Playing ball was the only ability I had, and it seemed like I could express myself by walking to the plate, knowing that there were hundreds of thousands of fans watching me. It gave me something all the money in the world couldn't have given me.

Necessity, the maxim goes, is the mother of invention; but in the case of the Negro leagues, it was also the prelude to invention. For it was in black baseball that American player participation in winter ball began, as well as the first league expansion programs, both of which were to become important aspects of major-league baseball. And there were additional precedents, notably Effa Manley's role as a team co-owner and league executive at a time when women were allowed in boardrooms only to serve refreshments or take dictation.

Mrs. Manley is now retired from the active sports scene. She lives in Los Angeles and is the co-author of *Negro Baseball . . . Before Integration*.

EFFA MANLEY

Before my husband, Abe, became interested in baseball, there were these 12 Negro teams barnstorming all over the country, depending entirely on their booking agents and the whole system was ridiculous. The western teams were the Kansas City Monarchs, Chicago American Giants, Birmingham Black Barons, Memphis Red Sox, Indianapolis Clowns and Cleveland Buckeyes. The eastern teams were the Homestead Grays, Pittsburgh Crawfords, Baltimore Elite Giants, Cuban Stars, Philadelphia Stars and New York Black Yankees.

Then, when Abe entered the picture, he got all the eastern teams, except for the New York Black Yankees, to go along with him to form the Negro National League around 1935. They agreed on the condition that he'd put a team known as the Eagles in Ebbets Field in Brooklyn. Each of the teams gave him two ballplayers and then he got more men. This is something the major leagues are doing today with expansion teams.

The next year, the western teams got together and set up the

Negro American League, and then the New York Black Yankees came in with us.

That first year we played in Ebbets Field, but we drew a very small crowd on opening day. What's funny is that I had sent invitations to all the important people in New York and they all came. Mayor LaGuardia threw the first ball and stayed for the whole game. The police commissioner and a bunch of his men were there, too. It was a very distinguished group but small. See, we were in strictly Dodger territory and that's all the fans were interested in; they weren't interested in Negro baseball. As for the game itself, it was terrible. We had bad enough luck to get the best Negro team for our opponents, the Homestead Grays, and they beat us 21 to 6, something like that. Home runs were a dime a dozen, and I left about the third or fourth inning.

Then, the next year, we moved to New Jersey, where a semi-pro team was playing. Now a man named Tyler, who had a place called Carlo's Chicken Shack—the most delicious fried chicken you ever tasted,—also had a semi-pro team there. So Abe proceeded to negotiate with Mr. Tyler to buy his baseball franchise and one of the players on that team, Ray Dandridge, the third baseman. I think he offered $5,000 or $10,000. I really don't know, because we never talked finances.

Well, Tyler permitted Abe to move into his territory, with Ray Dandridge being the prize of the package, and Ruppert Stadium in Newark became our home park for the rest of our baseball life. Abe made the arrangements with the bosses of the Yankees; he knew his way around.

You know, one of the things I got the biggest thrill from happened back when we first got the team. I was very upset about the fellows not having any work in the winter, so I made this contact in Puerto Rico (Puerto Rico, like Cuba, has always been very baseball-conscious) through a friend in New York who told me that if we sent the team down there, he'd keep them busy. I got Vic Harris, manager of the Homestead Grays, to go along to manage the team, and they went there as the Brooklyn Eagles. There were 13 of them; seven were my ballplayers and the other six were men Vic had gotten together, and it was quite a team. They proceeded to win the pennant in Puerto Rico and were received with open arms. The Bacardi Rum people gave them a trophy, which they brought back, and it's now in the Baseball Hall of Fame. After that we had no more problems with the guys not having work in the winter. Some of them got $1,000 a month; all the good ones had to do was contact the proper people.

As for our team, we always had a very good ball club. Abe was a genius at picking ballplayers. Any time he heard about someone good, he went to see him. We had one guy Abe heard about in upstate New York. Abe went to see him and liked what he saw, but the boy couldn't leave because he was on parole. I contacted the parole board and they said that he couldn't leave under any conditions, that he had to spend two more years in New York. Actually, I think the man who had the ball club there didn't want to lose him, because he was such a good player. Well, I've always been one of those people who believed that you have to know someone who knows someone to get anything done, so I contacted our New Jersey parole board, which contacted the New York parole board. The New Jersey board agreed to take the fellow in such a way that New York couldn't refuse to turn him over, and he turned out to be a wonderful ballplayer, a big help to the team.

Salaries? Back then, I think our payroll was about $8,000, and that was for about 16 or 17 men. A fairly good salary was $500 a month, but not everybody got that; some got a couple of hundred. It was according to what you signed the guys for, how many dependents they had, deductions and what have you.

We made sure we used the best of everything. We always had a nice bus and our stuff was manufactured right where the majors had their stuff done. The Wilson ball was adopted by the league.

Abe went with the team everywhere. It was his hobby and he wanted to see them play. He always stayed right at the hotel with the ball club, and if it was an important game, I stayed right at the hotel, too. We never went to a white hotel or some other hotel that was a little higher priced. In my book, the Negro hotels were all right.

But there were also some very hard times. In our case, the thing that saved our lives was that Abe's money was enough to hold us over. We actually dropped $100,000. You see, Abe had made his money earlier as a numbers broker. He had the Philadelphia-Camden territory sewn up until the gangsters moved in. Then the local prosecutor, who was a friend, told Abe to get out of town, because with the gangsters moving in he'd have to clean up the numbers. So Abe came to New York. But anyway, he had the money, and when he went to the bank every first and fifteenth, the payroll was ready and waiting for the ballplayers.

There were other teams that had hard times, too. I understand that Wilkerson actually mortgaged his home to keep his Kansas City Monarchs. And Sonny-Man Jackson had to come in with money to save the day for Cum Posey and the Homestead Grays. To tell you the truth, all the teams saw hard times. There were many occasions when they had to get outside help.

Yes, I attended all the league meetings, and my voice was heard as often as Abe's. There were other teams that had double representation, but none were wives. We had one of those perfect partnerships: I could not have done what Abe did, which was to get the teams together, and I don't think he could have done what I did, which was to take care of all the business details. Running a ball club was, believe me, quite a bit of work.

Yes, they may be using Negroes now, but in my opinion, they don't look as good as the players we had back in Negro baseball. The reason they don't compare with our old-time ballplayers is that they're depending on schools to teach baseball. But baseball is something you're born with. And those kids we used to have came up with just a stick and a ball in the back yard. There just aren't any Oscar Charlestons, Dick Lundys, Joe Williamses or Satchel Paiges today. Joe Williams' fast ball was so fast they called him "Smoky Joe" and "Cyclone Joe." And Satchel, when he had two strikes on a batter and two outs at the end of the ball game, he would turn around and call the outfield in before he threw the ball. Then he threw that fast ball that he knew he wasn't going to miss. It was like the ballplayers said: "You can't hit what you can't see."

Prejudice? Well, one of the excuses they used to give for not using Negroes was that they weren't good enough, and what happened? They went in there and broke an unbreakable record, Babe Ruth's home-run record.

Unlike other professional sports of the thirties, boxing was one that was not completely segregated, and thus several notable black fighters emerged during that decade, among them Joe Louis, Kid Chocolate and Henry Armstrong.

Armstrong's story reads like a version of *Somebody Up there Likes Me* or *Rocky:* the kid with no chance who, through preseverance and determination, becomes the world's featherweight, lightweight and middleweight champion and the only man to hold three world titles simultaneously. But, on a deeper level, is another story, that of a young black *athlete* encountering a wall of segregation and managing, by virtue of his position, to put a few chinks in that wall.

Today, Henry Armstrong lives in St. Louis, Missouri, where he is associated with the Herbert Hoover Boys' Club. He is also an ordained minister.

HENRY ARMSTRONG

It was '29, the year we had the big depression here. I'd been working on the railroad for three months, but I wasn't getting anywhere, because every time I'd get a check, I'd have to pay bills and the money would be gone. Then one evening a very strange thing happened to me. Somebody threw away a St. Louis *Post-Dispatch,* and all of a sudden, a little wind came up and took the paper apart. Well, believe it or not, the sports page dangled after me; then it stopped and opened up on a story: "Kid Chocolate, Cuban Featherweight, Wins in the Polo Grounds, Gets $75,000 for Half-Hour's Work." So I said, "This is for me. If he can do it, I can, too." The guys at work all said, "You can't do it; you can't fight. You're too small; you need to be big." See, they were thinking about big fighters like Jack Johnson and Jack Dempsey. But I said, "No, this guy weighs 123, and I can get up to his size, I know I can. And I'm gonna come back here in a Cadillac that I'm gonna buy myself." They said, "This little guy's gone crazy. Do you know what a Cadillac costs? It costs about $5,000." And I said, "Yeah? Well, I'm gonna buy it. I'm gonna bring that Cadillac back."

I quit the job and bought myself a pair of boxing gloves. I tried to be discovered by fighting in the streets, but no one would ever pick at me. Finally I got my chance to go to the YMCA, where I'd heard there were professional fighters who knew what they were doing. There was this one fella there named Harry Armstrong, who weighed 165, and he said to me, "You can't fight; you're a little fella." I said, "I've hit guys bigger than you and they fell," and he said, "Okay, put the gloves on."

Well, he knew all about fighting and he just jabbed me off. Then he said, "Look, when I jab, all you have to do is step over, let it go over your shoulder and then come back and hit me so you're hitting my weight and yours, too." He jabbed and I did what he said perfectly and he hit the ground. Then he said, "Okay, that's enough. I'm gonna train you." And that's the way we started.

At that time they didn't have any mixed matches. A colored boy couldn't fight a white boy and you couldn't fight a Chinaman here, so I knocked out a little colored kid at the old Coliseum on Jefferson Avenue and the next thing, I was ostracized. I couldn't fight a white boy and no colored boy would fight me.

So we went to Pittsburgh, and I was so good I was beating the professionals in the gymnasium. Then we went to Chicago, but all the promoters there said, "You better take that boy home; he's nothing but a kid. He'll be killed," and they wouldn't give me a fight. I said to Harry, "We'll make them regret it someday," and we came back to St. Louis.

Well, I went along for several days and then I began thinking about the '32 Olympics that were going to be held in California. I wanted to get into them and make a name for myself, and I told this to Harry. Now, his name is Armstrong and mine was really Jackson, but I took his name, since I had fought professionally in California and wanted to turn back to the amateurs, and we went as brothers.

It took us 11 days of hoboing to get to California, and when we finally got there, we went to one of those midnight missions where the bums go to get soup. We kept going to these soup lines, and Harry, having been a kind of fighter, would go out and get $3 for a fight and that would pay for a room for a week. But he couldn't really fight and he'd come back with his eyes and nose swollen, and since I'd sprained my arm, I couldn't do anything but shine shoes.

There were all these little towns, like Pasadena, Malibu Beach, Pismo Beach, just two or three miles apart, and when I got well, we jumped in these places and soon I was knocking out three or four guys a night. I got to the point where I was such a draw, we were making $25 a fight. Harry even put a skull and crossbones on my back, but the Boxing Commission made me pull that stuff off because I was scaring so many guys.

In the meantime, I got squinched out of the Olympics finals in San Francisco. The next thing was that Tom Cox, the fellow who owned my contract, sold it to a fellow named Wirt Ross, a professional manager. I fought quickly under him, and since I beat everyone in the professional ranks, the champion of the coast, George Ashford, wouldn't fight me, so they made me fight a little Indian boy up in Sacramento. I knocked him out in four rounds and became the featherweight champion of the West Coast.

Around '36, Al Jolson saw me fight and he purchased my contract for $10,000. Jolson gave me a great start, because as soon as he bought me, I was Mike Jacobs's first promotion in '37, and Jacobs was one of the great promoters of all time. He promoted Joe Louis, Ray Robinson, all the big guys.

Anyway, Jacobs promoted me in New York, and the first night in the Garden they put their best fighter in against me, the featherweight champion of New York City. Well, I had fought him on the West Coast and beat him that night, knocking him out with a left hook. I don't think we had even 4,000 people for that fight. But the next week I was brought back—that was the first time they ever brought a fighter back for two successive weeks—and we had over 15,000 that night. I fought Aldo Spalding and beat him bad.

Six months later I went to California and started going for the championships. It was my best year: I won the featherweight championship, and out of 27 fights, I had 26 straight knockouts.

Then what happened was that Barney Ross, the welterweight champion, said he'd fight me, since he'd run out of competition and I was the only one who was drawing. He weighed 147, so I built myself up to fight him. The morning of the fight, I got up and ate steaks for breakfast and drank water every 15 minutes to make the weight for the weigh-in. Well, I did, and I won the fight and held my welterweight title until about '45. I held my lightweight title until '39 and kept my featherweight title just long enough to win those other titles and hold them all simultaneously. You see, we did that as a kind of gag, because Joe Louis was coming along and he was drawing all the big gates and I had to have something different. Being a little fella, I had to have something big that would be a draw.

In '39 I fought the English champion over there and beat him in defense of my welterweight title. They gave me the Anglo-American Award, saying that I was the first Negro to go there and carry the banner of integrity. It was wonderful. They really honored me.

I was always thinking about breaking down prejudices. Back when I left St. Louis, I said, "I'm gonna break this thing down. I'm gonna make them want me." I'll never forget standing out in the cold in that old Coliseum in '29. That was the night I didn't have one fight. I had fought that little colored kid and knocked him out and I was out of it. There was nowhere to go. That hurt me pretty badly, because I was ostracized, segregated. I was thinking in my heart then, "Why is this so? I'm human, just like anyone else." And, of course, whenever I had the chance to hit it on the head, I did it.

When I first went to California, they didn't allow a Negro to fight in Hollywood. So after I got big, after I won the three titles, I said, "If they don't put Negro boys in that stadium in Hollywood, I'm going to close it up." I would fight in Los Angeles at the Olympic Stadium, and people would save their money to see me fight. Sure enough, in six or seven months, that place in Hollywood went bankrupt.

Well, finally they came to my manager to get me to fight there and I said, "Yeah, I'll fight for you, but I'm going to fight a colored boy." They said, "Okay, anything you want." Well, I put some 30,000 in there that night and they had to turn away about 6,000 more. They went back into business for another six months, but California was too big for them and they finally had to close up.

You see, I wasn't a militant person. I didn't go in like a Dr. Martin Luther King. I did it through my fighting ability. I said, "If you're going to segregate, I'm not coming. If you want me, you've got to break it down," and they wanted me because I was a draw. I could make money for them.

Now, as far as the money I made goes, I was never flamboyant. I just took it all in stride. I bought nice things, Cadillacs and LaSalles, and had a beautiful home on the West Coast. But I never took to being high hat about it. I'd always help a guy and give to charities, things like that.

But if you don't have a good accountant, you're going to lose a lot. In my career, 15 years of fighting, I earned close to $5 million. But besides big taxes, I paid ten percent to my trainer and a third to my manager. And before I got my third, we had to take expenses off the top, like training camp, which sometimes cost $2,200 a week, and each of the boys with me, who got almost $50 a day. Then too, I was probably cheated out of a lot of my money.

So if I had this to do all over again, I'd probably keep the books myself. So much money got away from me, so much. I shouldn't even be working now. I should just be sitting down, taking it easy, doing whatever I want to do.

Few people have had as broad a range of professional sports experience as trainer Eddie Froelich—hockey, baseball, football, major leagues, minor leagues, American League, National League, *ad infinitum.* **In this memoir, he shares some of his experiences during the thirties, as well as valuable insights he acquired.**

Mr. Froelich, whose most recent position was with the Chicago White Sox, is now retired and lives in Evanston, Illinois.

EDWARD FROELICH

As a trainer, my main responsibility was to put 25 men in the best possible condition at the manager's disposal. I strove to do this from the first day of training to the last day of the season. And I always weighed the risks of injury. For example, playing a player and possibly losing him for two weeks was a bad risk, so I tried not to take it, but sometimes I was overruled.

Part of being a trainer was making sure the players were in top physical shape, advising them about eating and sleeping habits, advising them even about life itself—about how to deal with youngsters and how to spend their first important money. There were many things I told them. Of course, injuries were the biggest concern—how to avoid them, how to treat them.

I was with the Black Hawks from '31 to the spring of '48. I was also with the Chicago Cardinals' football team in '34, '35 and '36, with the Brooklyn Dodgers in '37 and '38, and then with Kansas City in '39, '40 and '41.

Hockey back then was poetry in motion on a sheet of ice. A player who picked up the puck and started down the ice could carry it and pass it and then take a pass. If a player shot the puck from mid-ice, the fans used to boo. Then, all of a sudden, you'd hear them clapping. We used to come into New York, where the Rangers were a very strong team, and try to play for a tie so we could get a point, so it was that kind of game: one man in, shooting the puck across the blue line, most of the time from center ice. It would become obvious to the fans in the Garden that we were not taking any chances but wanted to get out of there with a tie and a point so we could get into the playoffs, and they—all 16,000 of them—would start singing the "Skater's Waltz." Have you ever heard 16,000 people sing the "Skater's Waltz?" It was really something!

I saw a lot of great players. We had, of course, the great Howie Morenz. He was past his peak when he came to Chicago, but he had the kind of greatness I've never seen since in a hockey rink. He had an electricity about him, the kind that when he was on the ice and picked up the puck around his own net, 20,000 people would come forward on their seats or stand up. I've never seen anyone skate like him. They used to call him the Babe Ruth of hockey.

No, the depression didn't affect the game. Of course, remember the price of tickets was correspondingly lower. The mezzanine seat, which is $10 today, was $2, box seats, $12.50 today, were $2.50, the first balcony was something like $1.50, and the top balcony was 75¢.

Salaries? Most of the players made from $3,500 to $4,500 a year. A guy like Morenz was making about $10,000, somewhere around there. Our top guy on the Black Hawks, Paul Thompson, was making $7,000; but guys like Tommy Cook were making only $4,000. Why? Well, everything was cheaper, and for many, many years, hockey players were terribly underpaid. First of all, I think there were nine major-league teams, and if a player didn't like it, tough luck: Go be a farmer or work for Sears and Simpson in Toronto. The players had to take it. Only since the World Hockey Association came into being have their salaries come up, and then they went overboard. I think the median salary now is $90,000 a year, with $10,000 in benefits.

Yeah, I was in Brooklyn in '37 and '38. The Dodgers were an old team then; a bad team, a cast-off team. When Durocher and MacPhail came in in '39, everything turned around for the better. But in the late '30s the team was known as the "Daffiness Boys" in Brooklyn.

Crazy things used to happen. It was the days of Babe

Herman, Wilbert Robinson, the fans, Ebbets Field. There was no other park like it and no other fans like them. It was a whole picture; no single element stood out. It was many things. The fans didn't go there to root for the home team; they went there to ride them. They used to call them the "bums," and that's what they meant. But you'd better not be a stranger and call them that; you'd better be sure you were from Brooklyn. And you'd better call them the "bums" in a certain way, as if way down deep you were really a Dodger fan but just didn't like the way they were playing.

What was it like to be with the Dodgers in those days? More than anything else, it was sad, frustrating. There was nothing pleasant about it. Of course, you look back on it and it's not as grim, but there's nothing pleasant about being in seventh or eighth place. I felt as if I didn't want to meet anybody on the street, as if when I had to go someplace, I had better go through the alley. Then there was the fact that everybody was making fun of the ball club. People in New York or Brooklyn never said, "How did the Dodgers come out?" They'd say, "What did the bums do today?" Which meant, What silly thing happened?

I'll never forget the time Herman hit a ball off the right-field wall and it wound up in a triple play. Dazzy Vance was on third, Chick Fewster was on second, and nobody was out. Herman hit one of these high ones, and it was a question of whether the right fielder was going to catch it. Just as it was coming down, it grazed the wall, and while Herman was coming around like hell, Dazzy Vance, who had gone up the third-base line, came back to tag up to make sure he could score if the ball was caught. In the meantime, Fewster had come off second base and he was going to score. The ball came and they had all three of them on third base! Then one of them made the mistake of stepping off, so they had two of them on and the other guy off and a triple play at third base. The story goes that in downtown Brooklyn that day a cabbie had his radio blaring away about the game when another cabbie pulled up next to him at a stop light and hollered, "How're they doing?" The first guy hollered back, "They got three men on base!" And the second guy hollered, "Which base?"

They used to say that things happened in Brooklyn that never happened anywhere else, and it was true. I remember being in spring training one year and players telling me all sorts of things about Brooklyn and Ebbets Field. I thought, "They're putting me on; it can't be like that." Finally opening day came, with the Giants and Dodgers, a big heated rivalry, playing each other. Bartell was the leadoff man. The first ball was pitched by Mungo. "Strike!" Bartell jumped out of the box to complain, and a tomato hit him right there, dotting the *i*. The first ball pitched; the guy must have been practicing all winter!

The next day there was an editorial in the *Brooklyn Eagle* about the rotten sportsmanship that some fans exhibited at baseball games, and what a sad commentary it was on the American public when these things happened. A couple of days later, the guy who threw the tomato wrote, "You are as crummy a bum as that Bartell is. What are you squawking about? I took the tomato out of the can, didn't I?"

After Brooklyn, I went to the Yankee organization in Kansas City and was there in '39, '40 and '41. Looking back on it, it was a pretty good thing. Kansas City and Newark, the two Yankee-owned teams, were considered the league powerhouses, and so we were regarded as the leaders in the American Association. We traveled pretty well, first class on trains, and stayed in the best hotels, and while we didn't get $24-a-day meal money, like they do today, everything about the Kansas City team was respectable.

Yes, a player had to travel the scale in those days. When a player signed a contract, the first place he went was a Class D league for $90 a month, sometimes $75 a month, and in some cases, as little as $50 a month—$50 a month! So he ate hamburgers and rode buses 500 miles from one city to the next, and he survived. But this is what he did when he wanted to make good.

Then, when he'd made good in D baseball, maybe he'd go to C, then to B, maybe skipping B to A and from there to AA. The American Association, the International League and the Pacific Coast League were considered AA. But the association was always considered to be a bit ahead of the other leagues. The

Coast League was considered a country-club league because they played sun games. A lot of the players, who would be just fringe players in the major leagues, preferred playing out there because they liked the weather and liked staying in one town for a while. They would play six days, with a doubleheader on Sunday, and then they'd have Monday off. They'd play 200 games; it was easy living and they liked it. But, you see, for guys who wanted to make it, the economics, the philosophy, the rationale was as simple as it could be: It was competition. They used to have 44 leagues in baseball—*leagues* every one of them, with six to eight teams. There was the difference—competition; it brought out the best.

In '34-'36 I was with the Chicago Cardinals football team. There was a good healthy rivalry between the Cardinals and the Bears, but the Bears were really the first team to gain prominence in Chicago, so they were the top dog. The Cardinals were not on a par with them from the early '30s on, when Halas began to assemble some real powerhouse teams. Our long suit was defense. We didn't have much offense and maybe we'd win 10-7, but the Bears were assembling powerhouses. They were coming on with great players, like Grange and Nagurski, all the talent you could possibly want; the team just kept growing and growing and growing.

Football was different then. Today a player plays defense *or* offense, or he plays on special teams. In the '30s the 11 guys played offense *and* defense. They played from the time the whistle blew until the game was over. Each player stayed out there while the other team pushed his butt all the way down the field to his goal line and scored, and he didn't come off the field. He stayed right out there while the other team kicked off and then he tried to push the ball down to the other end of the field. The only time a player came out of there was when he was hurt, and then he came back in just as fast as he damn well could. In those days, if he got hurt, he was released the next day.

When you ask me what it has all meant to me, I'd have to say I enjoyed it. But looking back, as I think about it, if I had it to do over, I don't think I'd be as serious about it. It used to be a grim thing with me. There was, there still is, so much emphasis on winning, and sometimes I punished myself a little too much trying to achieve that goal. I think about the times we might have lost four games in a row, and I couldn't eat or sleep, it was bothering me that much. But then I was the type of person who cared about what he was doing, and that's how it affected me.

One of the most interesting sports figures of the thirties was Thomas "Gumbo" Gibbs. A professional athlete, he formed his own baseball and basketball teams and toured the country with them, thus adding a unique chapter to the still-to-be-written history of black sports in the United States.

Mr. Gibbs is now retired from professional athletics, having been on the exhibition circuit from the twenties through the fifties. He lives in Chicago, where he is active in community sports programs and is writing his autobiography.

THOMAS "GUMBO" GIBBS

I was one of the greatest basketball clowns you'd ever want to see. On advertisements they called me "Tommy Gibbs, the Greatest Long-Shot Artist in the Business." I have stood from the foul line at the north end of the court and made a basket at the south end. From center court, it was just a regular shot for me. It was more or less just strength to push the ball that far. And in those days, you didn't have those one-handed jump shots.

We had what you call the "pepper game," balls going between your legs, rotating around your arm, spinning with your fingers. We brought the drop kick, the one the Globetrotters later picked up, to basketball. We would also do the run and lift. Sammy Gardner was about the tallest guy we had, 6'4". I was about the shortest, 5'9". Sammy would get into the center of the free-throw circle and we would crisscross the ball down, like what they call the rubber-band defense. Then Sammy would back up to the basket, I would hit the ball into him, make a jump, and he would catch me when I came floating in. Then I'd put the ball in and that would just kill the people. See, nobody ever worried about the score. They just wanted to laugh.

We always played local people, because it wouldn't have made sense to bring in other ball clubs when they wanted to have fun and see their own talent. Besides, they didn't have the money to bring in another club; what little money there was, they were going to give to us.

Even if we could beat a team by a thousand points, we never beat them over two or three. We would go into a town and see where we could make a thousand points and shut them out. But the score was always one or two points, and sometimes we'd have to play an overtime or something and the town was just tickled to death. See, if you killed somebody, you were never invited back. They wanted entertainment, not a runaway. They didn't want a stampede. So we would foul for a while, let them catch up, maybe miss a couple of baskets and let them get the rebound, then make a basket and that was it.

I had three teams: the Negro All Americans, the Negro All Stars and the Zulu Kings. We'd go into a town once and make pretty good as the All Americans, then change uniforms and go back in as the Negro All Stars, then put on some grass skirts, go back in and make some more money as the Zulu Kings. We wouldn't go back too soon, though, because people knew us.

The Zulu Kings got started because we were doing straight basketball and weren't making too much money. I came up with the idea from a fella named Dick Hudson. He always had some teams around him in Chicago that used to play donkey ball. He would go out to the stockyards or someplace, rent some donkeys, and they would play softball on the donkeys. One day he said, "Gumbo, I'm going to get some skirts to put on these guys and let them play like gals and that sort of thing." I thought about it, and I went out with him once with the grass skirts and then I went further than that: I painted my legs, and under my grass skirt I had basketball trunks.

We would go into the towns addressing ourselves as the Zulu Kings. We were fresh out of Africa and I was the interpreter. People would say "Good morning" and we would say "Ahooga," or something like that. That kept going until one night in Flora, Illinois, when we had the pots and spears and we got too close to one of the pots. One of the fringes on Red Flemming's skirt caught on fire and burned his leg. Well, that's when they found out we could speak English! They thought it was the funniest thing they ever saw.

The most popular team was the All Americans. I guess I put more into it because it was my first love. Those were the best ballplayers I ever had, and they stayed with me about five years. Then they started getting married and wanting careers and to make some money. They were having fun, but they weren't making any money with me. I don't remember one time a ballplayer came home with more than $50 in his pocket. Sometimes we'd have a dollar left after we paid a hotel bill. And sometimes I would have to call home for money to get to another town.

The average game was $35. Our guarantee was the first $35 plus 50-50, which meant we got the first $35 coming in the gate and 50 percent of what came in after that. Most times people would have to give us $4 or $5 to make up the guarantee. Our biggest gate in the '30s was $75.

See, the towns we would go into had small populations. When you would get into that town, people would get on the hotline and ring everybody who had a telephone for 25 miles around. And when that phone rang, everybody would pick it up and say, "Gumbo Gibbs is coming into town tonight with his basketball team." And then people would come out of the hills in wagons. Indians would come out wrapped in blankets, with kids, ragged and cold. I saw some of the worst sights you'd ever want to see. It was just pitiful.

We went to little towns in Iowa, South Dakota, and Nebraska. We were snowed in for a week in '38 in Marion, Nebraska. When we got out of the gym that first night, we could hardly get from there to the hotel, and they had to put us up for six or seven days.

Sometimes it took us three days to go 20 miles. Those are terrible times to look back on, but we enjoyed them then. See, we ate basketball, we slept basketball. It was just like dope: When you're hooked, you gotta have it.

One year I jumped back into the Midwest and East— Michigan, Indiana, Pennsylvania, Cleveland. Any time we went in, we played what they had: If they had a hardball team, we played hardball; if they had a softball team, we played softball. We weren't like the Globetrotters; they had their own ball club.

When we went into a town, we had to do our darnedest to win. A lot of times they would run in ringers on us, those semi-pro players, the Triple A getting ready for the majors. But we didn't care too much about that, because they couldn't do anything and we had a heck of a defense.

Besides all that, when we were playing in Youngstown, Ohio, they would have these amateur boxing shows, and while the basketball team would still be playing, I would be out getting us a bankroll; they would give me $25 for one of those little three-round bouts, which was a lot of money. I found out that I was pretty good. I won the Youngstown, Ohio, Golden Gloves Championship. So every time I went into Youngstown, if they had a card, I was on it. The minute I hit town, everybody wanted Gumbo.

I teamed up with a fellow they called the "Alabama Kid." His name was Johnny Reeves and he was one of the best pro boxers in Ohio. He was a light heavyweight, and at one time he was a contender. I was in his stable for a while, and when I would go through Ohio, I would fight on all his cards.

I had about 15 or 20 fights. Some of the guys I beat had been some of the top fighters, like Jim Kenny, from Germantown, Ohio, the state welterweight champion, Johnny Reeves's brother, who had beat some good boys, and a guy in Chicago by the name of Kirkpatrick, who used to fight out of the Savoy when they had amateur fights there. Kirkpatrick gave me a good fight, but I didn't get hurt. See, my big weapon was that I could hit hard. I couldn't stop anybody from hitting me, but when they got close enough to hit me, I got close enough to hit them, and that was the end of it.

I stayed out there so long, always hoping I'd hit the big bonanza. I knew it was there and I kept trying, but I didn't make it. I had a lot of people come to me and say, "I can do so much for you. I'll put your name up . . ." But I knew what could happen and I didn't want it to happen to me. Guys said they were going to make money for you, but if something happened to you, forget it, they got the money and you were in the baggage car. See, in those times there was no such thing as a rich black athlete, and I wanted to stay up there until the time I could make it big on my own. But I never did.

6
STAY TUNED FOR...

As noted elsewhere in this book, radio enjoyed a phenomenal growth during the depression era, and with good reason: Not only did it bring some of the country's greatest talent into people's homes; of special significance in the thirties, it was a free form of entertainment.

For those who tuned in each week to particular programs, the characters became real, distinct personalities. This was especially so in the case of Edgar Bergen, the Chicago night club ventriloquist with the wise-cracking, wooden-headed partner, Charlie McCarthy. The duo garnered radio's biggest audiences—audiences who truly believed that Edgar Bergen was one star and Charlie McCarthy the other.

It is difficult to pinpoint the impact of the Bergen-McCarthy phenomenon on American radio, if for no other reason than trying to do so is like trying to measure a mountain with a microscope. Suffice it to say that they brought entertainment and laughter to millions when such commodities were sorely needed and much appreciated.

EDGAR BERGEN

When talking pictures replaced vaudeville in the '30s, I went to night clubs and played places like the Waldorf Hotel, the Rainbow Room and the Hal Morgan Club in New York. Now, in the vaudeville years, Charlie was a newsboy; but, in order to play the night clubs, I had to put him in a top hat, tails and monocle, and those clothes were expensive. His top hat always cost around $35 and his full dress suit $125. And then on the radio it was even more expensive, because he had to have different clothes for different episodes.

I developed Mortimer Snerd when I played the Chez Paree in Chicago. I was bringing Charlie out two and three times for encores, but we had always thought of an encore as being something a little different, a "special," such as in vaudeville days when an actor would come out with a ukulele or something. So I devised Mortimer Snerd. I listened to the voice and it sounded stupid, so he had to be a boy who was stupid-looking but still likable. I sketched many versions of him on the tablecloths of the Chez Paree between shows. I then read up on phrenology, character analysis, and the features of the face, and Mortimer became a combination of weak features: low brow, receding chin, high eyebrows. He was scientifically stupid.

While I was still playing the Chez Paree, I went over and auditioned at NBC for Clarence Menzer. He said, "No, it won't go. The comedy isn't very funny." I said, "They're laughing at it at the Chez Paree," and he said, "Radio's different. It would only confuse them doing two voices." I said, "Amos n' Andy do other voices," and he said, "Well, that's different."

Later, while I was in New York, I got on the "Rudy Vallee Show." It was because Elsa Maxwell had thrown a party for the 400 at the Waldorf honoring Noel Coward, and instead of my pampering and flattering him, she got me to heckle him a bit with Charlie. Well, he liked it and it was a big success, so when they booked her on the "Rudy Vallee Show," they thought, why not book Bergen and McCarthy? They did, and that was the beginning of it, in December, '36. After I did three shows, the office agency, J. Walter Thompson, said, "How would you like to make it ten more and round it out to 13 weeks?" I said, "I'll take it," and it went right on from 13 weeks to 20 years on radio.

I established myself well enough on the "Rudy Vallee Show" that the agency and the sponsor, Fleishmann's yeast, wanted to do a big show on the West Coast, using motion-picture celebrities. It began in May, '37, and in three months it became the top-rated show in all radio. We paid many of the stars $5,000 to come on and do just ten minutes.

Don Ameche would open the show by saying, "This is the Chase and Sanborn Hour, with the —— orchestra" (we had two or three, but Ray Noble was with me the longest); then he would introduce the guest artist—singer, actor, comedian—and finally us, "Edgar Bergen and Charlie McCarthy!" After a break for a commercial, there would be a spot with Bergen and Charlie talking about school, holidays, and such. Charlie was the unruly boy, the rascal, and I was kind of pompous, stupid, but with elegance. Charlie would always outsmart me.

The exchange of dialog between us was so fast that sometimes people thought we were *both* talking. For three years I got mail asking, "Is it true that you speak for *both* you and this McCarthy?" We had form letters to answer them. Then Mortimer came along and it was the same thing all over again: "We know you talk for Charlie, but we can't believe you do it for Mortimer, too."

When the show went to an hour, Don Ameche would do a six-minute dramatic sketch with the guest star, after which I'd come on with Charlie and the guest star and do a three- or four-minute bit. For example, Charlie might say, "So you're Clark Gable? Well, I think this town is big enough for both of us. We can make an agreement. If you won't wear a monocle, I won't wear a turtle-neck sweater." Then there'd be an exchanging of secrets on how they won the girls, and Charlie would say, "Of course, you know I'm giving more than I'm getting." A musical number would close the show.

The Mae West sketch? That was whipped up into a big thing, because part of it involved a little bit with Adam and Eve that some people thought was taking liberties with the Bible, and a few lines, which didn't sound bad in the script, but sounded dirty the way Mae read them. For instance, when Mae said, "Why don't you come up and see me some time?" Charles said,

"What for?" She said, "I'll let you play around in my wood pile." Charles said, "I'll have to have a little time to think it over." She said, "I like a man who takes his time. C'mere, big boy," or something like that. Or when Charlie asked, "Did you ever find the one man you could really love?" and she answered, "Oh, yes, lots of times." That was about all there was to it.

Afterward I went into hiding because I knew we were in trouble. People were calling the office and the agency about it. The net result was that our rating went up two points and radio censorship became a little tighter, especially on our show.

Oh, yes, they always had censors and we always used to have fun with them. For instance, if something was taken out, W. C. Fields, when he was on the show, would put in something that was worse, such as, "I stopped in for a little libation at the Pussy dePussy Café." The censor would say, "You can't say that," and Fields would answer, "What's wrong with a little kitten?" But Fields was just having his fun with him.

Fields was my favorite of all the comedians I worked with. We had great respect for each other. He sent me a fan wire after I was on the Rudy Vallee Show for about two or three weeks, complimenting me on my timing and my comedy. So when it came to Hollywood and the new show, he was one of the first people we requested.

His feud with Charlie started right on the first show: "Is that your nose, or are you eating an apple?" Then: "My little diminutive chum, I'll whittle you down to a shoe tree." The folks knew that beneath the rivalry they really liked each other, and it paid off well. I was very careful never to let Charlie win over Fields. If he had topped him all the time, it would have destroyed something there.

Fields was a good man, and we had some great comedy. He could write and he could play what you wrote for him. So when it came to a script for him, it would come twice as easily and with better jokes than if it were for some other person.

I was head writer and assemblyman all the time, although we would have one agency man there. It was very important for me to do the comedy that I liked and to see that Charlie and Mortimer kept their personalities. For instance, sometimes they'd want Mortimer to eye the girls, but he was supposed to be bashful and young; he just wouldn't do that. And then sometimes Charlie and I would have fights where Charlie would get sarcastic and insulting but he wouldn't be funny, and that had to be watched.

Yes, when writing, I had to think of Charlie as another person. We even had him there for rehearsals. Most of the guests would go along with Charlie because that was the fantasy, but there were two or three who were going to be above it, so they would look to me when Charlie was talking—and they got screwed up.

I really didn't know until it was all over how successful I was—how ministers up in Canada changed their services so there wouldn't be a time conflict with Charlie or how I was number one or two with the Boston Symphony, or how, when I had Mae West on, the girls at some Catholic school didn't listen but prayed instead, because they knew Charlie was in dangerous company.

Yes, Charlie did receive a degree, from Northwestern University: "Master of Innuendo and Snappy Comebacks; churlish in behavior, acid in conversation, wood-headed in all relations, willing to borrow any and all ideas from the person closest to him, and in all other aspects a typical product of his learning in America."

But, as I say, although I knew it was successful, I didn't know how successful until it was all over; I was always so busy writing next week's show.

"The story of mother love and sacrifice," the stuff on which dreams were made and soap was sold—this was the substance of the never-ending saga of Stella Dallas, as portrayed by Ann Elstner. She was one of the most popular and enduring of those constantly beset characters who didn't live from day to day but from crisis to crisis, and her fantasy world became a daily reality for millions of her sex.

Stella Dallas was on the air from 1937 to 1955. Following her retirement from radio, Ann Elstner Matthews opened the River's Edge Restaurant in New Jersey, which she and her husband ran until its destruction by fire.

ANN ELSTNER MATTHEWS

I was playing ten shows sometimes. I remember once I was on two different shows on the same day: I was at NBC for *Here Comes the Milkman* and then I had to dash over to CBS, getting there just in time to play my part. I was young enough then, but all those things did take their toll. Still, it was a stimulus. In one show I might be doing a commercial and in the next one I might be the star. I was very versatile, and I loved doing all sorts of different parts. I could always double in any show and did it often. If I had just a small part, since I was on the show anyway, the director felt I could handle another part, too. Later on, of course, the unions complained.

Let's see, I was in "Moonshine and Honeysuckle," a magnificent program, written by Lula Vollmer, who had written the Broadway play *Sun Up*. It was on from '30 to '33, for a half-hour on Sundays, and when daylight-savings time came, the people in the Midwest just went wild, because they couldn't get to church without missing the program; so they made the ministers change the time of their service. The thing about these episodes was that they always gave food for thought. It's too bad they don't have more shows like that today.

Later, Lula Vollmer made a three-act play of the program, which was the first time that had ever been done. We went out for two weeks in costume. In Canton, Ohio, we had ten mikes onstage because there were 5,000 people attending. They would come early with their children and bring supper with them. Then, after the show, while we were still in costume, the curtain would be raised and the audience would file onto the stage as if it were a reception. They'd be wearing tuxedos, overalls, and carrying their babies in their arms. We would stop and talk to every person. They'd say, "Oh, won't you come this Sunday for dinner? We'd just love to have you." All of them felt as though they knew us, because we had been in their homes every week on radio. It was the most wonderful feeling.

We went to visit the blind a couple of times when I was with "Moonshine." When I walked out, I said, in the voice of one character, "This is Cracker Gaddis from the mountain," and I heard the audience titter. Then I switched characters and said, "My name is Mary Jane Eliza Belle Suzanne Shoemaker Gaddis, but they call me 'Firecracker' for short. They call me that because I pop so when I get het up." The audience laughed, and I went on in that character: "I'm right purty in the moonlight; I don't show off much in the sun." Those were lines people knew and loved.

After that, I did "The March of Time," a news-type program. I remember the time I had to do Babe Didrikson and none of us knew how she sounded. At the dress rehearsal in studio 22 at CBS, a *big* studio, almost as big as the Toscanini studio at NBC, there were a lot of folding chairs. I unfolded four of them, ran and jumped over them, then rushed to the mike, breathless, to say my lines. The director said, "You've got it, Ann!" Anything for the arts!

I also was in the "Magazine of the Air." We did interviews with famous people, and one of the people we interviewed was Amelia Earhart, several months before she was lost.

Yes, I did shows that people now have never heard of and that are not listed in the radio books: "Hillbilly Heartthrob," in which I played the lead, a little mountain girl; "The Gibson Family," in which I played Mrs. Gibson; "Wilderness Road," in which I was Mrs. Weston, leading my family west; and "Renfrew of the Mounted," in which I played a lot of different roles.

Well, if we're going to talk about "Stella Dallas," I think it would be nice to tell what the announcer said every day, the lead-in: "We give you now . . . Stella Dallas . . . a continuation on the air of the true-to-life story of mother love and sacrifice, in which Stella Dallas saw her own beloved daughter Laurel marry into wealth and society and, realizing the differences in their tastes and worlds, went out of Laurel's life. These episodes in the later life of Stella Dallas are based on the famous novel of that name by Olive Higgins Prouty . . . and are written by Frank and Ann Hummert."

Twenty-five of us auditioned for the role of Stella. All we were told was that this was a mother who was not very educated and she had a daughter who was very wealthy. Actually, I didn't know how to characterize her. You see, any time I had to do a part, I went in cold. If my characterization was on the wrong track, they would tell me. Or I might say, "Will this voice do?" and they might say, "Well, we think it ought to be a little higher." So when I went in to audition, I listened to what they said about the mother and her daughter and I did the role as I thought that person was, and it just happened to come out right.

I loved Stella; I felt that she was a separate entity in my life, really. There were things I might do as Ann Elstner Matthews that I would never do as Stella. For example, I would never think of smoking as Stella, even though I did smoke, because I just think Stella wouldn't have smoked. I knew her better than anybody, better than the writers, because I lived her every day. Some of the incidents were far-fetched, but when I was on the air playing Stella, I believed everything that I said. For instance, in one segment I'm in the Sahara Desert looking for the sheik who has taken my daughter into his harem, and there's this terrific sandstorm and I'm saying over and over, "Lolly, Lolly, I must find Lolly." Well, I almost fainted, the whole thing made me so dizzy; I could actually *feel* that storm. You *had* to feel it, and you had to make yourself *believe* it, because there were lots of things that were pretty hard to believe.

I was quite good at knowing things Stella wouldn't do. One time the director got very strict and didn't want anyone to change anything. I went along with it for a while, but one day I told him, "I just can't say that. Stella wouldn't say that to Minnie Grady, her best friend. I just can't say it." He said, "You have to; we *cannot* change." Well, at the time, I had a maid who had been with me for years, and she served as a barometer. When she heard that show, she said, "Oh, Mrs. Matthews, I don't like the way they're writing the show right now. That was just terrible today. There's no sense you telling that to Minnie Grady. You know, she's your best friend." And sure enough, our rating went down a little.

"Lolly Baby?" The actress who played her was adorable, quite young, and had about three children. She came right into radio in my arms. She wasn't on the program very long, though, because she caught pneumonia and died. It was very hard for me. I never felt quite the same about the character after that; I just couldn't; this girl had been "Lolly Baby."

Stella was very unusual: She was daring, she was honest as the day is long, and she lived by the golden rule. You see, it wasn't so much that I was in the show, but the formula of mother love and the golden rule—you just couldn't beat that.

There's only one show I can remember missing in the 18 years we were on. I had a fever of 104° once and *did* do the program that time, but the other time the doctor made me stay home. However, I had the weekend to recover, and I was back at work on Monday.

I have no idea why the program went off the air. Why did NBC, ABC, all of the networks throw these things into the ash pile? We were first or second every week in the soap operas. Here were 6 million people who adored us, who would buy any kind of soap we advertised, who would believe us if we said black was white. This was really the power of radio; this was what we had built up for all those years. It was a terrible thing to just chop those programs. I suppose the owners got frightened when TV came in. But nobody needed to be afraid for "Stella Dallas." It was a wonderful part to play, and I felt that a part of me had died when we went off the air.

People say now, "What are you doing?" and I reply, "I'm busy as I can be with interviews and fan mail." Naturally I miss the program, but not so much, because I'm onstage for Stella all the time. I go into a store or some other place and I have to be introduced to people, because to them, I'm Stella. We may have gone off the air, but we haven't gone out of people's minds. I'm practically current. And that's what's important, I think, to keep current.

Two of radio's earliest enemies of evil were the Lone Ranger (1933) and the Green Hornet (1936), both of WXYZ in Detroit. As Al Hodge, former "Green Hornet" actor and "Lone Ranger" director, explains, these programs began with the most unlikely of circumstances and, as viewed by contemporary standards, the most restrictive of story lines. Despite these conditions, however, they achieved great success in radio annals, both characters representing archetypal heroes.

Mr. Hodge has been a radio, stage and television actor for more than 40 years (including a stint as TV's first interplanetary traveler, Captain Video). He now lives in New York City.

AL HODGE

I graduated from college during the depression, and the first job I got was with a stock company doing one-night stands throughout New England. It was an offshoot of the old Chautauqua Company, which would go into small towns and put up a tent. They would bring in a group, let's say four actors, for four succeeding Thursdays. The first act might be the band, consisting of four people and the magician who sawed his wife in half every night, followed by the Antarctic explorer with the penguin on each shoulder. The *pièce de résistance,* of course, would be the stock company from New York, with this terrible play written by one of the ladies in the company. And since the play had eight characters and there were only four people in the company, we'd all double up in the roles.

When this job came to its sad end, I went to Cleveland and worked as a writer in a rather interesting experimental project called "wired radio." It was actually the beginning of Muzak, where you received radio in your home either by telephone or electric-light lines. It would be like cable TV now, except that it was wired radio with a special receiver, and you paid for it just as you paid for your telephone each month.

The receiver had five channels: A (popular music), B (classical music), C (talk shows), D (news) and E (plays and drama). You could also call and have a special program made for you.

While I was in Cleveland, my boss happened to visit a friend in Detroit, who was writing a program called "The Lone Ranger." This friend persuaded him to stay on and become the head of the continuity department, and he in turn invited me to come to Detroit and join him on the writing staff. I did, and it so happened that at that time they were auditioning people for "The Green Hornet," which was simply an offshoot of "The Lone Ranger" (instead of Tonto, the faithful Indian companion, you had Kato, the faithful Japanese valet; instead of the great horse Silver, you had the Black Beauty car; and like the Lone Ranger, the Green Hornet never shot anybody), and it seemed to me that I should audition, too, even though I had gone there as a writer. And lo and behold, I became the Green Hornet!

In the beginning, I got $50 a week plus $25 for the repeat show for the West Coast. As we got a few more sponsors, the show paid a few more dollars.

Kato? He was originally played by a Japanese named Tokutaro Hayashi, who owned the Sukiyaki Restaurant in Detroit and had been doing some work for an industrial film organization. He played the part until a date, which you may remember, in December, '41, when we could no longer have a Japanese, and so, unfortunately, he lost the job. The day after Pearl Harbor, Kato became a Filipino. The part was played by one of our regular actors, who used a Filipino accent, whatever that was. I don't think they ever used the word "Filipino" in the script. We just deleted the word "Japanese" from what had originally been the phrase "faithful Japanese valet."

"The Lone Ranger?" That show began shortly after George Trendle, the owner of WXYZ, dropped his affiliation with CBS. As an independent, he decided to have programming, so he got together a stock company of actors and a studio hand and began to sell air time, becoming a big-time operation on a local basis.

Now, at this time, Fran Striker was writing "The Lone

Ranger," as well as some other programs, which were sent to a script library in Buffalo, New York. These were then advertised for sale in a trade publication, so that way, anybody who had a station and wanted a dramatic series could purchase it. Well, Trendle got "The Lone Ranger" script from the library and, of course, had to pay for it. So he said "Nuts to this" and hired Fran directly to write the show for something like $25 a script for five scripts a week. And then Fran also began writing "The Green Hornet."

I don't know how the man did it. He never wrote on foolscap or in longhand. You see, there was never enough time to transpose the script from other copy to the duplicating machine; that's how fast it had to be done. So he just put it right on the duplicator as he wrote it and then ran it off! The scripts for both shows were extremely clear. Trendle had very definite ideas about that. Any word that could be misconstrued as having another meaning was deleted. Of course, there was no violence and nobody was ever killed. We had to be very careful never to offend anybody.

Brace Beemer? No, he wasn't really that caught up with the Lone Ranger role, but he had a façade about him that was absolutely beautiful. He traveled around in this beautiful black uniform dotted with real silver studs; he had real six-shooters, and his holster had real silver bullets. Once, a *Life* photographer went to Brace's farm, where he kept three white horses, all named Silver, to do a story on him. He had taken some shots of Brace with the horses and they were walking back to the house when a rat suddenly made an exit from the barn, about 25 feet away. Without breaking stride or changing his expression, Brace pulled out his six-shooter, blew the head right off this rat, and said, "Every once in a while I get a shot at one of those SOBs." Now, you and I both know that on one of her best days Annie Oakley couldn't hit a running rat that far away. But Brace played it perfectly straight, and I had to admire the man for it.

You know that "The Lone Ranger" was actually the reason for founding the Mutual Broadcasting System? You see, the program's first sponsor was the Gordon Baking Company, which made Silvercup bread, which, with the great horse Silver, was a natural. The sponsor wanted coverage in four cities where it had bakeries—Chicago, Detroit, New York and Cincinnati—and since it wasn't a network per se, they simply leased lines from the telephone company. Now, they had to have a cue to end the program, so they decided that since it was for the mutual benefit, they would call it the Mutual Broadcasting System, and that's the way the whole thing began: WLW in Cincinnati, WLR in New York, WGN in Chicago, and WXYZ in Detroit.

Sure, sometimes you'd have a funny thing happen on a show. One of the funniest, for instance, involved John Todd, the bald, heavy Irishman in his 50's who played Tonto. We had brought a gal down who was pretty good but who had no experience at all. In her script there were directions preceding her speech that said "Fading on," which meant that she should start her speech away from the microphone and then move in toward it. But she insisted on reading the directions aloud. And in this particular spot she was playing a banker's daughter, while Todd was doubling in the role of the banker.

The script called for the banker to be shot and to be lying in the middle of the street in the western town. His daughter was supposed to approach and say, "Father, Father, are you all right?" And he was supposed to say, "Yes, I'm fine." But she insisted on reading, "Fading on. Father, Father, are you all right?" Finally the director said, "Look, just cross it off the script. It's all right, you know what to do. Cross it off."

Well, we were on the air, and even though she had crossed off the directions, they were still in her mind and she said, "Fading on," etc. That threw Todd, who then lapsed back into Tonto and said, "Uh. Me fine," and that blew our banker to smithereens!

Yes, I learned a great deal from radio. You see, I also did directing—"Challenge of the Yukon" was my first show—and eventually wound up as the director of "The Lone Ranger."

For instance, since radio acting is different from any other kind of acting, because you could express yourself only with your voice, you had to learn how to play a microphone. That meant learning how to make an entrance so that it sounded as if you were coming from a distance, plus the right amount of voice to use when you raised or lowered it, depending upon where you were in relation to the microphone, plus maintaining a balance against someone else's voice, which might be weaker or stronger than yours, and so on.

No, I don't think any of us ever really thought about the impact we were having or would have later on. We just had our own little stock company in Detroit, with the same guys playing on "The Green Hornet" who played on "The Lone Ranger" and "Challenge of the Yukon." I'm totally amazed at the number of people who listened.

Who's that little chatterbox?
The one with curly auburn locks?
Whom do you see?
It's Little Orphan Annie

So began the theme song for one of radio's earliest and most popular serials, "Little Orphan Annie." Following in her footsteps came countless other cliff-hangers, all with the same "tune in tomorrow for the next never to be concluded crisis" format. But, while such adventures may have provided hundreds of hours of thrills, chills and escapes from life for millions of children, it was not until Shirley Bell Cole (nee Shirley Bell), who portrayed Little Orphan Annie, attained adulthood that she finally escaped the demanding taskmaster that dominated her childhood—the daily radio program.

Beginning in 1926 on Chicago's WGN, Ms. Cole was that station's most frequently utilized juvenile player, appearing every week in different productions. When the station began "Little Orphan Annie," she was chosen from hundreds of aspirants for what would become one of radio's most enduring and endearing serials. Ms. Cole now lives in Glencoe, Illinois.

SHIRLEY BELL COLE

It was the winter of 1930 that the show began. I had a job when other people were out of work, including members of my family. My initial pay check was $50, and in '30, $50 was a lot of money. I remember my family helping out aunts and uncles who were having a very difficult time, and that went on for quite some time. From that initial $50, I went to $80 a week. I don't remember the next pay slot. I do know that when the union, AFRA (the American Federation of Radio Artists), came into being, we received only base pay, scale. If money had been a secondary factor, perhaps I would have said, or my parents would have said, "Shirley's the lead in this show, she's important enough, she's going to have to get above-scale salary." But I was in no position to make that demand, so I took it.

My whole life revolved around the "Orphan Annie" program. It was a grind. You went to school, you went to work, you came home, you had dinner, you did your homework, you went to sleep, you got up in the morning and so on and it was a way of life. But it was all I knew, and it was necessary that I continue. I didn't think of it in terms of something I enjoyed doing; it was work. Like somebody would go to a job, any kind of job. Like, let's say, a secretary might say, "Yech, I can't stand this, I wish I was doing something else, but I've got to do it because I want to eat." Okay?

You didn't even have time to be ill. Everything depended on your voice. You had a contract to fulfill and you couldn't call in sick. Rain or shine, come hell or high water, you were there. The nature of the business was that, man, you couldn't afford to be sick; you couldn't afford to be anything but there. So, for the most part, I worked with or without a voice, with or without a temperature. There was no question of did you want to or did you feel up to it. You signed a contract; you were there and you did it—even on holidays, such as Labor Day, Memorial Day, Decoration Day. Anything but a Saturday or Sunday, you worked, period.

When it was time to renew my option, it never occurred to me to quit. It was the other way around; you wondered if the sponsor was going to pick up the option every 13-week period, which was the way the show ran. You wanted the job, needed it, and while you knew you might someday do something else, you never thought too much about it, because all your energies were focused in one direction.

The pattern of the program was really fantasy. For example, Annie lived down on the farm with friends of Daddy Warbucks, Mr. and Mrs. Silo, and they took care of her, almost like foster parents. But every so often Daddy Warbucks would come and take Annie on a trip with him, because, after all, how many adventures can you have on a farm? You didn't have spies, or pirates, so Daddy Warbucks would take Annie on trips around the world—China, or anywhere else in the Far East, or Africa, just as in the comic strip itself, and this is how the story evolved.

To do justice to the episodes, you had to imagine yourself hiding behind a bush or in a dark alley watching the villains and heavies and then hopping into a taxicab, which just happened to be there so you could follow them. The idea of being stranded on an island, looking for food, seeing a boatload of villains landing from a pirate ship and not wanting to be discovered because they might kill you, waiting for Daddy Warbucks to come and rescue you—this kind of thing was fun.

But there were all sorts of hazards. Heavens, it was a very costly procedure when you were at the tail end of a show and you would blow a line. You felt just terrible. There was not much they could do to correct it mechanically, and you just felt as if you had cut somebody's throat. If it was bad enough, they would do the whole thing over. This is where all the physical and mental anguish would come in: that you *don't* make mistakes, that you *must* do it letter perfect each time. Let somebody else blow a line, but let it not be you.

On the live shows, if somebody dropped a script or you had the pages mixed up, you'd jump around and put your finger on the line so the person could see it and let him read from your script. But you learned. You learned how to talk over a frog in your throat, if you were lucky; you learned to turn pages quickly; you learned to go in and out of a studio quietly without rattling a doorknob. And you learned to be very sneaky—if I may use that term—because everything you could do quietly was acceptable. If you made noise, forget it.

You see, there was no margin for error. At this point in the script, your voice should sound this way, and at another point it should sound that way, and they wanted this ability to reproduce an attitude or a sound—which really made you a little robot. I always referred to myself in later years as "the good little robot." You pushed a button, I did this; you pushed another button, I did that. It wasn't like theater, where there was some spontaneity. They wanted the spontaneity, but you had to place it at a certain point in the script.

I can't remember any of the fluffed lines that were humorous as such; but, if something struck somebody as funny while you were doing something mysterious and serious, and while everybody was chuckling under their breath you were trying to hear only what you were supposed to hear, well, that was discipline.

Mrs. Silo (Henrietta Tedrow), Mr. Silo (Jerry O'Meara), Daddy Warbucks (Stanley Andrews)—these adult voices came from the theater. Andrews was replaced by another Daddy Warbucks when he went out to California and became a movie and television actor. In later years he did the part of the Old Ranger on "Death Valley Days."

After I began "Orphan Annie," a talent pool for children was begun by a woman named Mrs. Foley. She started the Jack and Jill Players. From this group came such people as Frank Adams, Jr., who did Skippy, Billy Idelson, who did Skeezix, and Irene Wicker, who, before she became the "Singing Lady," did the part of Lillums, Harold Teen's girlfriend. This goes back to 1931, the very early days of radio, when they dramatized all the cartoon features.

Later, as I became older, I was kept in the background because the sponsor didn't want me seen, since I was no longer the ten-year-old Annie. The program ran for nine and a half years, you know, and the sponsor was afraid that somebody would find out that "little" Annie was not a kid but a young woman, and that would be horrible; it would spoil the image. So what the public didn't know didn't hurt them.

The show ended in the summer of '40, and that was my first vacation in all those years, because we had been on every summer. I had met my future husband that summer, just before I went on vacation, and we became engaged to be married the following Christmas. We were led to believe that the option would be picked up and the show would begin again in September. Well, apparently there was some hanky-panky going on because the sponsor decided to pick up another program instead, "Captain Midnight." I was working on that program, too. Once I became 18, they could not legally keep me on an exclusive basis for "Orphan Annie," so I proceeded to get the part of the ingenue in "Captain Midnight."

When we came back, they were already auditioning people for "Captain Midnight." The reason they did that I'll never know, because it misled everyone in the cast. We found out—later, of course—that they had no intention of using us, which I thought was a very underhanded thing to do. The whole thing was sickening. They could have said, "Look, this is it, we decided to quit, fine. We can't use you on "Captain Midnight," so we're going to bring in another character. Sorry, but we want another voice." But they were devious about the whole thing.

So the boom really fell. It was a great shock to me. What was I going to do? I still had a need to work. But, unfortunately, to most local producers of soap operas and other programs, I was Orphan Annie. I hadn't looked ahead and said to myself, "Someday this program is going to be off. You want to continue working in radio, so you'd better learn to do some other things." And while I did get some work, there was much I didn't get, because I continued to sound like Orphan Annie—not in the tenor of my voice, but in my attitude. I'd pick up a script and automatically respond in a certain way, because this was all I had done. So I didn't have too much of a career beyond the "Orphan Annie," "Captain Midnight" and a few miscellaneous parts.

I guess I kind of pooh-poohed it all for many years, because I think I was dissatisfied with having missed experiences in terms of growing up. Only in these past few years have I looked back and tried to be more realistic about it. Certainly it had to have given me satisfaction; otherwise, I wouldn't have stayed nine and a half years in such a demanding business.

Wave the flag for Hudson High, boys,
Show them how we stand!
Ever shall our team be champion,
Known throughout the land!

Jack Armstrong—the six-million-dollar bionic boy scout of keen intelligence, courageous spirit and indomitable will, who was just the kid next door. Or so every young radio listener fantasized.

For James Ameche, though, portraying Jack Armstrong meant not archetypes and adventures, but physical stamina and professional dedication. Ameche originated the role in 1933 and continued in it until 1936. He then went on to a variety of other radio leads. Mr. Ameche now lives in Tucson, Arizona, where he makes radio commercials.

JAMES AMECHE

The very beginnings of my radio career actually go back to my high school days, when I tried out for debating, oratory and school plays. My first run-in with radio was in Kenosha, Wisconsin, about '31. There were four of us: Ed Roberts, who later became the spokesman for Oscar Mayer, Walt Hardy, who became a successful documentary-film producer in Hollywood, Irving Wallace, who, of course, became a famous writer, and me. Our idols were the Marx Brothers, so we wrote a half-hour show we called "The Four Sparks Brothers." The local radio station allowed us to do this program on Saturday mornings—without pay, of course.

In the early summer of '33, there was a call that went out from Chicago. They were auditioning youngsters for the role of Jack Armstrong, selecting from all the high schools in the Midwest. They must have auditioned 600 or 700 kids, and I was lucky enough to get the part.

I hated our director for maybe six years of my life. He was

the toughest man, the most exacting taskmaster I have ever worked for in my life. He would put you over a line five, ten, a hundred times till he broke you down into a quivering mass of jelly. And he did this with everybody on the show. He had a vocabulary that would have done justice to the best in the navy. He'd hurl stopwatches, or whatever else he had, at your head. He was a wild man. His thing was, when you opened your mouth, he'd say, "I don't believe you, make me believe you." And after a while, you weren't going to open your mouth unless you were sure this man would believe what you were going to say.

"Jack Armstrong" started out six times a week across the board. And that was all I did at that time, because it tied up the whole day. The first year I did the show, I received the grand sum, for maybe 60 hours of work a week, of $59.50, though ultimately I got up to fairly good money.

We started off with CBS. At that time there were only 88-92 stations, and General Mills, which was the sponsor, wanted an additional 27 markets. So we had to make acetates, or ETs (electrical transcriptions); they were the big 17-inch discs that played at 33 rpm's. So three weeks before we did the live show, we used to record up at World Broadcasting in this immense room with a steel roof on the top floor of the Chicago *Daily News* Building. During the summer, with the hot sun beating on the roof, it'd get up to 115° there, and, of course, air conditioning hadn't been invented yet. We'd start at nine o'clock in the morning, and for a 15-minute show we'd work till noon, sometimes till 1:00. That's how long the director took with every one of the shows.

Now, the ETs had to be as perfect as you could make them, and many times you would hit what we called "jonahs," where you'd stumble or make mistakes, or the sound-effects men would make a mistake, and you'd cut and start all over again. I remember, one Monday session we worked till about 12:30 and didn't get it, so we came back Tuesday morning and started in again. We still didn't get it for three and a half hours. Finally, by what was maybe the 20th take, we got right up to the closing announcement. We had done it! Now, in that session we had a delightful stock actor named Henry Sachs, and he was standing with his back to one of the tubs of water we used for sound effects in those days. He was watching the announcer read the closing commercial when suddenly he moved one foot back, hit the edge of the tub, lost his balance, and fell in, with this huge splash and a loud yell of "Wow!" At that point, our hearts just dropped: We had to start all over again.

So those were the mornings. In the afternoons we'd get about 45 minutes or an hour for lunch and then start right back with that day's live show for the network, working steadily from about 1:15 to 6:15. By the time the end of the day rolled around, we were exhausted.

As far as mistakes on the live broadcast went, you just picked up, went on and got a little hell from the director after the show. I remember one incident, though, with Babe Ruth, that was really something.

It was in the fall of '33 that General Mills signed Babe to do a commercial on behalf of Wheaties. He was then the idol of the world; that was the year he pointed to the stands and hit a home run against the Cubs in the World Series. Anyway, the director said, "Now Mr. Ruth, would you mind running through the commercial so that I can get timing on it?" Well, Babe ran through it, and when he got to the phrase that went, "So, boys and girls, don't forget to ask your mother to buy Wheaties so she can make these cookies," pronouncing it "kookies," with an *oo* sound, the director pushed the talk-back button and said, "Mr. Ruth, excuse me for a moment, but that word is 'cookies.'" Babe says, "You don't have to tell me what cookies are; I grew up on them." Fine. A few minutes before airtime, the director says, "Mr. Ruth, may we go through it again for timing, please?" So Babe proceeds to read the commercial, and again he says, "So, boys and girls, don't forget to ask your mother to buy Wheaties so she can make these kookies for you." And again the director patiently pushes the talk-back and says, "Now, Mr. Ruth, please, we're just about ready to go on the air. Don't forget that word is 'cookies,' not '*kookies*.'" And Babe says, "You don't have to tell me; they're my favorite food."

We're on the air, and Babe gets to the phrase and says, "So boys and girls, don't forget to ask your mother to buy Wheaties so she can make these kookies." Well, he stops, takes maybe a three count and says, "I'm a son of a bitch if I didn't say 'kookies' again!" Now, this was in '33, when if you even *thought* 'hell" or "damn," you would be exiled to Siberia! The amazing thing was, though, that General Mills didn't call the Chicago office from Minneapolis, nor did the New York office call, and as the weeks went by, there was not one letter or phone call that came in. It was as if Babe Ruth could never say a thing like that. It was fantastic!

You must remember that radio was in its infancy. There was no such thing as having sound effects on records, because no such animal existed then. Every sound effect that was done was done live. And over at WBBM, which was the CBS outlet in Chicago, we had two sound-effects men who were geniuses of their time. They had a vast basement storeroom, which covered about an acre of ground, and in it were thousands of things they created out of their own imagination to duplicate sound effects. Every day they went down there to bring up whatever they needed. On the "Jack Armstrong" show, because there were so many sound effects, I don't think we ever used less than two sound-effects men, and in some sequences we had as many as four.

The program was immensely popular right from the start. It became the number-one daytime show and remained that way for years and years. I'll relate a story that shows how popular it was. The first time we ran a promotion was in the late fall of '33, after we'd been on only for a few months. It was going to be a three-week promotion, and we used to give away code rings and different prizes. Well, before the first week was out, every grocery store in the nation was sold out of Wheaties, so they had to stop the promotion, since there was no way they could supply the stores in such a short time. So the next time they ran the promotion, they had to station freight cars, filled with millions of Wheaties boxes, around the country to keep the stores supplied. And that was during the depression, and those prizes cost money: You had to send in a dime with three box tops in order to get the gift.

No, it was no big thing to me to be Jack Armstrong. I was so immersed in my work, I couldn't have cared less. I was just interested in getting through each day and doing whatever I had to do without taking too much of a beating from the director. See, back in those days, they didn't allow any publicity to be released on any of us, so nobody knew who Jack Armstrong or Billy and Betty Fairfield or Uncle Jim were. When they'd put a picture of Jack Armstrong on one of the Wheaties boxes, it was a composite of many, many faces, so he was actually faceless and therefore totally extraneous to me as a person.

Obviously I enjoyed doing what I did, or I wouldn't have tolerated the pressures so long. About '36, I started branching out and doing other things. By that time we had gotten to the point where the networks didn't have the morning sessions, so I got into soap operas and other programs and began playing leading-man roles. Then, in '38, I left the show and moved out to Hollywood, because I decided that leading-man roles were now my forte.

Why Hollywood? Well, you see, Chicago was the original hub of radio in the late '20s, early '30s. The reason was that the networks were divided into two legs: the eastern leg, which fed the eastern half of the country, and the western leg, which fed the western half. And because programs had to be sent over telephone lines in those days, it was much cheaper, in terms of line charges, to originate a show in Chicago than on the East or West Coast. Now, in '36, the coaxial cable came into being, so, gradually, you could originate a show anywhere in the nation and it didn't cost any more or less. And that was when Chicago's power began to dissipate and the shows started moving to New York and to the West Coast.

The value of radio? Well, radio was theater, but it was more than theater; it was theater of the mind. It opened vistas to people. They instantly produced their own sets, created their own characters. If there were 20 million people listening to a show, there were possibly 20 million sets and 20 million different characters. Each person, in his mind's eye, saw what he wanted with the voices and the sound effects and the music creating the illusion. This is why it was such a formidable era of entertainment for people. In the old days, the sets the human mind created were far greater than anything Hollywood or television could create.

Next to talk-show hosts, television's newsmen and program announcers are the media's rising stars. Indeed, in many cases, the news anchorperson is already the risen star. But it wasn't always so, for nearly half a century ago, when the news broadcasting business was beginning as a serious medium, there were no such things as anchormen, news commentators or in-depth reporters. Rather, there was one person who did it all.

As an announcer for rural radio stations, Herbert Morrison did do it all—reporting, newswriting, newsreading, even advertising copywriting. And because of his coverage of the Hindenburg disaster in 1937 at Lakehurst, New Jersey, a whole new aspect of on-the-air news reporting and broadcasting was born, one that, in Morrison's words, "opened up the gates for newsmen."

Today Mr. Morrison lives in Morgantown, West Virginia, where he works as a media consultant and teacher. In addition to his on-the-air activities, he has been president of the American Federation of Television and Radio Artists (AFTRA) and has run for Congress on the Republican ticket three times.

HERBERT MORRISON

My career started on Friday, June 13, 1930, which was the only Friday the 13th of that year. I had gone to Fairmount, West Virginia, to apply for a job as an announcer on WMMN. The call letters stood for Matthew M. Neely, who was then senator from that state.

Back in those days, they didn't give you a fancy written audition; they just gave you a program to announce, and the station owner would call up a lot of his friends and say, "How do you like this fellow? Does his voice sound all right?" If they said yes, he'd hire you. It was only logical. After all, if it sounded good enough on the air to the people who were listening, then that was good enough for the station owner and manager. So you were hired on the spot, and that's the way I got my start.

I was supposed to get $100 a month, but part of that had to be in merchandise from advertisers who couldn't afford to pay the station in cash. Remember, this was the depression and the advertisers were fighting for survival. So I got clothing from a store and meals from a restaurant. It was like the old days: You took things by the barter deal. I don't know how many stations did that, but I think a lot of them did. Things were pretty rough.

As an announcer, you did just about everything: You played records, you wrote your own copy (even your own commercial copy), and if you had entertaining ability, as I did—I played the guitar and banjo—you might also incorporate that into your shows. You had no set hours, no regular slot for your newscast. The station usually had two or three announcers, and the time would be evenly divided up among them.

As far as the government was concerned, the technical jargon was more of a concern to it than the copy you put on the air. The station had to obey the FCC rules on how much power it had, what its frequency was, if it stayed in its frequency, whether it overmodulated, things like that. The announcers just had to use common sense. You *never* swore on the air, never said anything obscene. Those were the general rules.

As far as news sources go, radio people were at a disadvantage then because they had no other source of news than newspapers, and the newspaper people objected to your reading their paper on the air. So whenever you used a news story, you had to rewrite it to make sure there wouldn't be anything earmarked as the newspaper article. Or you had to call around at the police station, the fire station and gather what you could.

We established good relations with the state, local and county police, the sheriff, the fire captains in the various communities, the political and labor leaders in the area and, of course, the nurses in the local hospitals. And, of course, the schools would tell us when they were closed, due to bad weather, and the mines and mills would tell us whether they were operating. So we became a source of information. Still, it was rough: Your sources of news were limited, your personnel was limited, you couldn't send a man out to cover a story and you couldn't spend a whole lot of time yourself digging up one.

When you were working as a joint announcer and program man, you didn't have time to do any in-depth reporting. In fact, there was very little in-depth reporting at all, because there just wasn't the time to include a long, involved, investigative story. That's the reason newspapers finally didn't object, because you whetted the listeners' appetite with maybe just a headline or a couple of minutes on a story.

A newscaster in those days had no particular status; he wasn't any bigshot or anything. You were looked upon as a broadcaster and that's what you were, because stations couldn't afford to have a man exclusively for news.

The Hindenburg disaster? That happened in '37, when I was an announcer at WLS in Chicago and was assigned to cover special events. In 1936 we had covered the flood in the Mississippi Valley, down around Memphis. American Airlines had flown a group of us newsmen in to report on the flood damage, both for public relations and public service. We came back with a story for the Red Cross appeal, and since the airline was cooperating, well, naturally that kind of publicity never hurt anybody.

Then, when that was over, American told me about the Hindenburg's first anniversary flight on May 6 and asked if I'd go down as their guest and watch it come in. You see, when the Hindenburg landed at Lakehurst, American would be the connecting service that flew people to New York or other parts of the United States, and they wanted to advertise this service.

I said yes because I wanted to prove to the station that you could cover an event by electrical transcription—in other words, that you could make a record and fly it back. That had been a dream of mine for seven years. So when the station decided to send a man down there, Charles Nehlson, one of the finest engineers a man could want, and I took the recording equipment to Lakehurst. Well, I had been talking for about eight minutes, telling how the ship's motors were just holding it for the men on the ground to grab hold of the ropes that had dropped out of the nose. I was describing how beautiful it was, when suddenly the explosion occurred. I knew then that tragedy had struck and that it was my place to continue talking and describing the crash. Racing through the back of my mind was the thought that this wasn't happening. But I knew it was, and I also knew I just had to continue on and make sure that we got an accurate report of what happened. Then I ran down and helped with the rescue work for a few minutes and got hold of some of the people who were burned and interviewed them. Later we also interviewed people who had jumped. We were kept real busy for a total of roughly 40 minutes.

We used a Presto recorder. The transcription was made on a 15-inch disc with 15 minutes on each side. The recording head was on a gear arrangement, and as it recorded, the head moved from the center of this gear to the outer edge of the record. If you stopped the motor, the needle just stayed right on the record, so you didn't have to reset it.

When we had accomplished everything we could, American flew us to Chicago. We arrived at dawn and, of course, immediately went to the studio. We didn't know if we had anything for sure, because the explosion had been so tremendous that the needle had jumped from the recording head and back down into the acetate record. So it wasn't until 7:00 A.M. that we found we still had good recording quality.

The program manager was against the station's putting it on the air; they had never used records on NBC. But Lenox Lohr, the president of NBC, said, "We'll waive that rule and put it on," and that was the first recorded voice on the network.

It began a new type of newscasting, because it opened the door for recorded broadcasts. Before, they had to have everything live—live music, live voices. If you wanted the president, you'd have to go to all the lengths of putting in telephone lines and broadcasting direct from the White House. After the Hindenburg broadcast, the first voice on the network was mine. The second voice was Neville Chamberlain's, with his famous Munich speech. It was put on in London around the middle of the day (early in the morning here). The third voice was President Roosevelt's. So the three of us broke the ice and made it possible to have interviews with so many more people and a greater variety of sources. The networks didn't have to get it live. They could call up the president on the telephone or send a microphone down there and play the recording on the evening news.

It had been proven that you could go out with disc-recording equipment, get a story and get it back to the station without any complicated installation of wire services several weeks in advance. This led to the development of better transcribing equipment and eventually brought tape recorders into faster production.

That '37 broadcast really opened up the gates for newsmen.

It was in the thirties that the power of radio as a means of communication was realized—and at no time more so than on that memorable night in 1938, when Orson Welles's broadcast of a "Martian invasion" resulted in a full-fledged national panic. This incident and others that illustrate the growing influence of radio are recalled by former announcer Dan Seymour.

Following his career in broadcasting, Mr. Seymour went into advertising, where, prior to his retirement, he was president of the J. Walter Thompson Agency. Mr. Seymour lives in New York.

DAN SEYMOUR

In '35, the year I graduated from Amherst, I needed a job badly, not only because I had worked my way through school, but also because I had, quite fortunately, acquired a wife, who's still with me 40-odd years later. I wanted to go into the theater, because I had been a drama major, but theater jobs were few and far between, and when someone suggested that radio might be a course that would eventually lead to the theater, I pursued that.

I was recommended to a gentleman in New York named Esty, who was the head of the William Esty Agency, and he in turn sent me up to WNAC in Boston. I had applied for any kind of job, and John Shepard, the owner of the station and the Yankee network, said that the only job open was for an announcer. I really didn't know what an announcer did, and he, in his rather gentle New England manner, said, "Damn it, an announcer reads," and surely I must have learned how to read up there at Amherst. So I read for him and was hired on two weeks' notice. I stayed there for a little over a year.

During that time I had a good education, not only in all the phases of operation of a radio station, but also in all phases of production, as well as announcing and acting. The station functioned as a very small business run by a group of people interested in this new-fangled thing called radio that was beginning to take a very real form. In fact, it had already gone through its infancy and was about to burgeon into the very glamorous life it had in the '30s, '40s and early '50s, when television began to replace it. These people at the station were primarily engineers, the ones who had conceived this means of communication. They were entrepreneurs in the sense that they were trying to find ways to subsidize the communication. That, in turn, led to entrepreneurial salesmen who tried to entice people to use radio, instead of newspapers, for advertising. And you had a group of mostly young people who were interested in the acting and emoting part of radio, and along with them, a smattering of very good ex-vaudevillians. They were the salt and pepper in the mix. Then there were the very talented musicians who early on found that radio was a wonderful means of communicating in their art form. In Boston, for example, we had not only Koussevitzky and the Boston Symphony, but also the Boston Pops, with its great leader, Arthur Fiedler.

And out of all this were developing a lot of new techniques for coverage of events. It was a period when the networks were beginning to cover the fights in a new and interesting way, and when you had in-depth communication on all sorts of public events. Admiral Byrd was at the South Pole and he would broadcast back to the United States once a week or every other week.

You began to realize the political power of the medium. For example, when I was in Boston, James Michael Curley, one of the most gifted orators of all time, was running for governor. He and John Shepard had been very close friends for years, and John made room for him almost any time Curley wanted to be on the network. I'll tell you an anecdote about that. At that time we didn't have control rooms; there was just a little red light that said, *On the air* or *Off the air*. Curley had always been notorious for the fact that he never kept any kind of time, probably with more justification than anyone I know, because he adlibbed everything. He never had a note in front of him. He would get started and then would talk and talk and talk. I was assigned to be the announcer as well as the production man in charge of all the Curley broadcasts out of our studio. We arranged a signal between us, with my fingers going up at five minutes, then four, down to half a minute. It worked fairly well until one night, just about two nights before the election, when he was going great guns and I got to five minutes. He shook his head, and when I got to four minutes, he shook it again. Then he reached into his pocket and brought out a wad of $100 bills because he was trying to buy more time. He kept talking, but in the meantime the red light had gone off and we were off the air. When he finished, there must have been $1,500 on the floor that he had thrown there.

No, there weren't that many restrictions in broadcasting, although there were restrictions that were growing by actual usage. You didn't create laws, you created patterns, especially in relation to the networks. For instance, John Shepard had two stations: WAAB, a local station, and WNAC, his main station for the Yankee network and the main Columbia Broadcasting System outlet in New England. Now, John was an arbitrary fellow. When Curley wanted to get on the air, John made it possible for him, even if it meant pre-empting a program. Well, the network was in an awkward position for many years and, because of the strength of the station, couldn't do much about the situation. But years later, in great secrecy, they were able to make another affiliation, this one with WEEI in Boston, also a very large station. They had a long debate up at Columbia as to how they would notify John. It was decided that John Carroll, in charge of station relations, would send Shepard a telegram reading, "The Lord is *our* shepherd, we shall not want." Well, that was the end of the affiliation with John Shepard and the Yankee network.

During the year I was there, I had an opportunity to do most everything that was involved in being on the air, including the timing and editing of a program, be it a dramatic show or a newscast. Covering events and reporting on them was another major facet of what we were doing. We were reporters and we would have to be jacks of all trades in a local operation, going out to cover a parade, a special event, a personality.

By the middle '30s most of the large radio stations had some off-the-air newsmen who covered events to be broadcast later, not in a live fashion as today, where you have a roving microphone. We didn't have the ability to tape at that time; all we had were some very bad acetate records and remote pickups for special events.

The thirst for news was beginning to be felt at that time. Maybe that isn't quite an accurate statement, because I never knew whether the thirst was there to begin with or whether the station stimulated it. For example, back in the fall of '35 we had a 15-minute show every night after the eleven o'clock news, the big news, and on that program we gave a report called "War Drums over Ethiopia," in which we detailed the events of that war. So radio stations performed a great service for their cities and developed into probably the most powerful communication arm in the community.

The networks were also becoming very sophisticated in the middle '30s. I'm talking now about the network news department, the news being fed out of New York. It was something we all did. When I came down to New York in June, '36, I had a news show every morning on WABC, which is CBS today. It was an early-morning newscast. I'll always remember the sponsor—Balm Ben-Gay, the rub. I was hired by the agency to do the commercial as well as the news, something we all did at that time but that subsequently stopped, except for rare cases.

It was different than in Boston, where you were very close to what was going on. Here there were many good professional news editors and you worked with them, doing far less in the role of news editor.

I don't want you to get the impression that I was a newsman, because I wasn't. Broadcasting news was just part of my work as an announcer on CBS. The news I did had to do with this particular program, as well as with early-morning programs, because when you opened the station, giving the news was usually your first assignment.

I don't know that my style was developed except by usage. It depended on the assignment. When I came to New York as a staff announcer, we were involved in almost every kind of programming. You went from the light to the dramatic to the very serious documentary to the very gay remotes at night, and I always felt that each one called for a different kind of attitude and feeling about your work. Maybe they were just nuances, but I felt you should sound a little different when you were picking up Guy Lombardo and his Orchestra than when you were covering a dramatic event. So one of the things I felt I had was a versatility in being able to become a part of the program I was involved in.

I was very fortunate when I first came to New York. At that time the most popular show on the air was "Major Bowes and His Original Amateur Hour," and Graham McNamee, the dean of all the announcers at NBC, had done it for many years. Then the show was transferred to CBS and every announcer in town auditioned for it, and I was very fortunate to win the audition.

Yes, I was purely an announcer. I introduced the show, and the major did the commercials. I think the show's appeal was one that's always been there—that of people getting up and performing and the audience either deriding them because they're bad or vicariously enjoying them because they're good, every once in a while knowing that they've seen a star in the making.

I never felt the major was the great showman everybody thought he was. I thought that he was a moderately good judge of talent, he had a very capable staff, and he had a very good commercial idea, which he took great advantage of.

A few years later I was sent to California by CBS with a program I had started in Boston for the Gillette Company, called "Community Sing," and it grew like Topsy. It went from a community sing to a point where there was hardly time for anybody to breathe in that half-hour. They added Milton Berle (it was his first network program) and he, in turn, added Jolly Gillette, the sponsor's daughter. We had Billy Jones and Ernie Hare, "The Happiness Boys," the "Mad Russian" and Tommy Cecil Mack, one of the great vaudeville performers. His act was built around the fact that he lisped; he would get terribly excited, throw up his hands in horror and scream, "Who'th ecthited? Who'th ecthited?"

Then I came back to New York and did a whole series of programs. As staff announcer, I was assigned to "The Mercury Theater" and was associated with Orson Welles for "War of the Worlds." He is one of the most gifted men I've ever known. He had started the "Mercury Theater on the Air" for CBS as a program from 8:00 to 9:00 on Sunday nights, which at the time CBS couldn't sell, because it was opposite "The Edgar Bergen and Charlie McCarthy Show."

The night of the dress rehearsal for "War of the Worlds" we had an announcer saying, "Flash! We interrupt this program to give you the following bulletin: The Martians have landed," or "People have landed in New Jersey." Afterward, Orson came to me and said, "That fellow doesn't sound right; you do it," which he had apparently planned all along. He knew exactly what he was doing; after all, my voice *was* that of an announcer. As a direct result of that broadcast, the networks had to comply with several federal regulations, among them one that an announcer could no longer say "Flash" or "Bulletin" on the air.

It's hard to describe the impact of that broadcast unless you were part of it. I spent all night answering telephones; we all did. People were completely certain that these things were happening. We tried to assure them that they weren't and they'd say "Don't tell me." The funniest thing that happened to me was that at 3:30 in the morning I answered one call from the mayor of Plainfield, New Jersey. He said, "Are you the jokers who put that Martian thing on the air tonight?" I said, "No, we're not jokers. However, we did put on the Martian program, but it was a dramatic program." He said, "I don't care what it was. I have two radio cars and they went up in the Watchung Mountains at 9:30 and I haven't heard from them since. Now, you get the hell back on the air and get them back for me!"

I knew we were having a problem about 20 minutes after we were on the air. You see, this particular break in the program took place at a very awkward time for people who were listening. I told you that Edgar Bergen and Charlie McCarthy were on opposite us. Their show would open with a comedy routine with W. C. Fields and Edgar Bergen. Then they'd break for a commercial, and listeners would turn the dial to hear what was going on on the other stations. Well, it was at that particular moment that they heard, "Bulletin! This is happening in New Jersey; these strange people have landed. Stay tuned and we will keep you informed." They heard that message divorced from the introduction to the program that said, "This is a dramatization tonight." It started to create a tremendous concern in the state of New Jersey and mounted and mounted, and soon Davidson Taylor, then the night production manager, appeared at our little "Studio One" porthole. Davidson was a tall, lanky fellow, rather cadaverous-looking to begin with, and now he looked more ashen than usual. He motioned to me and I sneaked out and he said, "We've got a problem: the phones. The switchboards are just jammed. People think it's real. What'll we do?" Well, Orson wasn't about to do anything. He was too great a showman. He sensed what was happening and reveled in it.

The next morning, there was a press conference called for about ten o'clock. We were all there, many of us having been up most of the night on the telephones. I was more concerned than the rest of the cast, because I was the only employee of CBS, along with the production man. Orson didn't show until about 11:20, and when he walked in, a red-lined black cape slung over his shoulder, like a toreador, you knew you were seeing the birth of a brand-new personality. Orson was a great showman and took complete advantage of it.

I think CBS's reaction at first was sheer disbelief, then consternation and, finally, jubilation, because of the great spotlight that was on us. Here we were, opposite the number-one show on the air, and we got the coverage we did. Certainly, as far as the cast was concerned, we were all behind Orson and were delighted. The program went from practically no rating to at least a respectable one.

My association with the "Aunt Jenny" program came about in '38 through an audition. I had worked for the sponsor, Lever Brothers, in Boston and had helped introduce the product that sponsored "Aunt Jenny": Spry. As a matter of fact, when we went on the air with the very first announcement for Spry, it caused a lot of consternation in Boston and we got a lot of very humorous calls. That announcement was, "Don't cry, little bride, don't cry, try Spry," and nobody knew what Spry was. You can imagine the nature of the calls we got. Finally, after two or three weeks of a teaser campaign of that nature, we introduced the product as an all-vegetable shortening; but, in the meantime, we were the talk of Boston. At any rate, I won the audition and then helped to pick an Aunt Jenny so we could go on the air. I was given a 13-week contract that, as I recall, lasted about 14 or 15 years. We were on every day from 11:45 to 12:00, with a repeat for the West Coast from 2:15 to 2:30.

The difference between "Aunt Jenny" and the other serials was that we told stories that would last, oh, anywhere from three to maybe seven episodes. One of the reasons we were a very successful daytime serial was that we broke the mold. You didn't have to listen every day, as you did with all the others. You could come in one week, be gone, then pick up a new story. The other reason for our success was that there was a great camaraderie between Aunt Jenny and me.

We had an imaginary set, Aunt Jenny's kitchen, that I would visit. Aunt Jenny would tell me a story; then we would talk about Spry and its uses. She would force her cookies or cakes on me with very little resistance on my part, and I would ask her, "How did you make it?" or "What was your recipe?" We gave recipes very successfully and even had *Aunt Jenny's Cookbook*. We had giveaways on the air that broke all records. Hundreds of thousands of people would write in for flower seeds or stamps. So it was a very successful program for many years. It had an enormous rating. We were always one of the top two or three daytime programs.

The original Aunt Jenny was a wonderful old lady named Edith Spencer, who had been a vaudevillian, and when she became Aunt Jenny, she was able to put away a little bit of money for the first time in her life. She didn't make a lot, but what she made was steady and more than she had ever had in her lifetime. Unfortunately, she died of cancer. The second Aunt Jenny was Agnes Young, who was one of the regular commercial characters on the program.

Some of our sound-effects men were great artists. They gave life to these shows in an extraordinarily inventive way. That was part of the whole period of radio I'm talking about. Everybody was as inventive as he could be, just the way Orson was when he changed the cast that night and told me to do the news flash. Or when we did *Les Miserables* on "The Mercury Theater" and got to the sewers of Paris. The sound man got together with Orson and they decided it was simple: Orson just told everybody, "We're going to put a microphone in the men's room and put on all the toilets." And those were the sewers of Paris in the background. It's that kind of inventive mind that pervaded the medium at that time.

During the depression, radio served a valuable function as a form of free entertainment people could enjoy in their own homes for the first time.

In the early days of radio, it was soon discovered that (a), people listened to certain shows more than to others and (b), they liked certain elements of those shows more than they did others. As a result of those findings, one of the most powerful aspects of the modern media scene emerged: the ratings system.

Archibald Crossley, principal architect of media measurement, recalls how that system began, starting with an advertisement-monitoring service and growing into a multi-million-dollar industry.

Mr. Crossley is now retired and lives in Princeton, New Jersey.

ARCHIBALD CROSSLEY

I started my own market-research organization in 1926, and we were primarily interested in studying the markets for goods and services. That was the new profession, of course. Radio was just a part of the situation in an effort to find out what advertisers were getting. There was no way of knowing how many people they were reaching, or who they were reaching, or when, or through what station. That was the communications side of marketing research. We were also interested in the kinds of products that should be manufactured, so we did a lot of product testing.

Then, in '27, an advertising agency asked us if we would use our field staff to monitor reception of a radio program of one of its clients. They wanted to know whether or not the program came through in each area, and, if so, how satisfactorily. We found a very curious situation. The networks were sending out programs at the same time local stores were putting on radio programs. This gave the local station the opportunity of either paying the network part of the money from local advertising or just accepting the money for national advertising. But what they did was to accept money from both the national and the local advertisers, thus putting on the local advertiser and robbing the network. And that was done in enough places so that the agency and the network got together and produced rebates for, the advertiser, since their advertising was not getting through at all.

Two years later, in '29, they asked me to do the same thing again. I said, "I think we probably accomplished something then, but I also think it's been reported enough, so there isn't much sense to repeating it. But how would you like to measure the number of people who are listening to the program?" And they said, "By God, can you do that?" I said, "Yes, I think so. If you'll give me a couple of days, I'll tell you." So I made some telephone calls and discovered that it was fairly easy to do. You just asked people if they had a radio set and what programs they heard, and you had the answers. The telephone was the best method, because we found that only a very small percentage of non-telephone homes had radio sets. This meant not only less cost but also that we could cover a wide area at one time without sending people around to homes.

Then, as a result of some work we did for Eastman Kodak, we got quite a lot of orders doing the same or similar studies. Sometimes we would concentrate on stations rather than programs, or on individual talents, and soon the agent who had asked me to do the original study, and then asked me to do it again two years later, suggested that I set up a standard subscription service, a regular monthly survey of what people were listening to. I went to the research committee of the Association of National Advertisers and tried to sell it to them, but they wouldn't buy it. So I advertised this survey on a subscription basis myself. As I remember, it was amazingly cheap, around $60 or $70 a month. It made history as the origin of ratings, a word we invented. We carried it ourselves for four years, and then a committee of advertisers, agencies and broadcasters got together. We agreed to work on a contract basis with them, which we did until '46.

We were chiefly interested at the start in what determined the size of a particular program's audience. One of our discoveries was the fact that the very popular programs, like "Amos 'n' Andy," would have "spill-over" to the next program on the same network and "spill-back" to the program immediately before, because people would turn on their sets about 10 minutes before "Amos 'n' Andy" came on and would listen to the end of that program. In addition, we found that if you were putting on a program at a certain time, that time might be very much better than another time.

Then we asked who in the family was listening and discovered differences among men, women and young people. Thus, if the desire was to reach young people, we would say that this kind of program would reach them better than another or this time would be a better time, and so on.

They came to be known as the Crossley Ratings, and in my opinion they came to be bought and sold on a basis of the points, as we called them, in the rating. The percentage points meant the percentage of people in the sample. We shied away from any projections into overall figures and usually let the agencies do their own work on that. Basically, a typical evening program should have had a rating of over ten points, with anything under that getting low. Sixteen percent was fairly good. If that rode up to 17 percent the next month, there would be a yell for joy from the advertising agency and a demand for more money by the talent. On the other hand, if the rating went down to 15 percent the talent might get fired. I had the experience of having various well-known talent call me up and say, "I've just been fired; what can you do for me?"

I can only say that it was unfortunate and unfair to use the sampling system rigidly in that way. There could easily be a variation of a point or two in a given month, more if there was a program that was simply getting very popular. I made speeches against this system and tried to bring it down, but I don't know if I had any luck in doing that.

The audio side of the programs made a great deal of difference, particularly with the announcer on the commercial. They were operated very differently from the way commercials are now operated on television. Then you had one company advertising through one program, so that we would make an analysis by sponsor and try to find out what people knew about that sponsor. It varied a great deal with the number of mentions of the sponsor on the air, the advertising of the sponsor in newspapers, etc. The number of times a commercial was aired was studied at great length. It was considered unwise to have too many mentions, with interruptions all the time. And you had a certain affinity to the sponsor. Smart advertisers were certain to have a tie-in with the program, like "The Palmolive Beauty Box Theater," so that the name was pounded home.

During these years the actual operations of our interviewing system expanded in many ways. First of all, we wanted to make a point of distinction between urban and rural areas. Another expansion was in the use of individual stations. We also did lots of special jobs, some on talent, some on testing of individual frequencies. At one point, instead of using the telephone, we used a mechanical device attached to a radio set to ask people what they were listening to. This little box had a tape with six or seven styluses on it, which would be kept rolling for a month. As the set was tuned to, say, WEAF at 6:14 P.M., the WEAF stylus would come down and make a mark on the tape. Then, if the station was changed to WJZ, the WEAF stylus would come up and the WJZ stylus would go down. So there would be all these tapes on a family's radio set, showing variations day by day, hour by hour, minute by minute, for a month. Of course, those tapes showed only that the set was used; it didn't show whether anybody was listening. So we made extensive studies comparing different sampling methods and changed our interviewing frequency to two-hour periods, eventually asking people what they were listening to at the moment.

Our mechanical recorder was operated about the same time Arthur Nielsen invented his. Nielsen's and several other recorders operated differently from ours.

Yes, I think I've been helpful along certain lines. I suppose the products I invented and developed would be considered a contribution, as well as my constant efforts at expanding marketing research, of which there was very little in 1918, when I started.

7
THAT WAS ENTERTAINMENT, TOO..

With the advent of talking pictures, one element of the live theater was clearly dying: vaudeville. As Joe Smith, one-half of the 73-year team of Smith and Dale (on whom Neil Simon's *The Sunshine Boys* is based), relates, the demise of vaudeville was as much a matter of technology as it was of finance. Some of the performers went on to radio, while others, like Smith and Dale, switched first to the movie studios, then to the night clubs. And in the end, what Mr. Smith describes as "the best medium of entertainment in the country" became only a memory.

Mr. Smith is now retired from the entertainment world and resides in the Actors' Home in Englewood, New Jersey.

JOE SMITH

By '33 or '34, talking pictures had come in and had killed vaudeville. For one thing, they could save money for the owner. It didn't need scenery or an orchestra; all a theater had to have was four walls.

Another thing was that a lot of acts couldn't work because of the microphones that were put in for the movies. You see, the sound of the talkies echoed against the walls and you couldn't hear anything, so theater owners deadened the walls and put in microphones for the vaudeville acts. Now that meant a lot of vaudeville acts couldn't work because the actors would have to stand in one place and talk in to the microphone—that's how stand-up comics got started—because if you worked without a mike, you couldn't be heard. And that meant we couldn't do the famous "Hungarian Restaurant" sketch, because it called for our walking back and forth.

So, when we didn't play vaudeville, we went into different things—comedy shows, revues, musical comedies, Earl Carroll's Vanities, Billy Rose's units. We played night clubs; we played Loew's when they came in; we did gambols for the Lambs' Club.

Between '30 and '32 we also made a lot of pictures for Paramount over in Astoria. They were two-reelers and we made them once a month. We always diversified the things we did in them—singing, dancing, comedy. We did the "Butcher Shop" sketch but not the "Dr. Kronkite" routine, because if we had done that routine on two-reelers, it might have gone to theaters where we were playing as an added attraction to the picture. Besides, we wanted to save it for night clubs and other places.

Then, when theaters started having two features, one running an hour and a half and the other maybe an hour, they didn't need an 18-minute two-reeler anymore, and that also killed a lot of vaudevillians.

One of the few features we made was "The Heart of New York" in 1932 from a show we had joined in 1930 called "Mandel, Inc." We made it at Warner Brothers and Mervyn LeRoy directed it. We also made "Manhattan Parade" at Warner Brothers, directed by Lloyd Bacon; we made "Nob Hill" at 20th Century Fox directed by Henry Hathaway; and "Two Tickets to Broadway," at RKO directed by James Hern.

Gangsters? Yeah, they had a part. They had night clubs and they had acts, and when you worked for them, they treated you wonderfully; they couldn't do enough for you. Waxy Gordon treated us marvelously. In fact, once when we went from

Washington to Pittsburgh on the train, with a drawing room he had given us, a waiter came in with a big tray of salad and a bottle of wine. I said, "You're in the wrong place, mister." He said, "No, this is from Mr. Gordon." Then one of Gordon's henchmen came in and sat down, and I said, "We're not hungry. It's only the morning." And he said, "I'm here to see that you eat it and drink the wine." Those were Waxy Gordon's orders!

How do I feel about it all? I think vaudeville was the best medium of entertainment in the country, but I don't miss it. Some people tell me, "We wish vaudeville was here. We want you fellows." Reminds me of a story: Once I was invited to a cocktail party that was given for the arts and sciences in Princeton at the home of Governor Byrne. He came over to me and we shook hands and I said, "I'm glad to meet you." He said, "Did you ever have that before?" I laughed and said, "Yes." He said, "Well, you got it again!" I knew then that he had seen Smith and Dale. That was from our "Dr. Kronkite" routine; the part where I'd hold up my hand and say, "Doctor, look at this!" and the doctor would look at it and say, "Did you ever have that before?" I'd say, "Yes," and then he'd say, "Well, you've got it again."

Yeah, when I look back, I've had a lot of fun. Charlie [Dale] and I were together from the start of the century, and there's been a lot of changes; but I go along with the changes. I don't go back and say, "Oh, I wish so and so was . . ." What's the use? Vaudeville just went out, that's all; you take it as one of those things, one of those things.

While depression-era movie studios emphasized escapist glamor and glitter, they also tolerated a few reality-oriented "experimental" films, like King Vidor's *Our Daily Bread,* which was about life in the depression, or *Hallelujah,* his earlier pioneering all-black musical film. In this way, Vidor recalls, directors who wanted to "make films that came from their own individuality" did so between the making of pot boilers and other, more conventional, films. Thus, by also satisfying their need for individual expression, directors like Vidor not only contributed some film classics but also expanded the artistic breadth of the American film industry.

King Vidor lives in California, where he now writes and lectures on American films.

KING VIDOR

I'd been trying to make a black film for about three or four years before sound film came along, and I had been repeatedly turned down. The reason I wanted to make it was that I had grown up in the South. My father had a sawmill in Texas, where I worked as a boy, so I saw a lot of black churches and homes. I just thought that the little villages and parts of the South I had gone through would make wonderful scenes for a film. Then when sound came along, I was in Europe and thought that it was the time to go back and do this film. I thought sound would really make the film, with singing and dancing and the music of the blacks.

Now, at that time, '29, MGM had made 50 films, but they were hesitant about making this picture. But I had made *The Big Parade* for them in '25 and it practically put them on the map, it was so successful. Then, in '28, I made *The Crowd,* and they had to feel that I might come up with something new and better. So that, plus the fact that I put my own money into the picture, sold them on the idea of *Hallelujah*.

Oh, yes, we ran into problems. We had to take the cast of New York actors, composers and musicians down to Memphis. And in Memphis, they couldn't come up on the regular elevator; they had to come up on the freight elevator. I had to get another hotel for them, and we had some trouble with some chauffeurs and drivers. Then we ran into problems about star treatment—who was to be called "Mr.," "Madam," "Professor," and so forth. Of course, there were more problems when we brought everyone to California.

Then we had trouble with the theaters. Some were afraid the film would attract a preponderance of black people and didn't book it. I had to go around and get reviews in Chicago, for example, to even show that there were reviews written. Then a fellow with a little theater booked it and was so successful that the big theaters booked it. This had never been done before, booking a film first in a second-run theater. They didn't even have little-theater circuits then; it was either big or nothing. In New York, the film opened in Times Square and in Harlem on the same night. Although I don't remember the exact reaction of the black press, I know it was favorable.

Billy the Kid, released in '30, was another film I spent three or four years trying to get them to okay. They were afraid of the violence, the fact that Billy the Kid was supposed to have killed 21 men. But they had a fellow they thought was going to be a star, Johnny Mack Brown, and I guess some other films of equal violence were made so they finally came around.

When we went to the Grand Canyon to shoot, the Grand Canyon looked like the Grand Canyon in both 70 mm and 35 mm: flat. The difference was that with 35 mm, you saw in peripheral vision, the eyes went out to the edge of the wide screen, while with 70 mm, you were looking at the screen but also beyond it; it was more embracing, as though it was wrapped around you, taking up your whole vision. There was no doubt about it: I was wildly enthusiastic about it. Fox and MGM each had 70 mm cameras, but since they were still paying for sound equipment, they abandoned the idea. There were only 12 theaters in the United States that could show a picture in 70 mm. Later, when Cinerama was a success, everybody came out with whatever equipment they had and started using it.

Our Daily Bread? I originally had in mind three themes: one about war (*The Big Parade*), one about steel (*The Crowd*) and one about wheat (*Our Daily Bread*). The idea of wheat came from my thoughts about farming. I had read a page in *Reader's Digest* that said the only answer to the depression was cooperative farming, the movement back to the farms. So that was the beginning idea, that people would put all their skills together and make the farm work.

Our Daily Bread was a follow-up on *The Crowd*. I used the same two characters, John and Mary. In fact, I tried to get James Murray for John again, but I couldn't.

Did I feel strongly political about that film? Well, it has been called "capitalistic" by the Russian government and "communistic" by the Hearst press, so it doesn't take a square-cut political stand. Now, in the early parts of the picture, when they try to keep the bank from selling the farm out from under them—that was my belief at the time. But I don't know even today, having seen the picture hundreds of times, just what the political slant would be. It does have some lines about the kind of law and system we were going to have, which is what I felt at that time. This was the depression, when people couldn't get jobs and didn't know where to go. So if you take a co-op, finding sustenance on a farm through working, but, well, I don't say that's the answer.

You see, it's more an artistic than a political film. The idea I had experimented with was the metronome, so my inspiration was purely the music and movement. The rhythmic ditch-digging scene is much closer to ballet than to politics.

It cost me $125,000 to make the picture. MGM turned the story down and RKO had an option on it but gave it up. I couldn't sell it, because they didn't understand that kind of picture. I had to go out and mortgage everything—the home, the automobile—to raise the money. I thought that much of the film. The only help I got was from [Charlie] Chaplin. He was a good friend of mine and one of the officers of United Artists, so through him I got the release, the distribution contract. I didn't care too much about whether it made a lot of money as long as nobody lost any money. But it's still running, and I still get a few dollars.

The Russian award for *Our Daily Bread* came when I was at the Paramount studio. They said it was the second-best award and the film would have had first place if it hadn't been considered a capitalistic film. And the Hearst press, on opening night, said it was a "pinko film." So, you know, you take your choice which one you want.

Yes, I thought we were going to win the Academy Award for it. We were told that afternoon. I was all set and moved the whole party, around 10 people, closer to the stage at an additional cost of $5 a seat; and then they gave it to *You Can't Take It with You* and Frank Capra.

No, I didn't turn down *Gone with the Wind,* exactly. What happened was that on a Friday morning I was given a stack of scripts to work on for David Selznick. They were talking about shooting in about a week, and I felt that it was a colossal chore; I wanted to do it when I had worked on a script for two or three months. I think I had just gotten out of some sort of script trouble and I hated the idea of doing scripts at night in between my other work. What I didn't know was that when a fellow like Willie Wyler or Victor Fleming was told, "We're going to start shooting in two weeks," they would say, "Yeah, that's okay," and then take two months before they started. But I wasn't smart enough to say yes and then stall. So I was going to turn it down.

Anyway, when I went in Monday morning, I saw that they had succeeded in getting Fleming to direct *Gone with the Wind,* provided I would go ahead and do the last few weeks on the *Wizard of Oz,* which Fleming was currently directing. I gladly took over the *Wizard,* because I didn't want to work under those other difficult conditions.

No, I didn't take any credit in that film; my name doesn't appear. You see, we had this policy in the Directors' Guild that a fellow couldn't come in and take equal credit when the other fellow had planned the whole picture—the cast, settings, all the conferences of pre-production. So we didn't want that; I didn't want that. But I liked the idea of directing Judy Garland, because outside of *Hallelujah,* I never got a chance to direct musicals.

I was pleased with the results of the scenes I directed. I certainly was pleased with "Over the Rainbow." You see, I'd seen a lot of musicals and I didn't think the actors knew what they were doing; they just stood before the camera and sang. I thought it would be good to have some sort of movement in the singing. Ordinarily, one never gets satisfaction from bits and pieces of a film, and I've forgotten the other scenes I directed—the cyclone scenes, for instance—but I still get a kick out of "Over the Rainbow."

Northwest Passage? We shot only the prologue of the book, you know. The things I was interested in were the scenic, photographic parts, a great bunch of men or long lines of boats, anything moving rhythmically. *Northwest Passage* had all of this, and I looked upon it just as I did digging the ditch in *Our Daily Bread,* the rhythmical movement of people, again ballet. It was a chance for me to put a lot of myself into that story.

We talk about actors expressing themselves, but directors have the same need to make films that come from their own individuality and not just a story that somebody wrote. I used to be very well aware that I had to make "pot-boiler" films, like *Stella Dallas,* so that I could occasionally make experimental films or films that affected me personally. See, there were two kinds of films: the film that came from inside, that came out of your own gut—and those are the ones I used to suffer the most from, trying to keep their original purity and intention, trying to keep them from falling under the studio conglomerate action and criticism—and the ones you did because the studio wanted something. Take *Street Scene* and *The Champ,* for example: I thought, I'll do *The Champ* as a box-office studio success and *Street Scene* as an experimental success, so if one goes over and the other doesn't, it'll keep my box-office artistic name at a certain level.

As far as sex goes, people have lost sight of the fact that before the Hays office came along, films were very heavily accented with sex and glamour. I was probably the only one at

MGM not going in that particular direction. They didn't make films with actual nudity, but the films were very erotic. The Hays office was simply to appease women's clubs around the country and to keep them quiet so that the pictures wouldn't be heavily censored and cut to pieces. The Hays office was superficial in a way; and it was political. It was the industry policing itself.

I remember that David Selznick had to fly to New York and call a meeting of the presidents of all the film companies to be able to get the last line in *Gone with the Wind,* when Gable says, "Frankly, my dear, I don't give a damn." But I don't think it adds anything to the film for actors to get into bed with their clothes off. I think it's probably better suggested, and that's what we used to do.

Irving Thalberg? You have to look at him in light of the fact that he worked on a new picture every week. He was not David Selznick, who made one picture at a time. Thalberg didn't sit on the set; he didn't write any scripts. He was so busy in the office that he never came onto the set. He was an entirely different type. The way to work with him was to tell him your idea and get his approval, then go ahead. He let you alone until he saw the finished rough cut of the picture, and if there was something he wanted you to do over to improve it, he might suggest it. A lot of people don't have the guts to remake some parts or change an actor in the middle of a picture; but he did.

He was a remarkable man, remarkable in that he was making 50 pictures a year at MGM and was in charge of a lot of big stars and big directors. That was his bigness: It wasn't in individual scenes; it was his insight. You'd tell him your idea for ten minutes and he'd say, "That sounds good. Go ahead. I'll see you in four months." Or, "It'll need a little more. Why don't you get_____ for it and we'll make a contribution to it." He saw himself as executive in charge of production. He didn't worry about time or money.

The thirties was a rich period for Hollywood's miscreant monsters and mad scientists. And while Frankenstein, Dracula *et. al.* were providing a deliciously terrifying escape from a depressingly torturous reality, a third menace was making its appearance on the screen—in a film that would be named in a 1977 American Film Institute poll as one of the ten all-time greats: *King Kong*.

The simian stunt man for *King Kong* was Carmen Nigro (stage name Ken Rody). He began his career working with Hoot Gibson and later worked with Tom Mix, Walter Brennan, Bela Lugosi and Boris Karloff, appearing in such films as *Murder in the Rue Morgue, Gorilla at Large* and *Mighty Joe Young.* Mr. Nigro made his last movie appearance in the 1964 film *Thunder Row.* He now lives and works as a security guard in Chicago.

CARMEN NIGRO

In Hollywood in those days, there were only three fellas working in gorilla pictures: Charles Gemora, a fella named Van Horn and me. Van Horn worked for less money than me because he had two or three brothers and they all took turns in one suit, whereas I had to "go to action" alone. It ranged anywhere from $25 to $100 a day, depending on the stunt you were doing. See, we never had any insurance, since the cost was so high. But where the script called for real acting before the public, the moviemakers always called on me.

In 1930 Michael Todd, Sr., was my manager. I heard they were going to make *King Kong*, so I took my suit out and kind of repaired and fixed it. I already had the gorilla suit because I'd made *Ingagi*, played a small sequence with Lon Chaney, Sr., in *The Unholy Three,* and made a few other pictures. Then they quit making jungle pictures for a while and I stored my suit away.

The suit had cost me about $3,500; it was made out of five, six pairs of skins. With the head piece, two sets of extension feet, and two sets of extension hands, it weighed about 150 pounds. That meant that I could stay inside the suit 20 minutes at the most.

I auditioned for *King Kong*. Merian C. Cooper, the chief executive of RKO, was well satisfied and wanted to use me. But Ron O'Brien, the cartoonist, tried to sell him the idea of using all animation. Cooper won, though, so I drew a contract. Frankly, I didn't care what he did and what he used, as long as I got paid from the time the picture started to the time it was released. I drew a salary of $150 a week for a year and ten months—$7,000 though I actually worked only about ten months solid.

That was me who was filmed on top of the Empire State Building, which was a model structure eight feet high with a fake background. I had ballet shoes covered with fur to look like ape feet and suction cups on the bottom of those shoes so I could stand on the dome, which was four feet high. Fay Wray was a model, too, like a Mattel toy. The airplanes I was catching were miniature planes (the real planes were projected onto a background curtain). They were on a real thin wire and were propelled by little gas-pump jets. The Sixth Avenue El was all a scale model. Most of the shots were filmed in a studio on the RKO lot.

I'd consider *King Kong* a classic film. But I had no idea it'd be on television or anything like that. If I had, I would have drawn up a different contract and retained royalties or something. I think I deserve just as much money as the star did for doing the work.

In the past couple of years, everybody's been making movies about *King Kong*. I wish them all the luck in the world and hope they have success.

King Kong, to me, is past performance. I'm not living on past performance. Right now I feel very happy to be doing the work I'm doing. I'm trying to stay out of the limelight as much as possible. For a man of my age, I need the rest.

The expression "cliff hanger" wasn't just Hollywood hyperbole; it was an accurate description of those weekly movie-serial installments that left the hero often doing literally that—hanging from a cliff, waiting to be saved before it was too late. Of course, when rescue did come, it was always at the beginning of next week's episode. Thus would pass each segment in one of the most colorful and entertaining aspects of Hollywood's B-movie industry in the thirties.

The master of such machinations was Spencer Gordon Bennett, who, after working on such serials as *The Perils of Pauline,* and *Pearl White* in the twenties went on to become a genius of suspense and special effects with his directorial efforts in the thirties and forties. Recently dubbed "King of the Serials" by a major film publication, Mr. Bennett is now retired and lives in Hollywood.

SPENCER GORDON BENNETT

In the thirties I had a bonus arrangement at Pathé and my salary averaged $750 a week. My job was to send episodes to a committee in New York, which voted on them as they came in, and then processed them for distribution. They voted the episodes "excellent," "good," "fair" or "poor." Now, if it was excellent, I would get $3,000 for that episode. I think there were only a couple of serials that were voted excellent, the action was that good.

The Pathé committee wanted to make sure that kids would be thrilled, and I used to test that when I was cutting the serial. Before the final cut, I would get all the kids from the neighborhood, and have them tell other kids, to come on a certain Saturday morning to our studio, where they would see a picture for nothing and then have ice cream and cake. The first time I did that, I had a crowd of kids, but when the picture went on, they were quiet. The serial went through all the thrills, but there was no excitement from the kids. I figured, "Jeez, there must be something wrong." Then I found out what the trouble was: The mothers had told their kids that if they made any disturbance at the studio, they wouldn't be allowed to go there anymore.

After I heard that, I said to them, "I think you don't like my serial." They said, "Oh, we do, we do." I said, "Well, when you like it, let me know, and when you don't like it, let me know, too." From then on, it was pandemonium, and I could tell how good the serial was by the kids' reactions.

These kids loved action. When you stopped and talked, they weren't interested; in fact, they weren't too interested in the story line, either. They loved action, chases, suspense, stunts, cars going off cliffs, or, as they called them, the "cliff hangers."

My forte was trickwork. The new directors today don't know how to do that stuff. I used to do a lot of it; that was part of my life as a director. I had a variety of ways to do tricks, like wrecking a real Rolls Royce that cost $36,000 in front of your eyes. I'd do it this way: Pretend there's this crossroad out in a suburb and you've got a chase. The Rolls Royce is being chased by a police car. When it gets to the intersection, an "n.d." car—that's what we called a nondescript car—comes out on the right, going to the left, just for the purpose of forcing the Rolls over a little bit. So the Rolls has now swerved out of the camera line to the place where the wreck's going to be. As it goes out of the picture, I follow behind it and keep panning. But I have a replica of it that looks as if it had actually made the impact. Now, this is all in one shot, no editing or anything. And as I pan over, you get the terrific crash, bang and everything else, so it appears as though the original Rolls is wrecked. Then I pan over and dolly up close to my leading man, who is positioned in the wrecked Rolls, the original having been driven by a double. The entire trick cost only $100—the price of having the wreck towed out from a wrecking yard. You take a major picture today; they'll go ahead and wreck the $36,000 car and maybe a stunt man will get hurt in it. When I did these tricks, it would take me two or three days to go over all these low-budget shots.

Also, I used to try to put the audience in the position of the actor. In other words, instead of taking the long shot and showing the stagecoach going off the cliff, I used to get a long shot and then put the camera in the mock-up stagecoach and shoot so that *you* were going down. That was the way to get the thrill in stunts, putting your audience in the situation. That's the best secret of good action. And, of course, the leading man would jump out of the stagecoach. Then, in the next episode, you'd recap about 50 or 100 feet of film and then have the climax. Those serials were as effective a draw as magazine serials were.

The number of episodes to be in a serial would depend on the exhibitors. They would say, "We'd like to have four 13-episode serials." That would be one a week for every week of the year. Or sometimes they'd want only ten, because they'd be filling in with a comedy, a short or animation.

As far as the westerns went, sure, every western story had a certain sameness about it. Twisting them around was about the only thing you could do. All the western actors had perfect horsemanship, and we made darn sure they were capable of reading the lines intelligently. We almost had a stock company in these westerns, the actors were so nearly type-cast. One would play a sheriff and you'd see him walking along the street and you'd say, "Sure, that's a sheriff." And then the same heavies would be in there. That made it so easy for the director; you could usually get a first take with these fellas.

Republic was the best studio in the business out here for action pictures. They used to have a great miniature department. The miniatures they put in the serials I did gave them a big-production effect. But at Columbia, where I made a lot of stuff, it was terrible. The sound men were not up to snuff at all, and their traveling shots had to be done over and over because they couldn't keep them in the camera.

Ken Maynard? I did about six or eight pictures with him. He was over his peak then and going downhill, drinking pretty badly in those days. But for his type of acting, he was still accepted. I used to have his double, Cliff Lyons, do all the long shots for me before Ken got there and leave spots where I was going to cut in for his close-ups and dialog. It made shooting a little difficult, but, fortunately, I knew cutting. If I hadn't, I couldn't have made these pictures.

Heir to Trouble was the first picture I made with Ken. In it, he plays a miner who gets a letter from an old friend saying he is sending a boy out to him. The miner thinks, "Fine, I'll have him work in the mine." But the boy turns out to be a baby boy. So Maynard's famous horse, Tarzan, takes care of the baby while he works. For example, to give the baby a meal, the horse pulls a rope that releases a gadget that sends eggs down a chute into boiling water, also turned on by a gadget. Then, when the horse finishes that meal, it goes over and rings a bell in the mine that means dinner's ready, and Maynard comes in.

When I was handed the script, I said, "People won't accept it." But Maynard said, "Yes, they will. They love this kind of stuff." And he was right. It went over so well that he asked me to make more, and so I made the others.

You see, when I first got into the business, I wanted to learn every angle of it to get experience. The fact that I could make an expensive scene for little or nothing was something most directors didn't understand. They never went in for that. But I made a study of it. Then too, I used to cut my pictures in the camera, just as I would edit in the cutting room, and that saved a lot of money for the company, which was usually on a low budget.

Directors now? Those who are making these $26 million blockbusters *spend* money to see how much they can spend. If they bring in a film that's budget or under, before they even look at it they say, "This can't be good." And if it's $4 million over, they say, "We've got something good." But that extra $4 million is not evident on the screen.

Ranking alongside the Hollywood superstars of the thirties were another group of box-office draws: two mice, a dog, a dog-man and a duck. No ordinary menagerie, they constituted the base of what was to become a leading source of entertainment in the movie industry: the Walt Disney Studios.

Ward Kimball, who was for many years one of the studio's top animators, recalls the evolution of those characters, as well as the work that went into some of the most popular movies ever made—*Snow White and the Seven Dwarfs*, *Pinnocchio* and *Fantasia.*

Mr. Kimball, who also led a very successful Dixieland jazz band (The Firehouse Five Plus Two), is now retired, spending much of his time traveling with his wife and working on his life-sized nineteenth-century railroad. He lives in Santa Monica, California.

WARD KIMBALL

I saw my first Disney cartoons quite by accident during the depression in Santa Barbara, where I lived at the time. I was going to art school on a scholarship and was thinking about going to New York to become an illustrator. To pick up extra cash, I worked at the Safeway store on Saturday mornings, and when I was through there I'd walk up two blocks to the Fox-Arlington Theater, where they had the original Mickey Mouse Club. Now, this was the early Mickey Mouse Club, not the second one, and was a promotional gimmick to get the kids to come to the theaters on Saturdays. The name Mickey Mouse Club was just a title and didn't mean that Walt Disney pictures were shown exclusively, because they weren't being made in that number. But, like any other club, they'd call meetings and observe all the proper parliamentary procedures.

Being a musician, I was hired by the theater to lead the kids in the club who played instruments in a little march before the program. Usually there'd be five or ten kids and someone would be out of tune and we'd stagger through some simple march while the kids in the audience would boo because they'd want to get on with the show. For doing this I would get $5, which was a lot of money in those days, meaning 1933.

After our musical offering, I'd sit in the audience and watch the cartoons. I always liked them and began to notice the difference between the Disney product and the others. I noticed that not only were they in color, they really made you laugh by building a gag with movement that was a little more artistic. In one picture I remember, *Father Noah's Ark,* as the storm gathers, the animals all head for the ark. I was impressed by the fact that the giraffes loped like giraffes, the elephants lumbered like elephants, and the squirrels hopped along in their characteristic way. It was caricature of movement based on realistic observation.

Also, Walt's cartoons were the first to get away from the old episodical gag approach and to the story line. This was still in the days when a cartoon was a bunch of gag episodes strung together. Early animators would sit down to animate "Felix the Cat" and would say, "What'll we do now? Let's have him go up on the roof and get squirted with a hose." With Walt's cartoons, he worked the story plot out before the cartoon was made so there was a story on which to build gags. This was an amazing breakthrough in cartoon techniques in the late '20s, early '30s.

Yes, Walt was the first to make a sound cartoon [*Steamboat Willie*]. People could hardly believe it. To see Mickey beating on a rib cage or a bunch of pots and pans, as in *Barnyard Broadcast,* and at the same time hear the sound—that really drove the audience crazy. But after the novelty of sound wore off, Walt started putting in the plots, and the audience began looking for them. So that while sound changed the whole conception of comedy, it was Disney who was the first to discover its possibilities.

Incidentally, Walt was also the first to use color in cartoons. It was very expensive in those early days, but I think he got a special deal from Technicolor. They gave him a discount for putting in "Color by Technicolor," on the main titles and for years that was a big caption.

Anyway, we heard at art school that Disney was looking for artists. So I thought, "Well, why not go down and do these silly cartoons for a while, then pick up and go to New York and do illustrations for *Redbook* and *Cosmopolitan?*"

My mother drove me down to the Disney studios (we had just enough gas to make a round trip), and the receptionist there went off to show my portfolio to Walt and several other people. When she came back, she said, "They'd like to have you come to work next Monday," and that was that. I think I started on April Fool's Day.

I was one of the first of the influx of new young artists who were art-school-trained or had taken art courses in college. Milt Kohl, Frank Thomas, Ollie Johnston, all of us came in within a few months of one another, and it was mainly this group that in time really changed the course and quality of artwork in the cartoons. We went a little closer to the realistic approach that Walt wanted and got away from what we used to call the "rubber-hose school of animation."

In those days, you have to realize, Mickey Mouse was a formula. His head was a circle, his ears were almost circles, his body was a circle around his hips, and you just connected these circles with two lines. If you had a big close-up, you drew the circles with a silver dollar, a medium close-up would be a half-dollar, a small shot would be a quarter, and so on down to a dime. It was so mechanical. Then, gradually, beginning in '34, we began to make the characters a little more pliable. When Mickey smiled, his cheeks would go out beyond the circle.

You know, I've been accused by young film buffs of the desecration of the century, because I was the one who changed Mickey's eyes from those little black-rat turds with the pie cuts in them to circles with pupils. It was just a fluke, because at the time I was designing a program for Walt's two-day party he threw for us at Lake Marconian after we finished *Snow White*. On the cover of the program, I had Mickey addressing a golf ball sideways, but he had to look out at you, the spectator, and in those days, if you rolled Mickey's black eyes into the corner, it looked funny, since you couldn't get direction. Now, all the other characters had the stock design for eyes: round eye balls with black dots for pupils. So I changed that just to make the thing look better. By God, there was an explosion from the comic-strip and other departments that I can still hear. But Walt said, "Yeah, I kind of like it." So that was the change in Mickey.

Eventually Mickey fell into disfavor, because we were changing our characters to make them more believable and we couldn't find plots and stories for Mickey. The duck always remained in favor because he was duck size. If you saw him in a living room or a yard, he was the size of a duck. Pluto the dog always acted like a dog. He was a gross caricature of a dog, but he was believable. The Goofy character was a man, even though he had a dog face. But Mickey, when you saw him in relation to the other Disney characters, he was three feet high, and who ever heard of a three-foot mouse?

By the way, the first time I ever saw Donald Duck was when I went to work there. He appeared in a picture called the *Wise Little Hen* in a minor role. All he did was quack and do a little dance with Peter Pig. While the Wise Little Hen plants her corn, she sings her song, "Who'll Help Me Plant My Corn?" Then, when winter comes and the corn is harvested, she doesn't give the Duck and Pig anything, because they wouldn't help her.

Right after that, a black-and-white Mickey Mouse film was made called *The Orphan's Benefit,* a classic where we were still doing the things that took advantage of Mickey's musicianship. We had Clara Cluck doing that clucking-hen opera aria, clucking style. We had Horace Horsecollar and Clarabelle Cow doing a ballet, and Mickey playing the piano. Donald Duck tries to recite "Mary Had a Little Lamb" but is immediately picked on by the little orphans, who are little mice in the audience. They throw stuff and he gets mad and blows up. "Okay!" he yells. "You want to fight?" and he bounces up and down. Overnight that picture established Donald's hot-tempered character, one jump from the *Wise Little Hen,* where he was just a duck, to this movie, where he became the feisty little duck.

The idea to put Donald Duck in *The Orphan's Benefit* came from Walt. What happened was that Clarence Nash, a milkman who came by the studio every day, stopped in and wanted to know if we ever had any need for voices. He did voice imitations. While he was giving Wilfred Jackson his repertoire, Jackson buzzed Walt and said, "Listen to this guy." Just to show that he had a voice, Nash recited in a duck's voice "Mary Had a Little Lamb" over the intercom. This gave Walt the idea to put the duck in *The Orphan's Benefit* and have him talk, trying to recite that nursery rhyme. Incidentally, Mickey's voice was Walt's voice.

Goofy started out as a character in one of the early *Barnyard Broadcasts,* in which Mickey does a radio show and the camera cuts to the audience, where there is this funny-looking doglike character clapping. Walt thought it was funny, so they cut to Goofy two or three times and got a laugh every time. Pinto Colvig, a story man, became Goofy's voice. Colvig was a crazy, corny guy who came down from Oregon; we called him the Oregon Apple Knocker. He played clarinet as a hobby and painted it yellow, playing it corny, like Ted Lewis. Anyway, Walt asked Pinto if he could talk with that voice and he said he could. They decided to call the character Dippy Dog, meaning a goofy dog, but that was too hard, since it was two words, so they settled on Goofy. Later they took him out of his aborigine state with his black body and long-limbed hose arms and put clothes on him. He became quite famous in our "How to Do" series: how to ride a horse, how to play golf, how to play baseball, how to play football. He was a man then, except for the face. Then, as he got more real and believable as a person, there was a big controversy over whether we should eliminate his ears. Some pictures had them and some didn't. I don't know what the final decision was.

Pluto was just a dog and had a few minor roles. His bark was by Pinto Colvig or Jim McDonald. But the role that made Pluto famous was the flypaper sequence, which I always refer to as a milestone in the new type of Disney approach in cartoons. I've forgotten what picture this was in, but it was a sequence in which some flypaper gets stuck on Pluto, and the more he tries to extricate himself, the more he gets caught in it. This could have been just a quick little scene but for Norman Ferguson, an animator who had come out from New York and had gone to work for Disney. He wasn't a great artist, but he had a wonderful feeling for timing and movement and would draw very quickly, getting the spontaneity of the thing. In this scene, Fergy's mind was racing ahead of his hand, and he kept adding and working out the sequence until it became a very long one. When Walt saw the first rushes he added even more business when he realized the possibilities. This was the first time you saw a cartoon character think and use logic in getting out of a predicament. It wasn't just a pie-throwing gag or a violence gag. Pluto really tried to use his head, and the more he tried, the more involved he got. It got big laughs because all of us had been in that same situation, whether it was flypaper or a thistle patch or pruning roses.

Pluto became Mickey's dog by the idea man's inventing domestic stories with Mickey and Minnie that called for a dog. I think the best relationship of the dog to Mickey was shown in a short called *The Pointer,* in which he was Mickey's hunting dog. It was a classic cartoon in color made after '36.

Minnie was in the early cartoons, when the animators began to get story-conscious. It was boy meets girl, boy is flustered by villain, the villain being Peg-Leg Pete, the caricature of a cat, who is always trying to get into Minnie's pants, so to speak—which I always thought was weird, because here's this big fat cat fooling around with this little mouse. But that didn't seem to make any difference in cartoons.

Walt had a self-censoring mechanism as far as all that was concerned. He was naive as far as dirty jokes were concerned. He had this built-in, Midwest, bible-belt sort of mechanism. He didn't say, "You can't do that"; we just sort of learned what we could and couldn't do. In the early days, of course, we showed outhouses in the early Mickey cartoons. Or a cow would run and her udders would flop around. Then the Hays office got a little tough, and all of a sudden it became obscene to show a cow with udders. The movies began to get very prudish. You'd go through these crazy periods, hills and valleys, of censorship.

Snow White? It was a gamble. It was done under financial duress because it cost a hell of a lot of money. It was going to run over a million dollars, and hell, we never spent that amount on anything. So Walt had to shop around to pick up the money and he finally got it from Gianini, of the Bank of America.

Gianini went out on a limb and took a risk, the climate in the thirties being that the picture would never hold up. The thinking was that people wouldn't sit still for an hour and a half; the bright colors would hurt their eyes; they'd walk out of the theater. There were dozens of reasons advanced why Walt shouldn't make a cartoon feature.

But Walt managed in *Snow White* to build a believable story that, with all the grossness of the caricatures of the dwarfs and the crudeness with which *Snow White* was animated, managed to have a hell of a lot of "heart." I was at the premiere, and when Snow White is stretched out on the bier and those dwarfs doff their hats, go up to the little slab to pay their respects and bow their heads, my God, you could hear the whole audience weeping real tears! I mean even big stars like Clark Gable had tears streaming down their faces; hard Hollywood tycoons were crying. A cartoon had never done this before. Walt knew then that the gamble he had taken had paid off.

We did the live action for *Snow White* using different people for models. Nestor Pavia, who was the villain in a local play in Los Angeles called *The Drunkard,* did the playback of the witch. But the animators didn't trace him; they just watched him and went beyond. In the '30s there was a funny baggy-pants Follies comedian by the name of Eddie Collins, a little guy. We would go down to the old main street burlesque house on Friday evenings just to see Eddie work in the blackout comedies. Eddie had this quality about him that made you like him as soon as he walked onstage. He was a little round-faced guy with a little cap and a mouth that went from here to here and a tongue that was 11 feet long when he let it out. Walt wanted to get Eddie to do live action for some of the seven dwarfs, especially Dopey, so we did, and there were a lot of gags based on him. For Snow White, we used a teenager, Marjorie Belcher. That was a hell of a name for such a sweet girl, but she became Marge Champion later on. At any rate, we stayed a little closer to her, because Snow White wasn't a gross character. Even though her face was made into a doll, we didn't caricature her too much.

While we were working on *Snow White,* drawing all this sweet stuff, we used to draw other stuff as a sort of release. I drew this view of Snow White with her legs spread, but not so you're looking in, with all the dwarfs lined up waiting their turn, with their joints out. I think Doc had tweezers on his or something, and Grumpy had this big, gnarled oak-tree limb and was the only one not facing her. He was facing away, still being belligerent about it. I don't know where the original drawing went, but it was reproduced, and by the time we got into World War II, every male riveter at Lockheed or at the shipyards had one in his wallet. I remember people coming up to me and saying, "Hey, you work at Disney. Have you seen this?" And by the time I saw it, somebody had added the title "Snow White and the Seven Truck Drivers," which I thought was pretty funny. I never would have thought of that.

Oh, yes, I was involved in *Pinocchio*. There was no problem with financing, because *Snow White* had made a few millions. It made six times its original cost, so we had the banks on our side.

I was put in charge of Jiminy Cricket. I hated the character because, first of all, the cricket is an ugly insect. How do you caricature, make lovable, a Disney-type character of a cricket that has funny saw-tooth legs and looks like a grasshopper? So my first crickets retained some of that insectlike quality, but each time Walt said, "No, it's not warm enough." What he was trying to say was that it wasn't cute enough. What we finally developed was a cricket that wasn't a cricket but a little man with spats, and coattails coming to a point like wings on a cricket. He had regular arms and gloves with three stripes on them, in true Disney tradition. His head was an egg-shaped blob with no ears, two little slits that represented a nose, and eyes that didn't bug out like a cricket's. Instead, he had small eyes, like the rest of the characters. Finally, he had a tall silk hat and carried an umbrella. I went through hell and fire to get that character. I mean, usually you want a caricature of something or someone. But what could I caricature with this? I wasn't caricaturing an insect; I was doing a blob who talked. So even though Jiminy Cricket with Cliff Edward's voice has turned out to be one of Disney's top characters, it was artistically and esthetically an ungratifying experience as far as I was concerned.

Yes, I was the art director on *Fantasia*. My favorite sequence was "Dance of the Hours"; I think that was a classic. I worked on what I consider an inferior sequence, the "Pastoral" sequence, with silly centaurs and centaurettes, and also on the section where Bacchus comes down the hill. But the really great stuff is the "Dance of the Hours" and "The Mushroom Dance."

Fantasia bombed. It was a *failure* when we made it and Walt felt awful. It was in the red for four years. Walt gave them Fantasound, but nobody had done fourth-dimensional sound back then. *Fantasia* was ahead of its time. People weren't ready to accept the higher forms of art! Audiences said, "Stick to your funny cartoons." Then, much later, the acidheads in the college towns began to discover the movie and it started to catch on. Now that film is being run continuously all over the world.

Yeah, I was one of the contributors to the Disney image. But be sure that that's explicit; because his genius was taking a bunch of artists who on their own couldn't draw their asses—egotistical guys, temperamental—Walt was able to take all this and mold it into the Walt Disney approach.

Anybody who names Clark Gable or Errol Flynn as the strongest and bravest character of the silver screen's golden era is off the mark. For such stars pale in comparison with the man who had the brute strength and unfailing wit to defeat his villainous foes every time: Popeye the Sailor.

Gordon Sheehan was one of Popeye's artistic creators. He also developed a number of other Fleischer-studio characters, as well as contributed to the company's two pioneering feature-length cartoons. In this memoir he recalls, not only the technical bases for the pop art of Popeye and company, but also a good deal of the human comedic side of a truly three-dimensional operation.

GORDON SHEEHAN

When I graduated from The Pratt Institute in Brooklyn in '32, the depression was on. That meant that it was very difficult to get any kind of job in the art line, especially the commercial art line. So I pounded the sidewalks of New York for months till one day I heard of this film studio at 1600 Broadway, owned by the Fleischer brothers, that hired beginning ad artists to do tracing and painting and learn the animation business. I went up there, as I had gone to a hundred other places, and fortunately at that time they were taking on artists because they were experimenting with a new character, Popeye the Sailor.

Max Fleischer and his brother, Dave, had started off in the silent days of films. When sound came in around '28, animated cartoons started to become popular, because then they could show the little characters dancing, talking, singing. Their character Betty Boop was just right for this particular era. She was originally a cute little dog character but the Fleischers decided to humanize her. The little ears became little earrings, the fur became little curls, and that's how Betty evolved.

Betty was made up to be a sexy little character. While as a rule they changed the costume from picture to picture, she usually wore a miniskirt or a low-cut dress. She was nicely curved with prominent bazooms, long eyelashes, jewelry and all the cosmetics that were needed to make a gal sexy.

Betty was mostly a song-and-dance girl, and that's what she did in every picture. There never was too much of a plot to her stories, although there was a lot of versatility. In each picture she played a different role.

Normally her color wasn't pure white; it was a little off-white. The studio was very fussy about the coloring of the Betty Boop cells and wouldn't let me paint any when I first went there. It could be done only by experienced girls, some of whom had been there five or ten years.

You see, in all animation there are usually three cell levels to save on the amount of tracing and painting. For instance, if the feet were to remain stationary but the head and arms were to move, the feet would be put on a bottom cell, the head a cell on top of that, and the arms on top of that, on a third cell. Since there were three levels, each cell had to be different in tone, otherwise there would be a little jump. So, starting with white on the top cell, each cell down would become a little grayer. They had a special paint they called "Betty-white," and for the top cell it was "Betty-1," for the next cell "Betty-2," and for the bottom one "Betty-3."

Mae Questel was the voice of Betty Boop and then she also became the voice of Olive Oyl. When she was in the heyday of recording Betty Boop, Loew's State Theatre on Broadway used to give her top billing in their vaudeville program.

Betty was a star. She was so popular a weekly radio program featured her. Betty Boop dolls and novelties were big sellers in stores like Macy's and Gimbel's.

Now, at the time I came along in '32, the Fleischers had been experimenting with this little sailor character that had been running in the comic strips. It was drawn by a Chicago cartoonist named Segar, who had originally started with a strip called the "Thimble Theater" about 1917-19. When Popeye was introduced in '28, he crowded out the other characters. So instead of calling it the "Thimble Theater," they started calling it "Popeye the Sailor," and he became very famous. At that time Fleischer and Paramount, which released the Fleischer cartoons in the theaters, were looking for a new character and thought they'd give this little fellow a try. They weren't quite sure that he would be as successful in the movies as he was in the newspaper strips, so they decided to put in Betty Boop and let her co-star; if Popeye couldn't carry the film by himself, she would carry it through. It turned out that the pilot film—which, by the way, was the first one I worked on at the Fleischer studio—was so successful that Paramount immediately wanted Max Fleischer to do a series. They ordered 12 cartoons for the coming year, which was quite a big order

The plot of the first cartoon has Betty Boop as a hula dancer at a carnival to which Popeye has taken Olive Oyl. Of course, there is a series of gags on him throwing balls at dummies, winning dolls, ringing the bell and that sort of thing. And naturally Bluto, the villain, who became Pluto in the later Popeyes, has a contest with Popeye with all these little games. Then, while Popeye gets up onstage and starts dancing with Betty Boop, Bluto steals Olive Oyl. But she rejects him and so he ties her to the railroad tracks. When Popeye sees all this, he goes after Bluto, and of course they have a good old fight. Finally, after doing away with Bluto, Popeye pulls out his can of spinach just in time to stop the oncoming train and rescue Olive Oyl.

I imagine the biggest reason for Popeye's success was that the cartoons were full of action. In the early cartoons, people wanted to see action; that's why we put in so much violence, fighting and running. Popeye never sat still. He was always up to something and was usually doing something good, even though he beat up a lot of people. There were an awful lot of complaints in those days about too much brutality, but Popeye was always doing it for the good of somebody. He was basically a benevolent character. Also, violence wasn't uncommon in those days. In fact, if you look at most of the early movies, the old Buster Keatons, the Keystone Kops and the others, there was a lot of violence, and it was something that was accepted.

Most of the fellows who worked on the cartoons never gave it a second thought. They were interested in getting laughs from the audience.

What we would do was take a script after it came from the story department and we would "story-board" it. In other words, we would make sketches of each scene on 8" x 10" paper and pin them up on the walls so that we had a visualization of the continuity of the picture. Then every member of the animation department would go through the picture scene by scene, and anybody could suggest anything they thought would add an extra laugh or make something a little more interesting. The outcome was that we usually ended up with a pretty darned good and funny story.

The original Popeye voice was done by an old vaudevillian named "Pepper Sam": I don't know what his real name was. After Popeye started getting a little prominent, Sam got kind of a big head and wanted more money and prestige and became a bit troublesome, so he was replaced by another character, who was just passable.

Now, when I first went to work at Fleischers', I sat next to a fellow named Jack Meyer, who preceded me there by a week or so. Jack came from a theatrical family and was always doing imitations of Ed Wynn, Joe Penner, Baron Munchausen or whomever. Jack was doing his Popeye skit at lunch one day when Dave Fleischer was showing some guests through the studio and happened to hear him. He called Jack into his office that afternoon for an audition, and Jack came through with the goods and was given a contract.

Jack added quite a bit to the Popeye character, because he not only did the voice but also worked on story plots. In addition, he really studied each film. In those days the voice was sometimes done after the picture was photographed. Jack would run through the silent version of the film and see where he could add adlibs without any obvious mouth action on the character's part. He got in a lot of gags and jokes of Popeye talking to himself, which made him much more interesting. It humanized him.

Speaking of Jack humanizing Popeye, there's a funny story

about him. In '38 the studio moved from New York to Miami, and Mae Questel didn't go with us, because she was raising a family in New York, so one of the girls from the Betty Boop radio show was picked to do Olive Oyl. Well, she and Jack met in Miami and, after becoming romantically involved, were married. The Miami papers had a big headline, "Popeye Marries Olive Oyl!" It was a big news item throughout the country.

Another interesting side effect of Popeye's film popularity was that his King Features syndication in the newspapers increased about three or four times. After that, King Features wanted Max to try their other characters to see if he could do the same thing with them. He experimented with such characters as Barney Google and Henry the Bald-headed Kid in various shorts, but none of them jelled like Popeye.

In '39 we did about six or eight Superman cartoons, but they weren't successful, either. They took too much drawing and didn't go over well at the box office. I think they were ahead of their time. People weren't ready to accept the human character moving around, and in addition, they were laughing at the wrong times. Of course, there were also a lot of flaws in the drawing. It was very difficult to emulate a human being, compared with drawing a rounded, animated figure.

Little Lulu, on the other hand, was quite successful. She was originally drawn as a one-panel feature by a woman cartoonist in the *Saturday Evening Post*. We did our first Lulu in '40 and made several after that. But she was a limited character. Being kind of a bratty child always getting into trouble, her story range became repetitive.

Other Popeye characters? Well, there was Wimpy, who was in the newspaper strip before Popeye. They tried him out in the regular animated cartoons, and he had such a different personality that he caught on and made a very good addition to the series. Whereas Popeye used gruff, almost vulgar language, Wimpy was an old gentleman who tried to speak the king's English. He was a sedate character and didn't move around very much, but he was also very crafty, always trying to wheedle somebody out of something, usually a hamburger or the money for it. Wimpy was always in a supporting role because there wasn't enough to his character to write an entire story.

Of course, there were other characters used in the strip, like the Sea Hag and the Jeep, which was a character that could foretell things by wagging its tail. Then the Fleischers developed a few characters of their own, like Popeye's father and the three or four kids who looked like Popeye. So from time to time they would be introduced, but they were used only once in a while.

The Fleischers were very creative people. Dave was more the showman and music man and also a very good director. Max was an artist and cartoonist. He trained a lot of the animators in the '20s and '30s who became pioneers in Hollywood. He was also quite an inventor. He probably had a hundred patents on different things. About '35, he invented a system for what he called third-dimensional animation, long before Disney had developed his multiplane camera set-up. In Max's process, all of the animation was shot through a vertical piece of glass, which was attached to a lathe bed. Behind this bed was a six-foot revolving aluminum turntable, on which artists in the background department would build sets of buildings, trees, and landscape. Then, as the pictures were shot, one or two at a time, the turntable would revolve, so that if Popeye was walking down the street, the background also moved, and it had a three-dimensional effect.

There was another important invention that Max made in animation—the Rotoscope. It was invented in the '20s and used with his Koko the Clown cartoons, which meant that it was drawn from actual photography. The scene would be shot in live action first and then, after the film was developed, projected onto a frosted glass, and the outlines would be traced on paper, so that you got very realistic action.

Max used the Rotoscope process to very good advantage when he made the full-length animated feature *Gulliver's Travels.* Around '37, Disney came out with *Snow White and the Seven Dwarfs,* and when it opened in New York City, it was a tremendous hit. Naturally Paramount noticed and wanted Max to do a feature picture right away, one that they felt could get in on the action.

A lot of stories were considered. I remember that the studio was asking for ideas, and anyone who worked for the studio could make suggestions, send in sample scripts, etc. I don't know who chose *Gulliver;* I imagine it was Max himself, because it was probably one of his favorite stories. Then too, he might have had the Rotoscope process in mind. You see, all the animation in *Gulliver's Travels* was hand-drawn, cartoon style. But Gulliver was a realistic character, so for each of his scenes a photograph of the live action was made and then traced onto paper with a few variations, of course, to animate it.

It took a little over a year to do that film. We started it when the studio moved to Miami in September, '38, and it was released at the New York Paramount in December, '39. During that time the studio increased in size roughly tenfold. They had to import people from Hollywood, away from the studios out there, including Disney's. They got some of the key men who had worked on *Snow White* to come to Florida. Paramount just poured money into it. The sky was the limit, which was quite a reversal in policy from the old days before we went to Miami. I think they spent a total of $4,500,000 on the feature.

As a matter of fact, the making of *Gulliver's Travels* was itself the principal reason for the movement and expansion of the Fleischer studio. By that time, besides making 30 or 40 one-reel pictures, they were getting into some two-reel color cartoons, and when they decided they were going to make a feature picture, they knew they'd need more and better working facilities. The ones that were available in New York were too prohibitive; so, since Max and Dave both owned homes in Miami Beach, and the state of Florida was then offering tremendous tax lures, that was the obvious place to move.

About a year after the film was released, the Fleischers began searching around for good material for a second feature and settled on a story, *Mr. Bugg Goes to Town,* which was later retitled, *Hoppity Goes to Town.* It was supposed to have been taken from a fairly well-known novel of that time—*God's Little Acre,* I believe. However, they changed the script around so much that there was very little similarity between the picture and the book.

The feature didn't do well. One reason was that the European and other world markets were big elements in the whole distribution process, and when *Mr. Bugg Goes to Town* was released, we were in the war, so there was hardly any foreign market. Also, people's attitudes had changed; they were starting to get serious about life and were hardly paying any attention to animated cartoons. In addition, the story line of *Mr. Bugg* was not as strong as that of *Gulliver's Travels*. Of course, *Gulliver* was a good, strong story to start with a few hundred years ago; but nobody knew this other story, and besides, it was contrived. They hired Hoagie Carmichael and Frank Loesser to write some nice songs about it and had famous names to record it, but the story just wasn't there. Interestingly, they had benefited from the experiences and boo-boos that had happened on *Gulliver,* so that technically *Mr. Bugg* was probably better. But it just didn't go over.

No, neither *Gulliver's Travels* nor *Mr. Bugg Goes to Town* are as popular with the public as the old Disney pictures. Disney had a formula for releasing his productions, then putting them away and re-releasing them when he thought the market was good. That way, they didn't pop up at different theaters all the time, and people didn't get tired of seeing them. On the other hand, the Fleischers sold the rights to their features, so you still see *Gulliver's Travels* on television around Thanksgiving and *Hoppity Goes to Town* around Christmas.

It was a wonderful era. It was an amazing time that never happened before and will never happen again. A group of young people got together to make these new things that were appearing in theaters. Most of us were between 20 and 30, and Max and Dave were only in their 40s. Even though the depression was on, it was a lot of fun, a wonderful experience. Of all the years I put into animation, those were the ones I remember most.

8
... AND ALL THAT JAZZ

The thirties were a rich and formulative decade for jazz and swing. For Lionel Hampton, who made a unique contribution to both kinds of music, it was also a decade in which there was profound social change—and he contributed in that arena, too.

Today Mr. Hampton, still a master of musical innovation, continues to perform, both in concerts and on records.

LIONEL HAMPTON

When I came to Los Angeles, I worked with Les Hite's band. We used to get arrangements from listening to guys like Duke Ellington, and McKinney's Cotton Pickers, the Casa Loma Band. We'd listen to their records and learn the arrangements note by note. I used to do the drum part.

Hite's band got to be very popular in L.A. and we always worked. We played for a lot of the black social events. They all had different kinds of clubs and were always giving parties. Most of the blacks in Los Angeles were at that time domestic workers—either maids, butlers, chauffeurs or housekeepers—for the movie stars. They controlled the stars' homes for them; they bought all their groceries; helped form the parties; helped prepare the dinners. To be a chauffeur or a housekeeper for one of the big movie stars, that was big stuff then. They were paid well, sure. Some of them had homes; in fact, some of the best black homes in California at that time were those of the domestic workers. Everything the movie stars would have in their homes, the help would have in theirs. The big black society leaders in L.A. at that time were the domestic workers.

So, since we were very much in demand, we always had good money coming down and our income was about $35, $40, $50 a week apiece.

Then Frank Sebastian, who owned the Cotton Club in L.A., gave us an audition and he really liked us. This club was more commercial than the Cotton Club in New York; it was the place where all the movie stars'd come, right across the street from the MGM studio. We had chorus girls, and Sebastian would bring out stars and headliners, like the Mills Brothers and Louis Armstrong. As a matter of fact, he was going to bring Louis *and* his band out to the club, but when Louis's manager heard us play, he liked us so well that he left Louis's band in New York and just brought Louis and his music out. We'd play some and then Louis'd come out and be the star. That was a great experience.

While we were playing with Louis, he asked us to do a recording session with him, and we did. The first record we made was "Memories of You," then "Driving Me Crazy" and "I'm Confessing That I Love You." At the studio, there were some vibraharps sitting in the corner. Louis asked me if I knew anything about that instrument, and when I said, "Yes, that belongs to the percussion family," he said, "Well, play me something on it." I just took the knowledge I had from orchestra bills and put it on the vibraharp, because it had the same keyboard, only the sound was more textured. That was the first time jazz had ever been played on the vibraharp.

I played with Louis for about nine months. He was the kind of guy who would always give me encouragement. Every night he would say, "Oh, man, you were great." Louis used to call me "Gates": "Man, you play the drums like a swinging gate; you swing your head off," he'd say.

After Louis left, I played again with Les Hite for a while, but I left him because I wanted to play vibes and he just wanted me to play drums. That was about '33. I spent a year traveling up the coast toward Seattle. I had a band with some good guys in it, like Charlie Grimm and the late Herschel Evans. We were playing for a booking agent and we would go to some towns and he would round up all the money and we wouldn't have any left. So I had to wire back to my wife's mother to send us some money to keep us going. But I kept on playing, because I wouldn't quit.

Then my wife took sick on the road around San Jose and had to go into the hospital, and her mother said for me to break up the band and go back to L.A. When I got back, I looked around and got a job playing for a guy in San Pedro, but soon I was working a little night club in Los Angeles called the Paradise, at Sixth and Main, near the depot where all the sailors would get their last beer before they went back to their headquarters in San Pedro and Long Beach. It was a sailor's place, all right: sawdust on the floor and beer for 25¢ a pitcher. One night Benny Goodman, who had heard about me, came in. He brought Teddy Wilson and Gene Krupa with him, and the next thing I knew I heard this clarinet playing behind me and the piano being played differently and the drummer playing differently, and there were Teddy, Benny and Gene playing behind me. That was just something unbelievable. Here was a guy I had always heard so much about. I idolized his playing, and here I was, playing with him and Teddy Wilson and Gene Krupa. This was just too much, especially after I had played with Louis Armstrong not too many months before. We jammed till about four o'clock that morning, and Benny asked me to make some records with them.

So I went out to RCA Victor in Hollywood and made a record with them called "Moonglow," and another, called "Dinah." That's how the Benny Goodman Quartet was born on records. Those records became so popular and caused so much commotion that Benny asked me to come and join him in New York, and I did. I stayed with Benny for four years. This was the first time that black and white had ever played together. You know, there was no integration in stage, music, sports; it was just unheard of. I think we did such a good job at public relations that it opened the door for Jackie Robinson to go into major league baseball, and for other black athletes and show-business people after that.

The public's reaction to the quartet was fantastic. I think it was one of the biggest applause-getters there was in the business. Sure, there'd be times we'd be playing a job and I would hear guys coming to Benny and saying, "What you got that nigger in there for?" And Benny'd say, "You say that again and I'll take this clarinet and hit you on the head with it." Some of his good friends would say it, too, you know.

When we played Richmond, Virginia, and Nashville, Tennessee, people'd ask Teddy and me, when we came in, if we were the water boys. We'd say (in high-pitched, pseudo-obsequious voices), "Yeah, man, we carry water. We're gonna drown you out." But it soon came to me that this was a pioneering job. This was going to change the social system of the United States.

I think the Benny Goodman Quartet was the greatest musical organization there ever was. It was God-sent with a message. It was a turning point for the social system.

We were serious; we attended to our business. We kept our hair combed, our shoes shined, our suits pressed. We were always on time; we weren't drunk; we weren't knocked out; we gave the best we could. We got along with everybody; we didn't carry chips on our shoulders. And all this was effective. Everybody liked us.

And for me, I had something I wanted to say, an individual thing I wanted to do, and I finally got into it when I got into the quartet. I was coming into my own then. I remember when I first started, Clare Musser, who was vice-president of a company that made bells and vibraharps, used to follow me around when we were doing five or six shows a day with Benny. In between, I had a set of xylophones always set up to practice on. He'd come by and we'd run through concertos, Mozart, Bach. He kept me up while I was getting my thing together.

You see, I got myself together. I continued to learn, even though I was playing professionally. I took the time between shows to take lessons from a guy named Freddy Albright in New York City, whenever I was there for a while. He was a great rhumba player on the xylophone. I would always go back to the xylophone and rhumbas.

I would also play classical music. That's what jazz is all about. It was like Bach had a beat to it. That's when I started developing and knew where it was for me. The classical was integrated with jazz. I had a piece we just recorded the other day that I wrote for the quartet, "Dizzy Spells," which was influenced by Bach. I realized that only after I wrote it.

Then, in '39, Benny took sick, had back trouble, and the doctor told him to lay off for a year. I was anxious to keep on playing, so he gave me his blessing and I got a band together. I found a lot of youngsters, trained them and turned them out.

I found Dinah Washington in Chicago, down at the Garrick Bar. Joe Sherman, the owner of the bar, took me to hear her. I invited her to come out to the Regal Theater, where we were playing, the next day. When she got through singing, I said, "What's your name?" She said, "Ruth Jones." I said, "Can I change your name if you join the band?" She said, "You let me join the band and you can call me anything you want to." So I said, "From now on, your name is Dinah Washington." It just came out of the sky like that.

Then a guy came up to me and said, "I really want to sing; give me an audition." I said, "Well, you can sing in the next show." He did and I liked him and hired him, too. That was Joe Williams.

My playing style created quite a stir. *Downbeat* and all of those magazines said I had too much showmanship. But I always say, "It's nothing that I rigged up; it's just the way I feel." If I feel like I want to sing, I'll sing and clap my hands, and if I feel like I want to dance, I'll dance. When I had my band, I used to jump up in the air and land on a tom-tom, and the public used to think it was the greatest thing. They'd tear up the house and applaud and applaud and applaud. I always like to give happiness to whatever I give, give a feeling to it, just put my whole self into it.

The thirties were hard times for sure, but not for everyone. Indeed, for a few they were actually good times. And for Earl "Fatha" Hines, they were not just good times but formative ones as well, for these were the years when Hines made his distinctive contributions to jazz and helped others who would later enrich the American musical scene.

From 1928 to 1940 Earl Hines led his band and played his piano at the Grand Terrace in Chicago. Today Mr. Hines is still making records and playing in clubs throughout the country.

EARL "FATHA" HINES

When we opened at the Grand Terrace, we had everybody. It was the "Cotton Club" of Chicago, seven nights a week. We started at 9:00, 9:30, and our first show was around 10:00. We had a very lovely clientele from the North Side, the Gold Coast. And we had the gangsters.

See, I had already had a reputation because of the radio programs. We had started on the radio with WENR. Emil Denmark and the Cadillac people opened up on the station. They turned the mike on, said, "You're on" and left it on. We just talked about the club, what was going on on the floor. It wasn't much of a radio show. But we had so much success with it that I was the first to go coast to coast—New York to Chicago, Chicago to California.

I was very fortunate in finding musicians who wanted to work. We had guys who loved to play, people you wouldn't know today: Walter Fuller, George Dixon, Cecil Irwin, Budd Johnson on tenor sax, Louis Taylor on trombone. Oh, there were so many. They got a kick out of driving the background for the guys who were playing the solo and then they got a kick out of his solo that made him feel like playing.

I had very good vocalists, too. There was Herb Jeffries, who finally wound up in pictures, Arthur Lee Simpkins, Valaida Snow. I finally wound up with great ones—Billy Eckstine, Sarah Vaughan and Johnny Hartman.

Billy Eckstine was working the Club DeLisa out here in Chicago. I had gone out to see a dancer who was going to close and whom we were going to put in the show. Before she came out, this young man came out to sing and I said, "Oh, good gracious, what a voice he's got," and besides, he was a very good-looking boy. So I said, "Would you like to come and join my band?" and that's how I got Billy.

Sarah Vaughan had won the amateur hour at the Apollo Theater. Anybody who won it got a week at the theater, so I went up to hear her. Just before Ella [Fitzgerald] came out, they put Sarah on, and when she sang, I said, "Oh, man, this is something." I went backstage and asked her if *she* would like to join the band, and she said yes.

At that time, you had only one type of music and it was swing. You didn't have all this modern music. There were many bands, but it was just one thing called swing. Benny Goodman, he made a reputation off of swing, but it was from the first four or five arrangements that he got from my band. We had recorded "Jersey Bounce." I'd been playing that for four years before Benny got it. But, you see, publicity in New York was stronger than publicity in Chicago, and it came out "Benny Goodman, the King of Swing."

What happened was that Benny was using arrangements from Fletcher Henderson and my man Jimmy Mundy. And when Jimmy left our band, we didn't know it, but he took those arrangements out of the books and gave them to Goodman. It was something that was happening. When you had big bands, you looked for something like that. People were moving, coming in and going out of all big bands. I didn't care too much about the fact that he took the arrangements, because he paid me back. But when they said Benny Goodman was the King of Swing from the tunes I had been playing, that's the part that didn't go over too well for me.

See, when guys were recording during those days, it was something that we liked to do, not knowing that we were going to make any kind of a reputation. We just went ahead and recorded. And, of course, by doing it, it was money for members of the band. As for me personally, I never paid much attention to that, because when I recorded, I recorded from the heart and that's what I wanted to do. I was tryin' to get as much out of the piano as I could. The money was for the side men.

Yeah, the '30s was a good time for me, a good time. We didn't know what the depression meant. See, after the gangsters came in, there was always money. They used to come into the club and the East Side would try to outspend the West Side. There were always guys comin' in there, trying to close us up at night, saying, "No more people," giving them a thousand dollars to run the club. So during the time of the gangsters in Chicago, there never was a depression as far as the clubs were concerned. We did all right.

My nickname came about this way. Ted Pearson was a radio announcer and a guy that was great at being an engineer as well. But he had a habit I didn't know anything about. The president of the network called me up and said, "If you like this guy you better talk to him, because we fired him twice and three times is a charm." So I went down there and talked to him between shows, the ones we used to put our broadcasts on. I said, "The president of the network called us up and said he wanted us to do a good show, so let's do a great show." But then, when we came off the intermission, the drummer said, "He's laying on the table." I said, "Oh, Lord, we've got 15 minutes before the broadcast." I got towels and ice and black coffee and everything else. Now, my theme song is "Deep Forest," and getting back at me because I reprimanded him, Pearson said, "Here comes Father Hines through the forest with his little children." I said, "Leave it in." That's how I got stuck with "Fatha."

The world of jazz in the thirties was just that—a separate world where the music was king, its attendants were musicians and its courtiers were all who listened.

During those years, Chicago was a center for jazz, with the Club DeLisa being one of its principal hot spots. Red Saunders was the owner of the now defunct club, and in this interview he describes its operation and some of the personalities who played there. Mr. Saunders still lives in Chicago.

RED SAUNDERS

In the early '30s, about '32, our band went to Kansas City and this is when I lived like a king. Kansas City was a little New York. It was the headquarters for all of these bands and all of these people, Andy Kirk and his Clouds of Joy, Mary Lou Williams, Count Basie, George Lee, Ben Webster, Lester Young, Hot Lips Page, Bill Dickerson, Jesse Stone. I got a chance to meet all these people. They were just budding musicians then, in their infancy, but with such brilliant ideas.

I stayed there about a year, and that was one of the bright spots of my whole career as a jazz musician. There wasn't much money at that time, so these men would go out and play one-nighters. But they lived in Kansas City, and when they were there, it was always just one big party. We had places where we would go to jam, and in our hotel a lot of musicians would get together and have big-band rehearsals. It was really great; so many beautiful experiences.

Back then, everything was tight. Musicians were making very meager salaries, $18, $20 a week. If they had a job making $25 a week, that was a big deal. One of the only places where musicians could really keep up with their craft was at house-rent, or Blue Monday, parties. That was where you could hear some of the best jazz in the world.

A house-rent party was a party to pay your rent. The people throwing it would have dinners and gambling and whiskey and girls, everything to get their rent together. There was no admission; the only charge was what you bought. Dinner—spaghetti, say, might cost you 25¢, and whiskey would be 50¢ a pitcher; but it was bootleg whiskey, so you took a chance at what you were drinking.

It was all word of mouth. See, the Prohibition law was so strict at that time that you couldn't put out any advertisement, because if you did, you would be tipping your hand. So at these parties they'd say, "Hey, don't forget to come to my party next week."

After Kansas City, I came back to Chicago, worked around for a bit and then went into the Club DeLisa in '35—and stayed there for 22 years. For that whole period of time, we were acknowledged as the best black show band in the country. We had a mammoth show, 16 chorus girls, seven or eight acts. We also did the Chez Paree, another big club in Chicago at that time, but whenever anybody wanted to let their hair down and see a good show with a line of girls, good dancers and good bands, they would come to the Club DeLisa. All the biggest musicians would be right there, because there were certain things they wanted to hear. The shows were tremendous.

Tuesday night we used to have celebrity night. You never knew who was going to come in: Louis Armstrong, Dizzy Gillespie, Erroll Garner, Lionel Hampton, Albert Ammons or one of the old blues singers, Chippie Hill, Billie Holliday.

Billie Holliday? Sure, I worked with her. It was just like her story. It was very unfortunate for anybody who got hooked like she was hooked. She was just a slave to this addiction. It was pitiful. She really didn't have a chance.

She got the name "Lady Day" from Fres; that was Lester Young. She called him "Fres" and he called her "Lady Day." They were like a marriage, 'cause they made so many records together. He admired her and she admired him.

Segregation? Sure, it was there in those years. No black musicians had the opportunity to play a radio station or the legitimate theater. That's where the good money was. All of those jobs went down the drain. You had a black union and a black president, but they were in cahoots with the white union and the white president.

There used to be territories back in those days. You couldn't play past Twenty-second street. If you did, one of the business agents or someone would beat you up or tear up your instruments or your union card. You couldn't do anything.

Segregation made the South Side independent; it made us create our own music. If people wanted to hear it, they would have to come down there. And that's what happened with Club DeLisa. But we always had an open-arms policy. When whites came, they were as free and welcome as blacks and were protected the same way. The musicians felt free and it was a brotherly thing.

Fats Waller, Louis Armstrong, the Cotton Club—these were among the people and places of the thirties that became legends to succeeding generations. In this memoir, Edith Wilson, the Chicago singer, actress and entertainer who was a part of that world, shares some of her recollections.

Ms. Wilson has been singing and acting for "50 years straight." She has played (or sung) everything from George Gershwin's compositions to the role of Aunt Jemima.

EDITH WILSON

I went into *Hot Chocolates* in '29. It was new to people, just like *Bubbling Brown Sugar* is today, and it was that sort of thing, bubbling over with songs. That's where I sang, "What Did I Do to Be So Black and Blue?" That was written for me by Fats Waller and Louis Armstrong. I used to black up my face. A fella came once to my door and said, "I have some roses here for Miss Wilson." I said, "Oh, thank you, I'm Miss Wilson," and he said, "You're not the Miss Wilson I'm looking for; she's a high yella." So he took the roses and left, and I was so upset. I sat down on the couch and sang: "Cold empty bed/ springs hard as lead / pains in my head / feel like old Ned / Oh, what did I do / to be so black and blue?" Such a beautiful song.

In those shows, they did things in three acts. Maybe in the first and second acts you just acted, but in the third act you came to a place where you got your song. "I'm weary this mornin'/ I don't feel so good/ Feelin' weary this mornin'/ I don't feel so good / da-da-da-da"—just go on like that. It would start with, "Well, this has been a terrible day for me. I wish Mrs. —— would come in," and then you would go right into it.

Fats Waller was just a grand fella, full of fun all the time. Fats, Louis and I did a song on the stage—"My Man Ain't Good for Nothin' But Love"—where we were advertised as "A

Thousand Pounds of Harmony." The three of us were good friends. I used to cook red beans for Fats that he loved. We used to ride together at night uptown from the theater and tell jokes and laugh. We had a lot of fun together. As a matter of fact, it was really a fun show.

I went to England with a show called *Blackbirds of '34,* in which I sang a song George Gershwin had written for me. He came up to The Plantation, where we were rehearsing to go to Europe. "Gotta have another song for Edith," he said, so he came up with "The Yankee Doodle Blues." I liked it right away and still sing it. It begins, "There's no land as grand as my land, from California to Manhattan Isle," and I used to do a little step with it. The newspapers wrote it up and said I must be Dixie's champion hip swinger, 'cause I used to shake my hips in the song. I really told them what I thought about Europe when I sang: "Europe's wonderful with all its ancient junk/ It's not as good as Kokomo and Kokomo's a dump/ I couldn't stay in London 'cause I couldn't stand the fog/ I couldn't stay in Paris 'cause I couldn't eat a frog."

Around '35 I went to Los Angeles with Jimmy Lunceford. I worked on the edge of town in a night club with him. He was strictly business. When he called a twelve o'clock rehearsal, he was there at a quarter to twelve, sitting on the seat with this long baton he had. Anyone who was five minutes late got fined.

I once did a show called *Lady Godiva's Horse* with an all-white cast. I never had insults or anything given to me because I wasn't the right color. I guess it's because I had such a long background in the theater and people had heard of me. I'm very grateful for that.

I worked the Cotton Club. At first I was there with McKinney's Cotton Pickers, before Duke Ellington got there. Duke had a little three-piece band uptown then. He was augmenting it and was going to have a bigger band. I don't want to take it on myself that I was the cause of his being there, but I'm the one who spoke up for him and suggested that the Cotton Club people hear his larger band.

I had a pretty good salary back in those days, but I didn't make as much as I had originally made. I got $250, $300 a week sometimes; then sometimes I got $175, but that was more money than anyone else was making. So I was able to have an apartment and a car. I was taking care of my family. I had sisters and I helped to feed and clothe them. I helped pay for the home down in Louisville. They hadn't had any hot water in the house. I'm the one that brought the tub in and all the water.

I think I've made a considerable contribution to each phase of show business. I've worked in bands, I've done shows, I've done radio, I've worked with schools. I've been working all my life, fifty years straight.

> While it's true that the roots of jazz are to be found in the black man's music, the playing and enjoyment of it has not been confined to one race. Indeed, as Art Hodes's memoir reveals, by the thirties, jazz had not only attracted white musicians but had also become the basis for a musical counter-culture.
>
> Mr. Hodes's career as a blues pianist began in the late twenties. Since then, he has worked in a variety of jazz-related mediums, as a radio-program host, journal editor, band leader, recording artist, writer and teacher.

Copyright © 1978 by Art Hodes. All rights reserved.

ART HODES

We were hit hard in the years following the Crash—very hard. In some places—"joints," they were called—there was work, but salaries were small. It was a time of scuffling. You did a lot of walking. There were times between meals and there were many times between jobs for jazz musicians. If you could find a job, you could have a band of six musicians who were good enough to be band leaders, a Bert Freeman on tenor sax, say, or a Gene Krupa on drums.

Louis Armstrong was scuffling at that time. He was a standout, but he wasn't making that big dollar. Earl Hines wasn't making that big dollar, either. Art Tatum was playing at the Three Deuces, and if he was making $75 a week, he was making big money. I doubt if he made that much. It might've been closer to $40. And these were the top performers, the top names in jazz.

How did you live? In the first place, most of us had no family; it was just you and you. And the music was so important to us, other things fell into place. If you ate, you ate; if you didn't, well, you made it. But somehow we did eat and we did have a car and we did get around and we listened to what we wanted to listen to.

There was no question about having a bank account or putting something away for a rainy day. It was just a question of following your star. You wanted to play music and that was it. I recall four of us going into a bar and saying, "Do you mind if we set up and play for you?" It wasn't even a question of pay; we just wanted a place to play.

I loved the blacks' music. It was the blacks who were the masters, the teachers. And, of course, Earl Hines was the best pianist. Anybody who played piano had to admire him. He had so much more to offer than any of us. When I first heard Earl, I felt like taking my piano and throwing it into the river. It wasn't a question of me not having rhythm, not being able to swing, not being fiery and all that. It was just that he had such message and ability. He had a lot of soul, a lot of spirit. He was the kind of guy who was always giving so much when he was playing.

Louis Armstrong was the best trumpet player. The first time I heard jazz records I heard Louis's Hot Five. He was doing his improvisations and they knocked me out. There were other great jazz trumpeters I liked to hear, too: King Oliver, who taught Louis and gave him a chance to play in his band; Jabo Smith; a fella by the name of Mitchell who worked with Hines. Oh, there were a dozen or so around who were recording who were good. They played a different style, a growl. They had something else going. Bubber Miley with Ellington, Hot Lips Page, these guys were fine, real blowers, good jazz players. But they all took their hats off when Louis walked on.

There were also blues players who were playing. Just like today, the Muddy Waters of that day were around, unknowns. In Chicago there was Albert Ammons, Pete Johnson and Mead Lux, the three piano players who played what they called "boogie-woogie" and became known as the "Boogie-Woogie Boys." There was also Pine Top Smith, and he played a different kind of boogie-woogie.

In Chicago in those days, every place had music. It wasn't a question of buying a television set and hearing the same music come out. Each place had a distinctive kind of music. For instance, in the Loop, the Chinese joints had bands, orchestras. Then there was the Savoy Ballroom on the South Side for hot jazz, or the Grand Terrace, where Earl Hines was working. There were also little clubs. On the South Side, there would be a barbecue place where they had a player piano, and you'd sit and listen to the player piano until some piano player came in and sat down and played. Mostly I went to places like that to hear these black performers who had come up from the South, uninhibited, playing the blues-style piano.

There were so many of them. Little Brother Montgomery was one of the first piano players I ever heard. And Big Bill Broonzy was one of the greatest blues people I ever met. He could really tell you about the blues; he was an artist. I don't think he ever made a dime. A man with all his ability, it was a terrible tragedy.

There was one fella by the name of Jackson. When he sat down at the piano, he could play you some blues like you never heard before. I heard him every night. But then he disappeared. When he came back, his gal and everybody had left him and he felt bad, so he played the blues. And then, about six months later, he disappeared again. The next time I saw him, he was dressed up, had a new chick and didn't play the blues. I said, "What's the matter?" He said, "I ain't got the blues." It was that simple. He was playing something else.

It was very civilized in those days. You could walk anywhere on the South Side, night or day, and be at ease. You were just accepted. There wasn't this unrest and these terrible feelings that are going on now among people. And they opened up to you. If you had the right vibes, they opened up to you; they began to act themselves, and you could really enjoy the scene.

The first time I sat down and played the blues, people laughed—and I would say rightfully so. But then one day I played in a gambling house that was all black and no one was laughing; they were listening. Because eventually I got the feeling of what their world was all about. It took me a while. I did a lot of listening, a lot of chasing. It was like going to school, matriculating. Your tuition was your admission and your teacher was working in some joint.

There was a whole clique of maybe 35 white musicians who

dug jazz and hung around the South Side and were studying, again by listening: Jack Teagarden, William Noone, George Wettling, Rod Cless, Red McKenzie, Floyd O'Brien, Muggsy Spanier, Pee Wee Russell. Davey Tuff played with Dorsey, Jess Stacy went with Goodman, Joe Sullivan went with the Bob Crosby Bobcats. Many of them discovered it all before I did. A few stuck with it, but most went the way of all flesh and decided it was more important to make it big.

Jazz was being killed right along. It wasn't just the Crash, there were many causes. Radio came in, and a five- or six-piece jazz band just didn't sound good on radio. But three saxophones, a Wayne King sound, filled the air better, and there were always some musicians who would take a job in a big band and sit there and read the charts, and when they had a chance to play hot for four bars, they would play. The rest of the time the hot men were the outcasts, sitting there playing fifth typewriter. Benny Goodman was one of those fellas who fit into that thing. So were the Dorsey brothers. And by fitting into that, they became band leaders. It was always a compromise. They'd say, "What we love to do we can't do. But we want to eat, and we want to eat well, so we do this and it pays." And so you had the little Benny Goodman jazz combo that would break out of the big band and so forth. They would get some kicks playing, but they stuck to business and did what brought in the bread. For the hardheads, like myself, who refused to go that scene, it became a little harder.

We were called hot men and we liked to play hot. You don't just want to sit back and wait for your four bars to come along so you can play. You want to play all the time. Big bands didn't do that—not those big bands, anyway. So those who wanted to went on and followed the golden trail and made the big buck. To me, it was a waste of time, a waste of my life.

The gangsters? Well, you must remember that they owned the clubs. If if weren't for them, we'd have been in bad shape. I wouldn't say they overpaid us or anything, but they provided us with a lot of work. See, in a way, some of them understood the music better than the cleaned-up people, because it hit them in the bottom of their stomachs.

My first employer, Dago Lawrence Mangano, a tough mobster, loved the pop scene. He'd write tunes, lyrics, that were slightly off-beat. He had a good banjo that he tuned as a four-string—you know, "My dog has fleas," one of those things. He could play it like a ukelele and he'd accompany himself. And this was a tough gangster, one of Capone's lieutenants, who was later killed!

When you worked their clubs, you behaved yourself, didn't notice what was going on. You weren't a reformer and you weren't mixing into it. If you stepped out of line, you had difficulties. There was a code of ethics in those clubs: If you saw, you didn't see; if you listened, you didn't talk. You'd see a bunch of big politicians drinking with the gangsters. Two sharply dressed women would come in and a little later disappear, and you'd see one man after another walk out of the room and come back. You'd put it together, you saw, but you really didn't see, you just kept your mouth shut. They called it "keeping your nose clean."

One fellow we called the Eagle was attracted to the hoods; he hung around them and they accepted him. But somewhere along the line, he decided he'd like to become a policeman and put in his application. One day I picked up the paper and there it was: "Eagle Found Dead." Maybe he knew too much.

Those people controlled that world. You didn't have to work in it. You could go to work for Jimmy Smith and his Cavaliers and play the ta-ta music and the cha-cha-cha and the Mickey Mouse, and maybe toward the end someone'd say, "Can you play a hot number?" and you got four bars and that was it; you had your evening. Well, that wasn't for me.

It's very simple: Jazz has been my life all the way through. It's a tremendous music. There's been a love affair between me and blues. The music was like a mistress and I worshiped it and I served it and it's done me a lot of good.

During the depression, jazz-blues musician Thomas A. "Georgia Tom" Dorsey went through the hardest of times. both pecuniary and personal. However, out of those experiences arose his interest in and dedication to a new form of American song: gospel music, or, songs of faith based on the New Testament.

Born in Villa Rica, Georgia, around 1900, Dorsey was the son of a sharecropper, teacher and itinerant preacher, and hence grew up with a strong grounding in the New Testament. As a young man he studied at the Chicago College of Composition and Arranging, and later became associated with musicians who became giants in the fields of jazz and blues—Ma Rainey, Bessie Smith, King Oliver and Lionel Hampton. It was about 1930 that "Georgia Tom" began to make a transition from blues to religious themes.

Copyright © 1978 by Thomas A. Dorsey.
All rights reserved.

THOMAS A. DORSEY

I had written some gospel songs in the late teens, but there was no market for them. The blues went out about '29-'30, and I had to get into something else.

I had been getting my gospel work together, making my arrangements and packing them away, when one of my friends, Reverend Hall, came out to my place and told me about this big convention in Chicago. "They say it's good down there and they're laying them in the aisles with one of your songs, ('If You See My Savior, Tell Him That You Saw Me.')" So together we went down, and it was true.

I met the singer and the orchestra leader of the convention

and they said, "We like this song; you got any more copies of it?" And when I said yes, they said, "Bring them down here; we'll give you a spot over there." So I took about 2,000 copies and sold them all down there, and I was in the gospel business from then on. That was about '29.

When I first started writing gospel music, I published it myself. With what little money I had, I got a printer and published it in one sheet. Some'd be too long; you'd have to publish them in double sheets, typed and everything, so I did that myself.

I got me one of the Baptist religious books that has the list of churches in it and their addresses, and with my briefcase under my arm, I'd go to the churches where they had rehearsals and demonstrate my songs. Nobody called them gospel songs, and I was almost thrown out of those churches. They said, "You can't sing the gospel, you got to preach the gospel." I said, "You're wrong, brother. I was taught by my father that the gospel is good news, don't care where you hear it, how you deliver it. This is poor folks' music, and gospel is good news; that's what the world needs." That's the way I got it going, for 10¢ a sheet.

I went from church to church, town to town, as far as you could get at that time, conventions and places like that. A big convention, like the National Baptist Convention, and they'd charge you about $20 to set up. But if you could get along, if you had any salesmanship or power over the audience, you'd get one of your songs sung there. They used to sing when they had places like the Chicago Coliseum, which would hold thousands of people. And with a little five-spot, you'd get someone to announce your song for you and tell the people to come in the back and get a copy at your booth. And that's where I made it. I'd sell four, five hundred dollars' worth of songs, and sometimes more than that.

Sally Martin was quite instrumental in my success as a song publisher. She went with me and sang the songs. She was easy to get along with and she wasn't money-crazy. Course, there wasn't any need to be money-crazy, because there wasn't much money at that time. Hard times were on, so we made the best of it. And she made good on it. I paid her well when we hit something big, and she finally opened up her own place.

When I went from town to town, the living conditions were bad. Nobody had any money in the depression. And the conventioneers didn't stay in hotels, like they do now. They'd stay in folks' houses. And they had to hustle for food unless they ate at the convention place. I didn't like that kind of thing; I liked to sit down quietly and I'd pay folks to cook for me.

My income in the '30s? Let's say it was fair. I got by. I was still living. Sometimes I didn't get all I wanted to eat, but I never starved.

Mahalia Jackson? She came on the scene later. Mahalia never was a blues singer. She had a good voice for it, but it was always church singing. I knew Mahalia; she was good, but there was no business for her. She heard me on some gospel show and said, "I want some of those gospel songs you have," and I said, "I'll teach them to you." We began to rehearse, and in about two weeks we had a repertoire that we could go into and do and we had a program and show when we started out. That was about '31. She wasn't as popular as she was in the later '30s, and I was kind of responsible for that popularity. I took her out on the road and traveled with her.

Traveling on the road with Mahalia was a lot of fun. We had a good time; she was friendly with people and people liked her. Sure we got along. You see, I think it's the way you handle yourself, the way you handle business and the way you handle people. We never particularly *wanted* for anything.

I got just about what I wanted during the depression because I didn't reach for too much. What did I want? Anything that came my way—anything. I was Ma Rainey's band leader for a couple of years, traveled the country with her. Then, when the blues business began to come back a little, I began to travel with many of the blues singers throughout the country. I was also a hunt man for a Chicago music publishing company and I found several stars. I did all their arranging: the late Monette Moore, Jamie O. Williams (that was Ink Williams's real name). So I always had something to turn to if another thing failed.

In '32 I took the job I have now in the Pilgrim Church. They wanted a gospel choir, so I went over there and rehearsed them about four months and then they hired me as the director, and I've been the director ever since. I don't know of anybody who ever stayed in a place that long.

I wrote "Precious Lord, Take My Hand" in '32 also. That's when my first wife died. I'd been out on the road, down in St. Louis on a gospel singers' tour. She was going to be a mother. Gus Evans, the assistant director of a church down in Memphis, Tennessee, drove me back that night and we got in about eight in the morning. I ran into the house, and they had never removed the body. The relatives met me at the door in tears, and I think that was one of the most shocking things that ever happened to me. There was a lovely bouncing baby boy there.

But that night the baby died, and I said, "Oh, heck, this is bad luck. I'm going back to my blues." But I didn't right then, and I think out of that sad ordeal came some of my best songs. That was the right time, the ripe time for gospel songs to make their appearance.

I wrote "There Will Be Peace in the Valley" some time later. I had been a widower for quite a few years. There was so much fighting going on in the world. They were looking for another world war to start any minute. And I was on a train, down in southern Indiana. We were going through a valley and I saw some sheep and they were calm, grazing. And near them were cows, horses, calm, all in the same pasture. And there were hogs down at the water, where a little brook ran through. And I looked way up on this hill, and there was a waterfall. The water was streaming down, shimmering down to the ground and into a little brook that ran peacefully out under the tracks to the tracks on the other side of the railroad.

The train stopped in that valley for a little while. I didn't know why they stopped it, but I do now. God stopped it to let me get my song, my message. I got a pencil and paper. Peace . . . peace . . . peace alone wouldn't make the title. Now, that place was a beautiful valley . . . water falling down, peace . . . "Peace in the Valley." Decided on it, put it on a copy sheet for the public stamp. Publishers picked it up. My publisher at that time was Hilden Rainsongs, but they turned it over to someone else and they made a lot of money from it. I don't know how much I made on that song. If I did, I wouldn't say, anyhow.

Someone'd come in and knock the back door down, thinking I still have the money!

That song was one of the world's best sellers, and it still goes well. Nearly every big artist took a shot at it.

My career? Well, when the depression was just coming, it was kind of dog eat dog: Eat if you could, starve if you couldn't. And it didn't get better till '36. But there was a lot to make me happy then. The depression kind of inspired me. It had a real feeling, and we wrote something that would fit everybody's condition. And then you got a different feeling. See, if a fella's in trouble, he doesn't feel the same as if he's walking down the street and it's a sunshiny day.

I think I've made a great contribution to the world—that's the way I figure—for there's people singing now about God that didn't even give a rap about Him. "Precious Lord" has drawn millions of people into the pathway.

I told you, gospel belongs to me. There were others, but I fanned it. I got behind it and advertised it and traveled throughout this country and Europe with it. We went through London, Paris, Tel Aviv, Jerusalem, Greece.

Gospel is good news and gospel songs have taken the world better than blues did. Gospel songs went around the world like wildfire. Why, I don't know: You have to ask God. One thing I do know: It was mighty good for me and I'm profoundly grateful. Gospel music has helped me to live; it helped me to get a new outlook on life and to get a new life. I believe God was directing me. If it hadn't been for God, I'd have been dead, with all the scraps I've been in.

9
A CLOSING MONTAGE

Today public-opinion polls tell us how we feel about everything from saccharine and sugar to celibacy and sex. While it has been only recently that we've learned how carefully our attitudes can be measured, pioneer pollster George Gallup points out that such information has been utilized for well over 40 years. Thus, as Dr. Gallup notes, while in the late thirties Hollywood was charting its cinematic-star appeal, radio was researching its "Enthusiasm Quotient," and even President Roosevelt was taking the public's pulse on foreign-policy decisions.

Dr. Gallup, the founder and president of the American Institute of Public Opinion, lives in Princeton, New Jersey, where he continues his work in the field of public-opinion research.

GEORGE GALLUP

In 1934, the *Literary Digest* dominated the public-opinion scene and had since 1916. As I recall, in '32 and '34 they sent out about 20 million postcard ballots for the elections. Their lists were made up of telephone subscribers and automobile owners, who at that time represented only 50 to 60 percent of the total population. They could send out postcard polls and get accurate results because there were as many working people in the North who were Republican as Democratic. I mean, there had been a slight difference, but there wasn't any real division or stratification on the basis of wealth in the Republican party.

Of course, I had the strong belief that with the coming of the New Deal had come a new stratification in the whole body politic, a whole new structure, with the poorer people going Democratic and the people with above-average income going Republican. Through my own polling efforts in Iowa, I had discovered this division, and as a matter of fact, the first test, the first use of sampling procedures, was in the '34 congressional off-year elections. We had to go through this test to prove to the newspaper syndicate that sold the Gallup Poll that it could be done. So '34 was experimental, a try-out period. It worked, and then later we became convinced that the *Literary Digest* predictions would be wrong. So in the middle of the summer of '36, we thought ("we" being young upstarts in the business and the *Literary Digest* being the great heavy polling organization with all the years of experience) that the only way to challenge them was to say that they were going to be wrong and tell the public why they were going to be wrong, actually giving the figures as to what they would find. We did it, and it was one of those stunts that really worked out beautifully. The important point is, we knew what they were going to find because we used sampling principles. (The way sampling principle works is that if you follow the laws of probability, you know that after you have polled from a true cross-section, whether a few hundred or a few thousand, you can be within 2 to 4 percentage points of the true figure.)

Yes, there were two other polls. Elmo Roper established the Roper Poll. As a matter of fact, their first publication, a weekly release to newspapers, was two or three months ahead of ours. Then in 1936, at campaign time, came Arch Crossley. So the three of us were in the '36 election, and all three polls conducted by this new scientific sampling method were on the right side and the *Literary Digest* was on the wrong side.

Now, at that time in history I was also doing many other things. I had started the first full-fledged copy-research department in advertising, which was an attempt to find out what kind of ads people read, which ones they saw and so on, and I also was involved in measuring the size of radio audiences. These were my main interests then, and shortly after that we got into the field of motion-picture research.

The first picture I ever worked on was *Gone with the Wind.* We worked for many years with David Selznick, the Disney organization, and Sam Goldwyn. The success of any motion picture depends chiefly on four things: one, the basic interest in the story idea; two, the casting; three, the publicity penetration of the picture, i.e., how many people know about it; and four, of course, the quality of the product, how well it's produced. So, through the years, starting with *Gone with the Wind,* we measured the penetration, how many people had heard about it, and of that percentage how many wanted to see it. With this information, we knew in the case of *Gone with the Wind,* that it was going to be big. The only other picture that has ever rivaled it is *Snow White and the Seven Dwarfs.* Incidentally, we worked on almost all of the great pictures from the middle '30s to the early '50s.

You see, people can tell us very quickly if they would like to see a picture based on Einstein's theory of relativity or whether they would like to see a western with 20 men shooting it out in some Wyoming scene. Right away people make their judgments on what they think a movie's about. Then, when you tell them the story line, you refine that first judgment, so people say, "That sounds interesting."

We did a lot of other very interesting things. For example, we established the first national radio survey procedure in the field of radio-audience research. You see, most radio programs then were built in 10 or 15 segments, and we would find out which segments had the greatest appeal with listening groups. We'd collect people and have 30 or 40 of them listen, making use of a concept that was later called the Enthusiasm Quotient, or "EQ." Based upon this type of survey research, Young and Rubicam, the ad agency by whom I was employed, found Jack Benny, Kate Smith and Arthur Godfrey, who all showed up well in these listening groups. Their spots were the ones on the segments that immediately sparked the enthusiasm of these listener groups; they were audience-pleasers. I wouldn't want to leave the impression that these people wouldn't have been successful if it had not been for this research, but research identified them as successful performers at an earlier point in time. Frankly, there was a commercial advantage in finding someone who was going to be a star before that person became generally known and accepted.

Strangely enough, I read now and then a piece in *Variety* saying that what the movie industry needs is more research, and I think to myself, "This is what they had and they've forgotten about it." There isn't anyone in Hollywood now who, to my knowledge, has any idea of what was done in those early days.

Roosevelt? I think Franklin D. Roosevelt made better use of polling data than any president before or since. He had a polling group he called upon constantly. A story that has never been printed is about the destroyers for bases. Before FDR made that famous speech, he talked to Eugene Meyer, one of the earliest subscribers to the Gallup Poll, who asked us to find out what the public's reaction would be. We reported back to President Roosevelt that the public approved of this idea; they liked it. This was supposed to be one of the most courageous speeches the president ever made, but he knew in advance the public's likely reaction.

We also found that the public generally was far ahead of Congress in seeing the peril of Hitler and that it was strongly in favor of building an air force at a time when the military leaders were opposed to it, convinced that air power would never play an important part in another world war. As a matter of fact, the public favored peacetime conscription almost before anyone proposed it. I think if it hadn't been for the poll results on conscription, it would have been defeated in 1940, a year after the war started in Europe. As it was, it passed Congress by only one vote.

I am thoroughly convinced that polls are, as Sam Staufer of Harvard once said, "the most useful instrument of democracy ever devised." I've seen how useful and valuable they are in times of crisis in this country, and I'm happy that I have been in a small way helpful in introducing this instrument. It's a matter of great satisfaction, obviously, but I believe I can add that it has never gone to my head.

Women in national affairs, government-sponsored medical care, beer as the American beverage — these are issues and images that have a distinctly contemporary ring to them. Yet, as Edward Bernays, a public-relations consultant, recalls, these were questions with which he was deeply involved as far back as the early years of the depression.

Mr. Bernays has served numerous government agencies and commissions, and has held professorships at a number of leading universities. He is the author of several works on the shaping of public opinion, and resides in Cambridge, Massachusetts.

EDWARD BERNAYS

Light's Golden Jubilee in 1929 represented a highly dramatic occasion in the life of America, because it came at the zenith of our economic power and strength. The building up of Thomas Edison as a god-head symbol for the technological progress that had brought this about was an idea the people of the U.S. responded to amazingly. This man had completely transformed society by the motion picture, phonograph, electric light, and the application of electricity to everyday life. That struck the imagination of the American people. Henry Ford had revolutionized life by gaining acceptance for the four-cylinder engine. These two men linked with President Herbert Hoover, regarded as a third godhead, were symbols who had helped bring about this prosperity. These three men participated in Light's Golden Jubilee's culminating event in Dearborn, Michigan. Justifiably fully covered by the "media," this event took place just before the stock market crash.

When the crash came it brought with it as much deflation as a soap bubble bursting. Nobody escaped its effects.

I remember coming to Detroit in the midst of the depression with a check of millions of dollars from General Motors, a client, to aid the National Bank of Detroit to reopen. The bank was important to the economy in Detroit. Jesse Jones of the Reconstruction Finance Corporation gave an equal amount in millions. When I arrived in Detroit with a vice-president of General Motors we drove from the station to the Book Cadillac Hotel. It was like driving through a devastated countryside, or in this case, cityside, everything looked completely bereft; front yards unmowed, fences unrepaired, houses in disrepair, a city laid low by the depression.

It was like a country devastated by an earthquake. But here, in addition to the earthquake's physical disaster, the earthquake also caused mental and emotional disaster to the people. Where could they look for help? There were no social security, no welfare payments, no Medicare or Medicaid.

Finally, Mr. Hoover, as a result of public opinion, decided to do something to increase employment. He decided to set up a President's Committee for the Unemployed, under the chairmanship of Arthur Woods, former New York City Police Commissioner and former Assistant to Secretary of War Newton Barker in World War I.

I was recommended for this Committee, and naturally, I accepted. The first thing I did was to emphasize to the other members of the Committee that the word unemployment carried negative implications. I said that we should not be the President's Committee for the Unemployed but that it should be called the President's Emergency Committee for Employment. That indicated its temporary nature and its constructive object. And so it was.

Mr. Woods let me proceed pretty much the way I wanted to. I had interesting and exciting adventures. For example, when the fields of Kansas were ready to be harvested, they needed men. I said, "One story over the Associated Press, the United Press and the International News Service will get them there." It did. Overnight men flocked to Kansas and its fields were harvested. To help dramatize what the Committee was doing, Arthur Woods one day talked to every governor by phone, asking cooperation. Of course his action gained public visibility throughout the country.

About that time, we also worked with the *Ladies Home*

Journal, to whom I said: "You have a powerful lever with your millions of women readers." There was no television; very little radio; and little airplane travel. The United States hadn't yet become "one room." The *Ladies Home Journal* was the nearest place to "one room" that American womanhood could be. I suggested, "Let's start a campaign that 'It's Up to the Women.'" I went to some of my economist friends with whom I was working for credit expansion. They wrote a platform for us for recovery which became the "It's Up to the Women" platform of the *Ladies Home Journal.* This platform outlined what women could do to fight the depression. All over the country women responded to it and helped to give the economy a boost. At the same time, based on confidence of public and private interest, the *Ladies Home Journal* printed the platform on slips which cereal manufacturers put in their packages to make women aware of the necessity of credit expansion. The movement swept the country, eliciting support from newspapers, magazines, and women's groups.

We worked in the mid-thirties with the Committee on the Cost of Medical Care. The Committee dealt with a very important problem, even more so than today. The Committee was chaired by a brilliant man who'd been President of Leland Stanford University, Ray Lyman Wilbur. This Committee explored the conditions of medical and health practices in the United States and made recommendations on how to improve them.

They engaged our professional services to bring the country to a realization of the problem and its solution. We recommended as one step, which they carried out, a series of hearings in different cities to arouse public interest and support for its findings.

The Committee also made separate studies of various phases of medical care: rural, urban, in-hospital, and the like. Each study was treated as a separate entity. We recommended a dramatic occasion for launching its final report.

Most Committee members were social scientists, sociologists, health statisticians and the like. There were also several members of the American Medical Association, who kept Dr. Morris Fishbein, then the editor of the *Journal of the American Medical Association,* informed about the Committee's recommendations. Fishbein in his life had done some constructive things for medicine. But he strongly opposed recommendations of the Committee for what he called socialized medicine. The week before the report came out, he wrote an editorial for his publication. He sent advance copies to many editorial desks in the United States. He stated social scientists knew little about medicine and deplored the Committee's findings. His one editorial made such a dent in the minds of editors throughout the country that it stopped medical progress until President Johnson, some 30 years later, landed Medicare and Medicaid.

When prohibition was lifted, the brewers of the United States retained us to advise them. What happened was this. There were many people still believing any drink with alcohol in it was linked with the devil. The brewers organized under Colonel Ruppert of Ruppert's Beer. One thing I believed would indicate their good faith was if they fought with the law enforcing bodies of the country to maintain sound practices in the sale of beer. By aligning themselves with law enforcement and virtue they were changing the public's attitude towards beer. We helped set up the United Brewers' Foundation to do this and to carry on other activities.

Our research found that countries with drinkers of high alcoholic content suffered more than those with drinkers of lesser content. We called beer the "beverage of moderation" because it had so much less alcohol than liquor. We asked a famed home economist from the University of Iowa to make a study of the recipes with beer used by the early colonials. She found George Washington liked beer cakes. She found other recipes of our colonial ancestors who used beer in them. The distribution of a pamphlet with these receipes helped modify negative attitudes towards beer.

The brewers at our suggestion cooperated with law enforcement officers to eliminate anti-social outlets of beer. We stressed the selling of beer in grocery stores so it would become a home drink instead of a symbol of negativism associated with the corner saloon. As I look back on it now, beer increased its popularity and decreased its negativism. That was 45 years ago. Beer has undoubtedly from a social standpoint helped to lessen alcoholism in this country.

The thirties were a turning point in America in that it was during those years that the first efforts were made to preserve and present our cultural and historical roots. The pioneer in this field was Alan Lomax, who, with his father, made the first oral-history recordings and then went on to make dozens of such recordings for the Library of Congress and commercial companies, while also producing an award-winning radio program.

Over the years, Mr. Lomax has continued to contribute to the preservation of American folklore through his writings, albums and research. He lives and works in New York City.

Copyright © 1978 by Alan Lomax.
All rights reserved.

ALAN LOMAX

At the peak of the depression, my family was wiped out and my father lost all of his money and was just down to a house, a Model A Ford, and a very small income. So my father decided to recoup the family fortune by going back into the field of folklore, which he had left some 10 years before. He contracted with Macmillan to do *American Ballads and Folksongs,* a panorama of American song. The ballads, cowboy songs, lumberjack songs, and spirituals had already been chosen, but my father felt that black secular song had been neglected and would be important for the book. So in the summer of 1933, he asked me to come along on his journey to be his driver and to carry the recording machine for him. We set out to get material both for the book and also for deposit in the Library of Congress, because he had by that time established a working relationship with their Music Division.

We headed for the Brazos Bottoms in Texas, with an Edison hand-wound cylinder phonograph. That was the only recording instrument that there was. Mrs. Edison had given that to my father for use on this trip. You recorded into a little horn and it mechanically registered the cut on the revolving cylinder.

The first place we went was called the Smithers Plantation near Huntsville. Somewhat reluctantly, the manager arranged for us to meet a group of his black tenant farmers at the plantation church that night. We set up the recording machine on the pulpit, set a kerosene lamp by it and recorded a couple of spirituals and then asked whether anybody knew blues or any other similar songs. Then a fellow named Blue got up. He was ragged as a jaybird. He said, "I'll sing it for you, but I want to put it on the phonograph the first time. I don't want to try out like you've had these other folks do. I want to sing my song right into that microphone." So we said, "But we need a rehearsal because we don't have that many discs." He said, "Boss, if you want to hear this song, you'll have to catch it the *first* time I sing it." And so we turned on the machine and Blue sang, "Poor farmer, poor farmer, poor farmer / They get all the farmer makes / His clothes is full of patches and his hat is full of holes / Steppin' down, pullin' cotton / from the bottom bolls / Poor farmer, poor farmer, poor farmer / They get all the farmer makes." And he went on in two or three other verses to depict the situation of himself and his fellows on this sharecropper plantation.

When the record was over, we played it back and there was immense joy in this group because they felt they had communicated their problem to the big world. "Well," he said, "We know when folks up there in Washington hear that one, they gonna come down here and help us out!" You see, at that point, these people were as isolated as if they had been in the Cape Verde Islands. They were subject to whatever the local law was. The Supreme Court didn't reach them. The blacks were totally at the mercy of local authorities. They didn't have any other way of expressing themselves, of getting their ideas out to the rest of the world. So, they weren't interested in our purpose about writing a book or studying folklore or any of that. That was absolutely beyond their ken. But they did see the machine and they did know that we came from somewhere else and they wanted those people at the other end of the line to hear what life was like for them. That's why they were singing for us; they wanted to hook into the big network. They'd all heard radio; they'd all heard records; *they* wanted to make a record; *they* wanted to get on radio; they wanted to get into the communications system.

That experience totally changed my life. I saw what I had to do. My job was to try to get as much of these views, these feelings, this unheard majority onto the center of the stage.

We took our recordings of spirituals and black music from the Brazos Bottoms and went up to a nearby black college. We wanted to share what we had with the blacks and see whether we couldn't work out some way for them to work with us. So we played our little cylinders for the head of the music department and the head of the English department in the office of the president of the local black college.

There was a total coolness to that playback. They didn't like those sounds. They were very polite, very pleasant, but our overture to them totally failed. It was partly because our approach wasn't exactly right, I think. We were just a couple of Southerners. But it was also because of the fact that black roots hadn't yet become acceptable to the masses of black people because there was so much pain associated with the development of black culture.

In the meantime, there had arrived the most important invention in communications of the 20th century, the portable recorder. The Library of Congress had bought the first battery-operated portable recorder and had sent it to us in Texas. It worked on two heavy 12 volt batteries, and consisted of pieces weighing about 500 pounds. It was my task to move that machine in and out of the back of our Model A Ford every time we had a recording session. My father was the producer and I was the recorder. It was a role I really loved, as you can imagine.

On our next stop we went to the Texas penitentiary to record secular songs. That first day we recorded "Go Down Old

Hannah," "Ain't No Mo' Cane on the Brazos," "The Gray Goose," "Long John," "Take This Hammer," and a dozen others that are now considered great American songs.

The people who sang for us were in stripes and there were guards there with shotguns. They were singing there under the red hot sun of Texas, people obviously in enormous trouble. But when they opened their mouths, out came this flame of beauty. This sound which matched anything I'd ever heard from Beethoven, Brahms or Dvorak. They sang with beautiful harmony, with enormous volume, with total affection. And this was the second stage of my conversion to my profession. I had to face the fact that here were the people that everyone else regarded as the dregs of society, dangerous human beings, people who were called every name, whipped, driven, brutalized, and from them came the music which I thought was the finest thing I'd ever heard come out of my country. They made Walt Whitman look like a child; they made Carl Sandburg, who sang these songs, look like a bloody amateur. These people were poetic and musical and they had something terribly important to say. "Go down old Hannah / Don't you rise no more / If you rise in the mornin'/set the world on fire." I mean, "Volga Boatman" was down the stream from that. So I had found my folks; I had found the people that I wanted to represent, that I wanted to be with. After that I could never have enough and still to this day, I can't have enough of finding and making more avenues.

We went from that prison across the South, visiting other plantations and other prisons. We went to Harlan County and I saw the conditions there. We recorded in the Kentucky Mountains and then we went to Washington. The Library of Congress gave us a little table in the cellar and a row of shelves. It was very dirty and dusty, but we had a place, a national repository for these recordings.

In about two weeks, we presented a program of recordings to the heads of all the Departments. The Library of Congress was a different place then, an old-fashioned place with gray-haired scholars, and about a hundred of them came and listened to us. We didn't know what they were going to say.

Now, these were electrical recordings with a good velocity

microphone and it was a very, very fine sound. So, for the first time, America could hear itself, because up until then, *no one* had ever heard these people singing. There had been poems about it, but ours was the first time the contact was made. Well, the Library of Congress gave us a standing ovation. And from then on, we were able to do what we needed to do with the Library's sponsorship.

We spent the next three months making *American Ballads and Folksongs* and then we took the book to New York, where it was well received. We went to conferences where my father told stories and I sang. Then in Washington, the same thing occurred and I became a kind of a singing lobbyist.

Skipping a few years of collecting and work of the same kind, I ended up as the person in charge of the Archive of Folk Song at the age of 21. And because of my work, I became the first oral historian. This came about because I asked people how they were feeling, what they were thinking, right after the singing was over. That way, I was able to get people to free associate and verbalize the feelings in the music. I sat at the tables of blacks and they told me about their anger, about the incredible things that had been done to them after the Civil War and Reconstruction period. I began to publish those thoughts as the headnotes about songs, rather than scholarly notes about variance, and to use that prose right off the record as a way of evoking the real feelings of the singers about songs.

One of the most fascinating people I recorded was Aunt Molly Jackson, the great Kentucky mountain ballad singer. Her annotation of songs became a whole biography and after that first day, I helped her tell her whole life in terms of the 100 or 200 songs she knew.

Leadbelly? I interviewed him in '35. He was a very difficult guy to interview. He sang, he was very pleasant socially, but he was also very close-mouthed. He'd been through too much, and he'd learned not to talk. But I was his young admirer. We lived together with my father for about six months and I became his confidante. Bit by bit, he told me his story and it was this biography of mine that was made into the recent movie. My father and I wrote his story, which was the first singer biography in America. I had read in the literature that folklorists were doing things like that in the Soviet Union, that they decided that the biography was the best way to learn what the songs meant. So I sat down with Leadbelly and tried to duplicate the Soviet method, and that was the real root of the oral history. Then I began with other singers in the same way. I met Woody Guthrie in 1939 and I recorded his life story along with his songs. That material was recorded by Elektra, but was rather poorly edited.

Then came the job with Jelly Roll Morton. Jelly Roll was not only a great composer and performer, but a man with a real sense of history. He had thought out very carefully the significance of what he had seen. During our interview, he sat down at the grand piano at the Library of Congress and told me his story, that of the first American jazz composer.

You see, while Aunt Molly was the mountain bard, and Leadbelly was a maker of the blues, Jelly Roll was the first jazz man who was musically literate. He wrote down his scores; he was very self-consciously controlling the total ambiance, just as Handel did. He was a programmatic music composer. The sound of the street went into his music; and as he reminisced, he recalled the influence of the multi-cultural background of New Orleans, illustrating at the piano as he talked. And here he was the first to depict the origins and rise of jazz in that city—all matters that are more commonplace.

Jelly Roll said that he had done it all, but he and I both knew that this wasn't the case. It was just his way of dramatizing his story. He said, "Me, Jelly Roll, I was there and I did it all." But "Jelly Roll" was just the symbol in his own mind of all the people of his period there. We recorded his whole life story. Then, as you know, it was published in an extremely successful volume of discs, that were the most-wanted discs of the world for a while. And later I spent three or four years building his recorded material into a book—*Mr. Jelly Roll,* the first true recorded oral history ever published.

During this same period, 1938-39, CBS invited me to make a series of radio broadcasts on American folk music for schools.

They wanted me to be the singer-narrator. I was to sing the tunes, and then the CBS symphony was to play an arrangement of one or two of them. But that struck me as old hat. In my contract I specified that I could have so and so many guests who would be paid such and such fees *and* that the Golden Gate Quartet, which was the greatest black singing group in America would be hired as the network's staff quartet.

So that year, I presented Burl Ives, the middle western singer, who had just turned up sleeping in the park; Woody Guthrie, who had come in front the West; Aunt Molly Jackson from the Kentucky Mountains; Leadbelly from Louisiana; Pete Seeger, the young New Englander with the five-string bango; and the Golden Gate Quartet representing the blacks; and myself from Texas. So the whole of American folk music was presented to schoolchildren of the United States. I also took my show to the Virginia mountains and Canada for other kinds of songs.

The program went on twice on Tuesdays, at 9 in the morning and at 3 in the afternoon for two years. I think there were 20 broadcasts each year. In those programs, the real American folk music got on the air. We cut past the fancy ballads. What we had were the songs of occupations, the songs of women, the songs of blacks, the songs of the prisons and we went into every school in the country.

When Aunt Molly Jackson sang like a real mountain woman, the CBS staff was shocked out of their minds by her caterwauling lonesome style. But we got letters from schoolrooms all across the South and the Southwest saying, "That's the greatest singer that's ever been on the air." She represented their style. The program I did with Woody Guthrie won the national prize as the best educational broadcast of the year. So, in those few years, suddenly the whole field was launched.

But while all this was happening, I felt myself to be just one of the thousands of people in New Deal Washington, who were really busy with the same task—finding out the richness of the country and working toward a more equitable American future. That's what we were really all doing, whether we were working on the economy or law, the theater, folk music, or building new communities. We were all united in this one main objective—to make sure that every part of the country, every sector, every aspect of American culture, every tradition was realized in its own way, on its own terms.

One of the most interesting of my roles then was to be a kind of entertainer and bard for this New Deal group and I spent a great deal of my time singing these songs at Washington parties. The liberals adopted these songs as their culture, it was their literature; it was the art of this new big democracy the likes of which nobody'd ever seen—a country of working class people, of farmers and minorities everywhere with a new, raw, exciting culture rising from its belly. This is what we all felt in our hearts.

Earl Robeson was a visitor to the archives then. He learned these songs, which he then made into concert pieces. Then taking off from that, he composed his great songs of the New Deal era. So, in that way, the archives became not just a place that stored culture and was concerned about the ethnographic survey of American music, but a live cultural center concerned about feeding back—stimulating the whole country. It was feedback with a perspective, the Whitmanesque, Sandburg perspective, that the people, yes, they had something to say—the people were worth listening to; and it didn't matter if they didn't speak or sing in the conventional way—the more they were to be heard. And so the archives played the role of representing the actual voices of the common man of America in the New Deal period.

Also during those years, we wanted to get out our field recordings but no company would have them. They would much rather have me or Burl Ives sing them. The real thing wasn't acceptable. But then Leadbelly got into some trouble in New York and was sentenced to prison. At that time, I was at Columbia on a graduate fellowship. I quit Columbia to become his defense committee to raise his legal fees. One of the ways I found money was to arrange a recording for him with Music Craft. That was in 1939 and they paid us $350 for this first commercial pure folk music album, "The Sinful Songs of the

Southern Negro." Then that same year RCA Victor asked me to make an album for them and I said, "You're crazy. But I have a man here who ought to do it." And so Woody then cut the "Dust Bowl Ballads" and that was the second commercial folk song album. Also that year I went through the libraries of all the commercial record companies and found all the old hillbilly and black records. I arranged for Victor, Columbia and Decca to release reissues. Only then did we arrange funds so that the Library of Congress could publish the field recordings from the archives.

Now here, I'm going to go back a little bit. Since I had been in the field most of the time, I had a different view of folklore than most of my colleagues who had largely studied folklore from books with some field trips. I had never been in the library. I had been with the people all the time and I had had to learn and understand the material because it was entirely in their own terms. One of the things that was very clear to me was that Americans were the first people who were able to voice the deep anguish, resentment, and sense of injustice that the working-class people of Europe and the Middle East had felt for many centuries. Whereas these people had made ballads about heroes killing dragons and giants, in America expression could be much more direct. For example, "The Buffalo Skinners"—the story of a dishonest boss whose crew killed him "and left his damned old bones to bleach in the range of the buffalo." Now that's an unprecedented song. There was nothing like it in all European folk literature. In America for the first time it was safe for the common laborer to be frank. When I got to England and collected the working-class material, I discovered that such kinds of ballads could put a man out of work for his whole life—just the rumor that even sang them. Folklore, I realized, had been a disguised form of protest against tyranny for many thousands of years, since the first big empires came into being. Thus when I found that a whole body of topical songs had arisen from the union struggles of the thirties, I welcomed this as the modern wave of the need for human beings to speak out about what was just and fair and equitable, to tell the story just the way they had seen it. I became a collector of union songs and songs of protest. And by 1940, those of us who were interested had a sizable corpus of 300-400 songs that were a new and completely American form. Nothing like it had existed in the history of mankind. Only with the New Deal did we get this upsurge of protest and song.

My colleagues in the colleges then didn't understand what was happening because they had not seen this fundamental point about the hidden symbolism of the traditional folklore material that they had studied. They hadn't been out in the field, they hadn't been there at that first session in Huntsville. Blue's song of protest about sharecropping in the Brazos Bottom grew right out of the spirituals that his folks had just sung to me. Folklorists made a sharp line of distinction between the traditional spirituals and pieces like Blue's new topical song. But for me, this American genre was the continuation of the genuine river of human tradition. But now it was right out in the open and saying exactly what the people had long needed to say. Some of the material was raw, some of it was crude, but it had a kick like a Georgia mule.

So out of this realization came the singing movement, with Pete Seeger and a whole young generation. The making of new topical social songs became a vital new element in American culture. And, of course, that has kept on blooming. It was the thing that helped to keep America alive during the fifties, when so many voices had fallen silent. Because by then the topical singers just kept on singing, they couldn't be silenced.

Man is a communicator. But now, because of technological inventions, communication has become the privilege of the few who own the broadcasting systems. We sit at the other end and listen to what they have us hear, so as a result the art of conversation has almost disappeared. We do something called 'rapping,' which isn't conversation, it isn't the rich old human thing. I mean I can hardly stand two participants in a contemporary conversational style; it's so flat emotionally, it's so lacking in fantasy, it's so uneloquent. It hasn't got any balls, it hasn't got the old delight in language in it. I have spent my life listening to the great talkers of this country—prisoners, mad old women, old coots who were the last of their kind whether they were lumberjacks or sea captains sitting at their feet and saying, "Tell me more, my God, enchant me for another hour." These people really had something to say and knew how to say it. They spoke superb English or Spanish or whatever. They had inherited the art of talking and they cultivated it. Now we're cut off from all that by the namby-pamby, styleless chatter of the Jack Paars and host of other standardized and censored network mouthpieces.

> There was probably no greater symbol of the seemingly limitless prosperity of the twenties than Samuel Insull. His financial empire was so far-flung that not even he could claim total knowledge of all his companies at a given moment.
>
> However, in December, 1931, as Samuel Insull, Jr., relates, his father's empire began to crumble. What ensued was a 17-year legal battle that provided headlines for much of its duration and ultimately left the Insull family devoid of any of its once fabulous financial resources.
>
> Mr. Insull is now a Chicago insurance broker.

SAMUEL INSULL, JR.

It's very easy to be a Monday-morning quarterback. Certainly if I'd known as much then as I knew a few years later, there are many things I wouldn't have done. But you must remember the atmosphere of the twenties. History didn't mean much; all that prosperity was going to continue and continue. Once I went to a big reception at the Continental Bank and this man came up to me and said, "Mr. Arthur Reynolds wants to talk to you." Reynolds was the number-two man in the bank. I went up to Mr. Reynolds and said I was the head of one of the Insull companies, which banked there. He said, "I know all about that. What I want to talk to you about is something bigger. Any time you organize a new company, we can give you another $21 million. All you've got to do is organize it. You don't have to conduct any operations, just get it legally organized on paper. You've got lawyers; just turn it over to them and the bank will give you another $21 million." This was the twenties psychology.

Our collapse? Well, the thing that precipitated matters for us was that about December 15, 1931, we ran out of collateral. The stock had dropped to ridiculously low prices, and in addition, there was a terrific public uproar. I had to go to the heads of the five Chicago banks, who immediately referred me to the bank officer who handled things when there was trouble. Then I had to make a trip to New York to see all those bankers.

The one thing I didn't have any worry about was keeping a job of some kind, because even in New York, banks that wanted my father out were very insistent that I stay. Their reason was that I was the only one who, as my father said, knew more about all the Insull companies than any one person.

It was a time when we were living from day to day. You could expect anything. I was just numb.

In the fall of '32 I was sent to Paris, where my father and mother were settled. They'd been gone since June, and when I left Chicago, there was no talk of any indictments. But two days before the ship landed at Liverpool, the indictments began, so almost immediately we took off from Paris, heading to Greece, because there were no extradition laws there. We kept my father in Greece as long as we could. As a matter of fact, the abbot of that monastery where they haul you up in a basket offered him sanctuary because he thought my father was being persecuted. But he just thanked the abbot and said, "No, that would be a living death." There's no record of that except for a conversation between my father and me.

Public sentiment about my father began to turn around when he started on his way home. Coming back, there were three people on the boat with him: One was from the Associated Press, one was from the United Press, and one was Jimmy Kilgallen, the father of columnist Dorothy Kilgallen. They were all cooped up on this ship for two weeks, and my father had to talk to them about something, so he just started out with a monolog on his days with Thomas Edison. Finally, when they were out in the middle of the Atlantic, Kilgallen said, "I think you're on the level and I think I can help you. But we'll have to break a rule. You'll have to give me an exclusive." A couple of days later, Hearst papers across the country carried the headline: "Insull Broke." And that was the beginning of the turn-around.

As for the federal-court trials, frankly, the only problem we had in the first one was to get enough space at the table for the counsel and the press.

Our attorney, Dwight Thompson, was a remarkable man. His

whole thesis was that here is a man whose entire career has been built up, so at the last moment is he going to turn into a crook? The day my father testified, he just ran away with the whole thing. It got going so well that Leslie Salter, the federal prosecutor, became so interested that he quit objecting.

Then I remember when the government introduced our income-tax returns. I was on the stand and Thompson made no objection. So Salter said, "Read off for each year the salaries and charitable contributions," which I did, the contributions being more than the salaries. When we were finished, Salter turned to his assistant and said in a whisper you could hear all over the courtroom, "You SOB! Why didn't you tell me that was there!"

Later, when we got well into the case, and Salter and I were in two adjoining urinals during a morning break, he said to me, "Hell, Junior, you men are legitimate businessmen, aren't you?" I said, "Well, Les, that's what we're trying to prove to you." And he said, "I'll be goddamned; I had thought you were just another bunch of crooks."

Later we heard what happened inside the jury itself. During one of the recesses, about halfway through the prosecution's case, one of the jurors, who was an ex-sheriff, said to his roommate, "You see all those dollies (seven tiered stands) with account books on them that they wheel in here every morning? Well, we probably shouldn't be talking about this, but you go over there during the lunch hour and see who wrote those documents." So the fellow did, and he said, "It was one or the other of the defendants." The ex-sheriff said, "That's what I suspected. This case is a phony. I've been dealing with crooks all my life, and the one thing they don't do is write it all down while they're doing it. So I don't care what the government says, this case is a phony."

Well, when the jury was marched out by the bailiff, they just wanted to say "Not guilty." But the ex-sheriff said, "Uh-uh. That just gets all of them in trouble. Somebody'll say it's a fix." So one of the jurors had a birthday, and instead they sent out for a cake and had a three-hour birthday party!

In the next federal case, the senior district judge, Judge Knox, from New York, came out to try it. He later said that he was sent out by Chief Justice Hughes to end this Insull thing one way or the other. The government finished presenting its case, and Thompson made a motion for a directed verdict. The judge said something and all the feds jumped to their feet and began arguing. But the judge said, "No, I know my duty. If a conviction came down, I'd have to set it aside. Mr. Bailiff, bring in the jury." Then he said, "I'm instructing you to bring in a verdict of not guilty."

The criminal part of the litigation was all finished by '35, but we still had a lot of civil litigation. My father's settlement was obviously moot when he died in '38. His estate was $4½ million in the hole. My case wasn't disposed of until June 1, 1948. Then I very simply gave a statement of my net worth and a check to match and that was that. I let them divide it up.

I stayed at Commonwealth Edison until January 1, 1939. I was never told to pack my bags and get out, but it was very obvious from the remarks that were made and reported back to me that I'd better jump before I was pushed, so I did. The reason they wanted me out was because of the Insull name. There was a complete reversal of feeling about it, a revulsion. It was a fact and you have to accept facts; you can't remake them. Bitterness? Why waste time on it? What's the point? It'd just upset my digestion.

"Those were wild days," remembers former FBI agent Virgil Peterson, and indeed they were. They were literally the days of cops and robbers; good guys and bad guys; G-Men and gangsters; shoot-outs between FBI agents and such public enemies as John Dillinger and Baby Face Nelson. It was a time when these government agents would establish a super-cop image that would last for decades.

Following his service with the FBI, in 1942 Virgil Peterson became executive director of the Chicago Crime Commission. In 1969 he left the agency and is now a writer, lecturer and consultant on organized crime.

VIRGIL PETERSON

I graduated from Northwestern University Law School in '30. There was a notice up on the bulletin board, a letter from J. Edgar Hoover asking for young, interested lawyers, and I put in my application. I took the examination, was interviewed and was accepted. I didn't know too much of what it was all about till after I got in training school. But then, of course, in 1930 nobody knew much about the FBI, since it had just started.

My first office was in New Orleans. Then, in '33, I was transferred back to Chicago, which was where everything was happening as far as crime was concerned. That was where Jake Factor was kidnaped by the Touhy gang. I worked on that case, interviewing Factor's relatives, his wife. There were all kinds of leads, and finally we located their hideout in Glenview, Illinois. I was out there with a lot of other agents, waiting for about 24 hours, since we thought they might come back, but they never did. We found three gallons of nitroglycerin buried in the back yard. Those were rough times.

In the early part of '34 I was on special assignment to the Bremer kidnaping case in St. Paul, and when Dillinger made his escape from the Crown Point, Indiana, jail in March, '34, I came back to Chicago and was assigned exclusively to that case until it ended.

There was no Bank Robbery Act at that time, so our jurisdiction in looking for Dillinger was the fact that he stole a sheriff's car and transported interstate commerce—in other words, interstate transportation of a stolen car.

The case was handled right out of the Chicago office as a regular assignment. I was assistant to Melvin Purvis, agent in charge of the Chicago office. Then, in early '34, roughly in May, the case was made a special assignment. Sam Crowley, an inspector, came out here to take charge of the case, and I was his assistant.

The Dillinger case was considered special work. Everything was in turmoil as far as working conditions were concerned. There were all kinds of false leads at different times, and some of the agents would be sent out in airplanes. Of course, those leads never developed into anything. Sometimes we put in almost 24 hours at a stretch. It was a terrific assignment, very demanding.

Then—I think it was on April 20—we got a call from Manitowoc, Wisconsin, that the Dillinger mob had been holed up in this Little Bohemia Lodge, so two planeloads of agents went up there in two private chartered planes, which held only six or seven passengers per plane. We landed in Eagle River, Wisconsin, 40-odd miles from the Little Bohemia Lodge, about six o'clock in the evening, more or less commandeered four cars, (we weren't terribly experienced), and started out for the lodge.

There was a long driveway up to the lodge, and dogs started to bark and the whole thing backfired. There was a lot of shooting and a constable was shot badly, I don't know by whom; it could have been one of the agents, for all I know. The Dillinger mob went out through the back, where there was a lake.

In the meantime, agents Jay Newman and W. Carter Baum and someone else were in this coupe when they heard that there was some excitement up at the Northern Lakes Lodge. They went up there and found Baby Face Nelson trying to grab a car.

Nelson grabbed a gun and shot Newman with a grazing blow on the side of the head, and Baum was hit right above his bulletproof vest and killed.

Now, we didn't know definitely that the Dillinger mob had escaped. We had the place surrounded all night, and the next morning we got tear gas in the place and captured the four women who were there; Helen Nelson, Marie Conforti, a girl by the name of Delaney, who was Tommy Carroll's girl, and a woman whose name I don't recall. They were tough; they were no Sunday-school girls. Helen Nelson was very quiet and didn't give the appearance of a moll. She was really devoted to Baby Face Nelson. She had to be very tough, though, because she was with him when he was driving all around the country and she had left her two kids with in-laws here in Chicago.

We came back the next day, and all I'd had in those 24 hours was some orange juice, toast and coffee. It was cold up there, you know, in that wooded area, with snow on April 20, and we weren't dressed for it, so Purvis took Ralph Brown and me back to Chicago.

Of course, there was a lot of criticism of Purvis, who was in charge of the case, and, I suppose, you always have a tendency to feel that criticism is unwarranted. But also, realistically, you knew with hindsight, things could have been handled differently. Of course, the bureau was in its infancy at the time and didn't have anywhere near the tremendous expertise it would have subsequently.

Then Sam Cowley came up here to be in charge of the case on special assignment. I remember his saying, "All we need now is the First National Bank to be robbed; then we'll really be loused up."

At any rate, on July 20, Cowley and Purvis had the conference with the Lady in Red (Anna Sage), together with Sergeant Zarkovich and Tim O'Neal from East Chicago, Indiana, and learned that she and Dillinger were going to either the Biograph Theater or the Marlboro Theater on the West Side. So we had to make plans for both places, and on Sunday, July 22, I was in the office, coordinating the two theaters.

That night we found out they had gone into the Biograph,

and we had that place covered. Right in front of the theater were Purvis, Sam Cowley, Ed Hollis, Charlie Winstead and a fellow by the name of Hurd from Oklahoma. When Dillinger came out of the theater and spotted them, he took it on high and they ran after him. He had a gun in his pocket that he was trying to get at when they shot and killed him. Right afterward, there were a lot of people trying to grab some kind of souvenir or something.

(As a matter of fact, up at the Little Bohemia Lodge, Emil Winnetka was selling bullets. He sold enough to have won a war. I don't know where he got all of them. He had Dillinger's father up there on exhibit, too. He was just a nice, simple fellow, kind of ignorant but harmless, from the backwoods of Indiana. Hubert, Dillinger's brother, was a cocky individual, on the arrogant side. He certainly wasn't what you'd call friendly. I suppose there was some resentment, but they brought it on themselves.)

Then, on November 27, 1934, Cowley and Ed Hollis were killed in Barrington, Illinois. You see, we had three agents in the home of Hobe Hermanson nearby in Lake Geneva, Wisconsin, because friends of Baby Face Nelson were there. Hermanson had gone shopping, and later, when a car pulled up in the drive, the agents came out, thinking it was Hermanson coming back. Well, it wasn't Hermanson; it was Baby Face Nelson, John Paul Chase and Helen Nelson. Here were these agents in their shirt sleeves unarmed in the front, and Nelson, I'm sure, was suspicious. He asked for Hermanson and they said he'd be back in a few minutes. Then the agents called Cowley, gave him the license-plate number, and Cowley ordered two more cars and they headed for Lake Geneva.

When they got up near Fox River Grove, Illinois, agents McDade and Ryan spotted Nelson's car coming toward them and they turned around and started following it. Chase, in the back seat of Nelson's car, began firing out the window, so McDade and Ryan pushed down the accelerator and shot ahead of Nelson. Ryan had busted out the back glass of the coupe and was firing at Nelson's car; water was shooting up from where he'd hit the radiator. Cowley and Hollis were in this old

Hudson, and they had whirled around, too, so that Nelson's car was between the two FBI cars.

Well, when they got to Barrington, there was a dead-end street. Nelson was an excellent driver—he'd driven one time on the old Robie race track—and he shot out on the side of the road by the Standard Oil filling station. In the meantime, Cowley and Hollis were coming, but when they got around the curb, they ran off the road and disabled the car 172 feet from where Nelson, Chase and Helen were.

Nelson and Chase jumped out of their car, and Chase used the hood of the car as a kind of barricade, while Nelson started shooting at the two agents. He was determined to get the bureau car, so he came right down the middle of the highway with a machine gun. The agents fired back, Hollis with a shotgun, Cowley with a machine gun, and hit Nelson, sending him down on one knee, but he kept on coming and he hit Cowley in the abdomen, which was a fatal blow. Hollis ran out of ammunition and ran behind a telephone pole and he was also hit, and Nelson went over and finished him off at close range.

Nelson was dying, but he got into the bureau car, and Helen and Chase joined him. They shoved their guns and stuff inside, Chase took the wheel, and they drove off. When Nelson was dead, they removed all his clothes, dumped his body on Mannheim Road and then called an undertaker.

When Cowley was killed, it caused the same shock as when Carter Baum had been killed, because these were high-grade people. Cowley was one of my closest friends, and we were both very friendly with Hollis. So there was grief. And the same was true of Washington headquarters. There was concern over the loss of such fine men. But there wasn't any time to postpone any of our activities. Things had to go on when one of those things happened. In fact, it created even greater motivation, because you were anxious to catch those responsible for killing agents.

The Dillinger case was pretty well cleaned up toward the end of the year, but other cases were just breaking. They'd solved the Bremer and Hamm kidnaping cases. The Touhy gang had been suspected in the Hamm case, but it was the Barker brothers, Volney Davis and Alvin Karpis who pulled that and the Bremer case, and they were subsequently convicted. (Freddy and Ma Barker were killed in Florida, and they got Karpis, too, I think, in Ohio.)

At any rate, in May, '35, I was transferred to take charge of the Milwaukee office, and it was one thing after another. We had one big bank robbery, a fugitive case, Ed Bentz. He'd been a fugitive for six years, one of the biggest bank robbers in the country. We had a cover on the mail and baggage of his girlfriend, Verna Freemark, in south Milwaukee for about four months. As a result of this cover, we found out that she was coming to get some trunks that had been shipped there. Finally we got permission to pick her up, and through her we found out where Bentz was living in New York. We sent a teletype there, and within 24 hours he was picked up. They'd been looking for him for six years. It was that kind of stuff.

Whenever I was in charge of an office, we had to go to Washington at least once a year, and we always had a conference with Hoover and all his assistants, people like Clyde Tolson and Ed Tamm, who's now, I think, a circuit court of appeals judge in Washington. That was part of the ritual. You always had to talk to those people. I was always very apprehensive, because Hoover was very demanding. But everything always went all right.

I had a lot of admiration for the way Hoover built up the organization into the finest of its kind in the world. Hell, he was only 28 when he took charge in 1924. Hoover had his weaknesses, though. It would have been much better from his standpoint—probably from the bureau's, also—if he had retired before he was 70. He stayed too long.

The dedication was part of the spirit of the whole organization. In the first place, they hired really top-flight personnel, dedicated people, whose character was beyond reproach in most instances. You felt that it was a privilege to be part of the organization and you wanted to do your best.

At the same time, though, I think there were certain things that needed correcting, too. The handling of personnel, the discipline was just, well, unbelievable. Maybe there were certain kinds of infractions that justified summary dismissal. But you'd have other things of not that serious import. Somebody, say, might do something that resulted in bad publicity, and even if it was done unintentionally, he'd be disciplined, which usually meant a transfer to an undesirable office.

There was always the feeling that Purvis was disciplined because he got all this publicity. He was in on everything for a while. He was there when they captured Pretty Boy Floyd and Volney Davis, and, of course, he got all the publicity on the Dillinger case. I don't know whether or not they were burned up because he got all this national publicity, but I think Purvis felt that was true, and he resigned.

You had no life when you were in charge of an office. Even when I was in Chicago, my wife-to-be came to Chicago and we planned to be married three or four times, but I could never get off. I didn't have much home life, either. I'd never leave the office during the weekdays before midnight, and sometimes it'd be 1:30 in the morning. Then I'd have to be back again by nine o'clock the next morning. Those were wild days.

INDEX

Ameche, James, 221–25
Amalgamated Meatcutters and Butcher Workmen of North America, 154–55; Fur and Leather Workers' Department of, 156–58
Arms trade, 18
Arvey, Jacob, 93–96

Baker, Newton, 11
Baldwin, Roger, 111–14
Baseball, professional, 171ff; blacks in, 174–80, 181; Edward Froelich in, 191–93; income of players, 193; Thomas Gibbs in, 198–99
Basketball, professional: Thomas Gibbs in, 111–14
Bennett, Spencer Gordon, 256–59
Bergen, Edgar, 201–05
Bernays, Edward, 306–09
Black cabinet, 55–56
Black(s): baseball players, 174–80, 181; in construction work, 53–54; and culture, 312; and Democratic party, 97–100; discrimination in boxing, 188–89; and labor movement, 151–53; lynching of, 116–18;

Affirmative action: first in federal government, 53
Agricultural Adjustment Act, 41; opposition to, 70
Agricultural Adjustment Administration, 16
Agricultural Conservation Act, 41
Agricultural Conservation Administration, 41
American Civil Liberties Union, 111, 113–14
American Federation of Labor, 26, 151, 154–55. *See also* individual unions by name.
Antilynching law, 118. *See also* Lynching.
Anti-Semitism: and Franklin Roosevelt, 87–88; and New Deal, 104; and State Department, 21; and students, 135
Antitrust laws, 89
Armstrong, Henry, 185–89
Artists: as cartoon animators, 260–68; and cartoon movies, 269–76
Arts, subsidy: National Endowment for the Humanities, 62

334 INDEX

and major league sports, 172–73; and music, 310–19; in professional sports, 196–200; and segregation, 118–22; wages and hours of, 159
Boxing, amateur: Thomas Gibbs in, 199
Boxing, professional, 185–89
Brain trust, 2
Brandeis, Justice Louis, 102, 104
Brotherhood of Sleeping Car Porters, 151–53
Brown, J. Douglas, 24–31

Cardozo, Justice Benjamin, 101–03; and social security, 29
Celler, Emanuel, 87–88
Censorship: Hayes office, 252–53, 265; of radio, 204
Childs, Marquis, 105–09
Civil rights: and David Graubart, 148
Civilian Conservation Corps, 8, 63–66; blacks in, 63; recreation in, 64; work of, 63
Cohen, Milton, 127–31
Cohen, Wilbur, 32–37
Cole, Shirley Bell, 216–20
Communist party, 113; and Hamilton Fish, 75
Congress: and depression, 67–68; pay reduction of, 78; and Supreme Court, 102; unity on Roosevelt proposals, 77; work compared with '70s, 79–80
Congress of Industrial Workers, 26, 154–55; Communist control of, 75; and United Professional Workers Union of America, 164. *See also* individual unions by name.
Cotton: contracts, 17–18; reduction of production, 41
Crash: *See* Depression.
Criley, Richard, 132–36
Crossley, Archibald, 240–43
Crutchfield, John "Jimmie," 174–80

Democratic conventions, 3, 91–92; Roosevelt-Smith rivalry, 83
Democratic party: and blacks, 97–100
Depression: action necessary, 77; American people in, 50; and blacks, 17, 121–22; Committee on Economic Security, 32; and economic crises, 2; and elderly, 32; and public relations, 307–09; relief organizations, 142; Townsend Plan to alleviate, 34, 123–26
Dickerson, Earl, 97–100
Disney, Walt, 260–68; approach to cartoon movies, 262, 264
Dorsey, Thomas A., 296–300
Dubinsky, David, 159–62

Early, Stephen, 6–7, 106–07
Eisenhower, Milton, 38–45
Elliott, John D., 123–26
Equity Guild: Federal Theater Project, 60–61

Farley, James, 2; and '32 campaign, 9
Farmers, 16–17, 38; and bank foreclosures, 112; and federal programs, 17, 41–42; tenant, 17

INDEX   335

Farm Security Administration, 41–42
Fascism: and Spanish civil war, 127, 129–30; and students, 135–36
Federal Bureau of Investigation: and Baby Face Nelson, 326–27, 328–29; and John Dillinger, 326–28; Virgil Peterson in, 325–31
Federal Emergency Relief Act, 17
Federal Theater Project, 57–62; children's plays, 58
Feinglass, Abe, 156–58
Fields, W. C., 204
Fish, Hamilton, 67–76; Dies Committee, 75; war issue, 71
Fleisher, Dave, 269, 272, 274, 275
Fleisher, Max, 269, 274, 275
Football, professional, 167; and depression, 168; Edward Froelich in, 194
Frankfurter, Justice Felix, 101, 103
Froelich, Edward, 190–95

Gallup, George, 301–05
Gallup Poll, 302–04
Garner, John Nance, 11
Gehringer, Charles, 171–73
Gibbs, Thomas "Gumbo," 196–99
Gorman, Patrick, 154–55
Gottfried, Carl, 63–66
Graubart, Rabbi David, 147–50
Green, William, 151, 155

Halas, George, 167–70
Hampton, Lionel, 277–81
Helstein, Ralph, 46–50
Hines, Earl "Fatha," 282–84

Hiss, Alger, 15–23
Hockey, professional: Edward Froelich in, 190
Hodes, Art, 291–95
Hodge, Al, 211–15
Hoover administration, 24–25
Hoover, Herbert, 2; and agriculture, 38–39; depression measures, 2, 69; leadership in depression, 82; as politician, 69; and repeal of prohibition, 68
Hoover, J. Edgar; and FBI, 330–31
Hopkins, Harry, 2, 49, 108
Howe, Louis, 2, 4–5

Insull, Samuel, 321–24; trials, 322–24
Insull, Samuel, Jr., 321–24
Interior, Department of: Robert Weaver in, 51–56
International Ladies Garment Workers' Union, 157, 159
Isolationism, 19–20, 85; and lend-lease, 85; prewar, 85

Jewish culture, 143–46
Jewish Daily Forward, 137, 159; and David Graubart, 149
Jewish vote: and Roosevelt, 94
Jews: and Communist party, 146; and Roosevelt, 87–88; and Socialism, 142–46
Jews, leftist: and Communism, 149; and Fascism, 149

Kennan, George, 21
Keyserling, Leon, 89–92
Kimball, Ward, 260–68

Kreindler, Hannah Haskell, 159-62

Labor: and Roosevelt, 36. *See also* Labor unions; individual unions by name.
Labor Department: and social security, 35
Labor law: and National Recovery Administration, 47
Labor movement, 151. *See also* Labor unions; individual unions by name.
Labor unions, 156-58, 159; and agriculture, 134; battles to organize, 154; boycott of Germany, 161; integration in, 135; organization of, 157-58, 164-66; and strikes, 132-33; and white-collar workers, 163. *See also* individual unions by name.
Landon, Alfred, 36, 70
LeHand, Missy, 12-13
Lend-lease: and Roosevelt, 85
Lewis, John L., 155
Library of Congress: and folk history, 317
Literature, Yiddish, 138-40
Lomax, Alan, 310-20
Long, Huey, 34-35
Lynching, 116-18

Manley, Abe, 181-84
Manley, Effa, 181-84
Matthews, Ann Elstner, 206-10
McAdoo, William, 11
McCarthysim, 75; and Roosevelt, 22
McCormack, John, 82-86

Mercer, Lucy, 12
Mitchell, Clarence, 115-22
Morgenthau, Henry, 7; and Roosevelt, 28
Morrison, Herbert, 226-30
Music: Art Hodes as blues pianist, 291-95; Benny Goodman and jazz, 279-80; black unions in, 287; blacks and jazz, 277; blacks and secular songs, 310, 312; blacks' segregation in radio and theater, 286-87; blacks and spirituals, 311-12, 319; blues players, 292-94; Chicago and, 292-95; Chicago gangsters in, 294-95; Chicago and jazz, 282-84, 285-86; Edith Wilson and, 288-90; folkmusic recordings, 318; gospel songs, 296-300; jazz, 277ff, 285-86; jazz and classical, 281; jazz as counterculture, 291ff; jazz and Louis Armstrong, 278-79, 292; Mahalia Jackson as gospel singer, 298; radio death of jazz, 294; recordings, 279, 283-84; salaries of musicians, 289-90; swing and Benny Goodman, 283; Tommy Dorsey and gospel themes, 296-300
Movies: awards, 251; and blacks, 248-49; cartoons, 260, 269-76; cartoon animators, 260-68; cartoon artist techniques, 270-72; cartoons and color, 261; cartoon feature films, 275-76; cartoon plots, 271; cartoons and

sound, 261; cartoon techniques, 274; cartoons and voice imitations, 263-64; classic cartoons, 265-68; costs of, 250, 259; classics, 248-53, 254-55; directors, 248-53; Donald Duck, 263-64; double features, 246; *Fantasia,* 268; *Gulliver's Travels,* 274-75; *King Kong,* 254-55; Mickey Mouse, 260, 262-63; *Pinnocchio,* 267; pot boilers, 252; serials, 256-58; *Snow White,* 262, 274; stunts, 258; talkies, advent of, 245-46; trickwork, 257; Walt Disney, 260-68; westerns, 258-59; *Wizard of Oz,* 251-52

National Association for the Advancement of Colored People, 115-22
National Industrial Recovery Act, 89-91
National Industrial Recovery Administration, 90
National Labor Relations Act, 113
National Labor Relations Board, 113
National Recovery Act: opposition to, 70
National Recovery Administration, 46-48
Nazism: and *Freiheit,* 144-45
New Deal, 1, 16-17, 21-23, 112-13; and blacks, 51-52, 97; and Felix Frankfurter, 103-04; opposition to, 91; spirit of reform running out, 49-50; theater, 57; and unions, 160

Newspaper Guild: and Yiddish writers, 140
Newspapermen. *See* Press.
Nigro, Carmen, 154-55
Novice, Paul, 142-46
Nye Committee on Munitions Industry, 18

Old-age insurance. *See* Social security.

Pearl Harbor, 85-86
Perkins, Frances, 2, 35
Peterson, Virgil, 325-31
Populism, 20
Prohibition repeal: and public relations, 309
Public-opinion polls, 301-05; Arch Crossley in, 302; Gallup Poll, 301-05; *Literary Digest* and, 301-02; Roper Poll, 302; techniques, 302-05
Public relations: Edward Bernays in, 306-09
Public works, 25; nondiscrimination in, 53
Press: conferences, 106-07; influence on government, 105-06; Marquis Childs, 105-09; and medicine, 309; and movies, 250-51; and news on radio, 227-30; opposition to Republicans, 72; in presidential campaign, 3; prowar, 75; and public relations, 306, 307; and Roosevelt, 6; and Samuel Insull, 322; and social security, 36. *See also Jewish Daily Forward, Newspaper Guild.*

338 INDEX

Race relations: in CCC, 63; in labor unions, 151–53
Radio: acting in, 214–15; announcers, 235–38; announcers as newscasters, 226–29; "Captain Midnight," 219–20; Chicago center of, 225; commerical sponsors, 240–43; Edgar Bergen, 201–05; electrical transcriptions, 222–23; and folk music, 315–16; founding of Mutual Broadcasting System, 213; "Green Hornet," 211–12; growth of, 201–05; and *Hindenburg* disaster, 228–29; and history programs, 310ff; "Jack Armstrong," 221–25; "Little Orphan Annie," 218–19; live broadcasts, 223; "Lone Ranger," 211, 212; Muzak, 211; news programs, 207; news reporters for, 233–35; and Orson Welles, 236–37; power of, 231–39; ratings methods, 241–43; ratings of shows, 240–43; and recorded broadcasts, 228–30; restrictions on, 233; serials, 211, 212, 216–20, 238; soap operas, 206, 208–10, 220; sound effects, 224, 238–39; theater, 225; violence, lack of, 213
Randolph, A. Philip, 151–53
Randolph, Jennings, 77–81
Rauh, Joe, 101–04
Rayburn, Sam, 39
Reconstruction Finance Corporation, 39

Recordings: of folk history, 310–15; of news, 228–30
Republicans: in '32 election, 4
Roosevelt, Elliott, 1
Roosevelt, Franklin D., 1–10, 11; and anti-Semitism, 13; and blacks, 56; campaign antiprohibition speech, 4; campaign, first presidential, 2–4; campaign style, 107; and Dorothy Rosenman, 14; "fireside chats," 6, 40, 106; first Hundred Days, 40, 78, 94; and Hamilton Fish, 67–75; and Hitler, 73; and Japan, 74; and Jewish establishment, 141; and polio, 6, 93–94; as politician, 68; and press, 29, 106–07; and public-opinion polls, 304; re-election as governor, 2; repudiated Democratic platform, 69; and Supreme Court, 84, 87, 107–08; and third term, 9, 13, 88; "war cabinet," 74; and Yiddish-speaking left, 143
Roosevelt, James, 1–10; as father's secretary, 6
Roosevelt, Sara, 5, 12
Rosenman, Dorothy, 11–15
Rosenman, Judge Samuel, 11, 13

Saunders, Red, 285–87
Scrap iron: and war, 21
Seymour, Dan, 231–39
Sheehan, Gordon, 269–76
Simon, Lewis, 57–62
Smith, Al, 1; betrayed by Democratic party, 69
Smith, Joe, 245–47
Social security, 33–37; 106, 166;

administration, 32–35; advisory board, 24; bill enacted, 32; board, 34–36; influence of law on Townsend Plan, 34–35; and Jewish Socialism, 142; plan, 26–30
Soil Conservation Service, 42–43
Spanish civil war, 20, 127–31; and Abraham Lincoln Brigade, 127, 130–31, 145, 149; and International Brigade, 127ff; and Jews, 145; and Loyalists, 134–35
Sports: trainers, 190–91. *See also* individual sports.
State Department, 15, 18, 20–21
Stone, Justice Harlan, 108
Strikes. See Labor unions.
Students: and causes, 132–36; during depression, 132–35; movements in '60s, 132, 136; support of Spanish Republic, 134
Supreme Court: and Agricultural Administration Act, 41; and court-packing plan, 91, 101, 107–08; and New Deal, 101, 112–13; and Roosevelt, 87; and Roosevelt programs, 84

Townsend, Francis E.: income plan, 34, 123–26
Tugwell, Rexford, 2, 89

Unemployment, 15, 33; and blacks, 52; in fur industry, 156; insurance for, 29, 166; and Jewish Socialism, 142; and relief measures, 2, 6, 25; and students, 132
United Professional Workers Union of America, 164

Vaudeville: demise of, 245–47
Veterans: bonus, 124; bonus march, 40; organizations, 19
Vidor, King, 248–53
Violence: complaints of, 271; lack of on radio, 213

Wages and hours, 46–48, 89, 157, 158, 159
Wagner Act. *See* National Labor Relations Act.
Wagner, Robert, 89–92
Wallace, Henry A., 38, 40–45
War production 30–31
Watson, Pa, 7, 30
Weaver, Robert C., 51–56
Weber, Simon, 137–41
Willkie, Wendell: Hamilton Fish opposition to, 72
Wilson, Edith, 288–90
Women: and wages, hours, 159
Working conditions, 157–60
Works Progress Administration, 16–17

Yanoff, Morris, 163–66
Yiddish-speaking left, 142–46